ROUTLEDGE LIBRARY EDITIONS: HISTORY OF MEDICINE

Volume 7

THE HISTORY OF PHARMACY

THE HISTORY OF PHARMACY
A Selected Annotated Bibliography

Edited by
GREGORY HIGBY AND ELAINE C. STROUD

LONDON AND NEW YORK

First published in 1995 by Garland Publishing, Inc.

This edition first published in 2019
by Routledge
2 Park Square, Milton Park, Abingdon, Oxon OX14 4RN

and by Routledge
52 Vanderbilt Avenue, New York, NY 10017

Routledge is an imprint of the Taylor & Francis Group, an informa business

© 1995 Gregory J. Higby and Elaine C. Stroud

All rights reserved. No part of this book may be reprinted or reproduced or utilised in any form or by any electronic, mechanical, or other means, now known or hereafter invented, including photocopying and recording, or in any information storage or retrieval system, without permission in writing from the publishers.

Trademark notice: Product or corporate names may be trademarks or registered trademarks, and are used only for identification and explanation without intent to infringe.

British Library Cataloguing in Publication Data
A catalogue record for this book is available from the British Library

ISBN: 978-0-367-08576-6 (Set)
ISBN: 978-0-429-02312-5 (Set) (ebk)
ISBN: 978-0-367-07561-3 (Volume 7) (hbk)
ISBN: 978-0-367-07565-1 (Volume 7) (pbk)
ISBN: 978-0-429-02139-8 (Volume 7) (ebk)

Publisher's Note
The publisher has gone to great lengths to ensure the quality of this reprint but points out that some imperfections in the original copies may be apparent.

Disclaimer
The publisher has made every effort to trace copyright holders and would welcome correspondence from those they have been unable to trace.

THE HISTORY OF PHARMACY

A Selected Annotated Bibliography

Gregory J. Higby
Elaine C. Stroud

Associate Editors
David Cowen
Marvin Fischbaum
William H. Helfand
Ramunas Kondratas
John Parascandola
Ernst Stieb
John Swann
James Whorton
James Harvey Young

GARLAND PUBLISHING, Inc.
New York & London / 1995

Copyright © 1995 Gregory J. Higby and Elaine C. Stroud
All rights reserved

Library of Congress Cataloging-in-Publication Data

Higby, Gregory.
  The history of pharmacy : a selected annotated bibliography / Gregory J. Higby and Elaine C. Stroud.
    p.   cm. — (Garland reference library of the humanities ; vol. 1366) (Bibliographies on the history of science and technology ; vol. 25)
  Includes bibliographical references and index.
  ISBN 0-8240-9768-8
  1. Pharmacy—History—Bibliography.   I. Stroud, Elaine Condouris, 1950– . II. Title. III. Series. IV. Series: Bibliographies on the history of science and technology ; vol. 25.
  [DNLM: 1. Pharmacy—history—abstracts. ZQV 711.1 H634h 1995]
Z6675.P5H53   1995
[RS61]
615'.1'09—dc20
DNLM/DLC
for Library of Congress   94-33279
                                                            CIP

Printed on acid-free, 250-year-life paper
Manufactured in the United States of America

General Introduction

This bibliography is one of a series designed to guide the reader into the history of science and technology. Anyone interested in any of the components of this vast subject area is part of our intended audience, not only the student, but also the scientist interested in the history of his own field (or faced with the necessity of writing an "historical introduction") and the historian, amateur or professional. The latter will not find the bibliographies "exhaustive," although in some fields he may find them the only existing bibliographies. He will in any case not find one of those endless lists in which the important is lumped with the trivial, but rather a "critical" bibliography, largely annotated, and indexed to lead the reader quickly to the most important (or only existing) literature.

Inasmuch as everyone treasures bibliographies it is surprising how few there are in this field. Justly treasured are George Sarton's *Guide to the History of Science* (Waltham, Mass., 1952; 316 pp.), Eugene S. Ferguson's *Bibliography of the History of Technology* (Cambridge, Mass., 1968; 347 pp.), François Russo's *Histoire des Sciences et des Techniques, Bibliographie* (Paris, 2nd ed., 1969; 214 pp.), and Magda Witrow's *ISIS Cumulative Bibliography. A bibliography of the history of science* (London, 1971–; 2131 pp. as of 1976). But all are limited, even the latter, by the virtual impossibility of doing justice to any particular field in a bibliography of limited size and almost unlimited subject matter.

For various reasons, mostly bad, the average scholar prefers adding to the literature, rather than sorting it out. The editors are indebted to the scholars represented in this series for their willingness to expend the time and effort required to pursue the latter objective. Our aim has been to establish a general framework which will give some uniformity to the series, but otherwise to leave the format and contents to the author/compiler. We have urged that introductions be used for essays on "the state of the field," and that selectivity be exercised to limit the length of each volume to the economically practical.

Since the historical literature ranges from very large (e.g., medicine) to very small (chemical technology), some bibliographies will be limited to the most important writings while others will include modest "contributions" and even primary sources. The problem is to give useful guidance into a particular field—or subfield—and its solution is largely left to the author/compiler.

In general, topical volumes (e.g., chemistry) will deal with the subject since about 1700, leaving earlier literature to the area of chronological volumes (e.g., medieval science); but here, too, the volumes will vary according to the judgment of the author. The topics are international, with a few exceptions, but the literature covered depends, of course, on the linguistic equipment of the author and his access to "exotic" literatures.

Robert Multhauf
Smithsonian Institution
Washington, D.C.

Contents

Introduction	vii
Part One: Bibliographies and General Studies	
1a. Bibliographies, Encyclopedias, Dictionaries	3
1b. General Historical Literature and Historiography	20
1c. National Studies	26
1d. Company Histories	43
1e. Biographies	54
Part Two: Special Subjects	
2a. Practice of Pharmacy	92
2b. Basic Pharmaceutical Disciplines	103
2c. Materia Medica (Drugs) and Drug Therapy	123
General	123
Pre-1600	133
Post-1600	146
2d. Laws and Regulations	171
2e. Professional Pharmaceutical Literature	184
Classics	184
Historical Studies	190
2f. Professional and Social Aspects	196
2g. Economic and Business Aspects	210
2h. Education	222
2i. Manufacturing (not including company histories)	244
2j. Equipment and Museology	254
2k. Patent Medicines and Quackery	285
Part Three: Pharmacy in the Arts	
3a. Architecture and Interior Design	289
3b. Painting, Sculpture, Graphic Arts, and Photography	292
3c. Creative Literature	308
3d. Music	310
Author Index	311

Introduction

Historical Background

In the ninth century in the sophisticated Islamic city of Baghdad, the occupational ancestors of today's pharmacists arose. Islamic scholars had revived interest in Greco-Roman medicine and added their own pharmaceutical knowledge. The resulting complex and elegant mixtures of drugs required the skill of a specialist. At those places where the Islamic world interacted with western Europe, emerging from the isolation of the Middle Ages, the concept of the separation of medicine and pharmacy was shared. These ideas took root earliest in Spain and southern Italy, where other advanced institutions transferred to Europe. Public pharmacies appeared by the 1100s. By the middle of the thirteenth century, the separation had become so common that Frederick II, ruler of the Kingdom of the Two Sicilies, issued an edict to that effect.

During the Renaissance, apothecaries became active members of the European guild system, usually aligning themselves with grocers and spice sellers or with physicians. By the seventeenth century, apothecaries began breaking away to form their own guilds, as their authority and power grew. This occurred in large part because of the growth in the number of exotic drugs arriving from explorations and from the concurrent rise in application of chemical techniques to medicine making. As pharmacy became an established part of Western society, it also influenced the broader culture. Pharmacists and pharmaceutical themes found their way into the arts.

From the mid-1600s to the mid-1800s, pharmacists were among the leaders in chemistry, making discoveries, writing textbooks, and designing new apparatus. Nicolas Lemery, Carl Wilhem Scheele, Martin Klaproth, Antoine Baumé, Carl Freidrich Mohr, and Henri Moissan are just a few of the most prominent pharmacist-chemists.

Apothecaries came to British North America in the seventeenth century, often practicing a mixture of medicine and pharmacy as had been the case in England. In sharp contrast with continental Europe, pharmacy as a occupation had a haphazard and disorganized development in the British Colonies and in the young United States. It was not until the middle of the nineteenth century that the infrastructure of the modern pharmacy profession arose—laws, literature, schools, associations, and so forth. At about the same time the modern pharmaceutical sciences—pharmacology, pharmaceutical chemistry, pharmacognosy, and medicinal chemistry—had their origins and began to influence how medicines were made. Mass manufacturing techniques were applied to pharmacy, first with basic ingredients in the mid-nineteenth century, and later in the next century with end dosage forms.

In the twentieth century pharmacists retained much of their control over the distribution of medicines, even though the responsibility for making them was being turned over to manufacturers. This began a decades-long search for a more complete professional role in the health care system. In recent years, the focus has shifted from drug information to patient counseling to "pharmaceutical care." The latter concept, still under development, places pharmacists in the position responsible for proper drug use by patients. The need and opportunity for this great shift in professional function came in large part from the great number of new drugs discovered and marketed since 1940. Whole new classes of effective medicines were introduced such as the antibiotics, corticosteroids, tranquilizers, antidepressants, antihypertensives, radioactive isotopes, and oral contraceptives.

The historical literature on pharmacy has dealt with these subjects in an uneven fashion. Some topics, such as the discovery and development of penicillin, have received a great deal of attention, while other subjects have been ignored. The economics of pharmacy, for example, is a field wide open for research.

Bibliography Guidelines

As a profession, pharmacy has a long tradition. An evaluation of the history of the discipline, however, is of more recent origin. To cover its history in a bibliography, we have drawn on many sources from a number of disciplines in order to compile a selective list of the major references in the field. The distribution of references among the various research areas is not even and shows some of the strengths and weaknesses in the development of the discipline.

The guidelines for including selections in this bibliography revolve around its intended use. *The History of Pharmacy* is designed for graduate students and teachers of the history of pharmacy, scholars in related disciplines who want an introduction to the field, and researchers in the history of pharmacy who would like to explore the literature for an area other than their own. In other words, this is intended as a selective guide to the secondary literature. The reader should expect to find a broad overview of the literature that emphasizes the most important and

Introduction

essential works. Some consideration is also given to availability of materials. Sources have been omitted because of their limited accessibility (dissertations are generally included in this category, unless they provide a unique resource). Unless otherwise indicated, we have personally looked at each reference to verify the bibliographic citation. For a particular topic, preference is given to good secondary sources that are synthetic and comprehensive with good references. Next come new editions of primary sources with descriptive, historical introductions, and commentary. And the third level of reference is the primary source when few or poor secondary sources are available. English-language works are preferred, with selections from other languages taken when English material is not available.

Three main sections make up this bibliography. The first section includes general studies that cover the field as a whole, including the historiography of the history of pharmacy. Part two deals with special subjects in pharmacy, and part three covers pharmacy in the arts. There will naturally be some overlap between these areas, and instead of using a system of cross-references, the complete citation is repeated in as many categories as are appropriate. In this way, the sections remain self-contained.

Each category in the general outline entails its own set of questions and criteria for inclusion. There was no attempt to make this bibliography comprehensive but rather to give the reader a good sense of the kinds of literature available by being selective. In the national studies section, for example, many of the French and German studies of pharmacy in particular geographic regions were omitted simply because there are so many of them, and their detail would not be useful for a first-time researcher to the field. Pharmaceutical company histories posed a different kind of problem in terms of deciding which to include. There are very few histories of pharmaceutical companies that step back away from the public relations angle to present an account of the scientific accomplishments of the company without the biases of the individual company's agenda. Indeed, most have been prepared primarily as public relations vehicles. Despite their shortcomings, these works have historical value, since many of the authors had access to company archives, and the facts and figures about the company are also useful.

The biographies section poses similar problems, since some of the biographical information is heavily biased. The number of good, analytical book-length biographies of pharmacists is rather small; instead, we find a large number of short articles written to commemorate the accomplishments of an individual. An attempt was made in the abstracts to alert the readers to unbalanced presentations. Another problem with biographies is who to include. Our criteria were that the individual not be living and that his major accomplishments were significant for pharmacy. Although we tried to make sure all the individuals were pharmacists, sometimes the individual's significance for the history of pharmacy took precedence over professional status.

Pharmacy has always been composed of scientific, practical, and artistic elements. References that are included in the heading "Practice of Pharmacy" reflect the state of practice at the time and the "art" of pharmacy. The scientific side of pharmacy appears in articles in section 2b—Basic Pharmaceutical Disciplines. A discussion of the scientific disciplines that have been required for pharmacy naturally overlaps with discussion of the education of pharmacists (2c—Education) and the development of products and techniques (2c—Materia Medica and Drug Therapy). This latter category, not surprisingly, includes more citations than any other. Because it stands at the core of the practice of pharmacy, across chronological and geographical boundaries, materia medica has had the longest tradition of evaluation in the history of pharmacy. A chronological division of the literature appears here, separating the classical from the early modern period. Before 1600, the Galenic tradition in Western medicine prevailed in determining the appropriate drug or therapy, and the profession of pharmacy was tied closely to the medical profession. As new theoretical and professional systems developed, and the Galenic tradition gave way to "modern" scientific studies of the materia medica, the profession of pharmacy took on more independence. Thus, 1600 is a convenient dividing point in the history of materia medica.

Societal structures as well as scientific structures have had their effect on the development of the profession of pharmacy. Legal constraints (section 2d—Laws and Regulation) have determined not only what the pharmacist can do but also how it must be done. Some of the results of these regulations are reflected in the pharmaceutical literature, such as pharmacopeias (2e—Pharmaceutical Literature). In this section 2e we have deviated slightly from the general goal of only including secondary literature. Section 2e—Pharmaceutical Literature: Classics includes primary sources in the development of pharmaceutical literature, while the secondary studies are placed in section 2e—Historical Studies. Pharmacists have organized themselves into state, regional, or national groups as they took on the role of professionals. Their endeavors in this area are covered in 2f—Professional and Social Aspects, while the practical economic side of the profession is covered in 2g—Economic and Business Aspects. Pharmacy's self-identity is also linked to the ways its practitioners are trained: references on this topic are in section 2h—Education.

Introduction xi

The practical side of pharmacy can be seen not only in the way pharmacists work on the local scale but also in the large-scale presentation of pharmaceutical products to the public. Large-scale manufacturing of pharmaceutical products is a subject that has implications for the scientific, economic, and social impact of pharmacy. The history of this general topic appears in references in 2i—Manufacturing, while histories of specific companies appear in 1d—Company Histories. Equipment that the pharmacists uses, especially on the small scale, forms an integral part of the study of this profession. Studies of the techniques and equipment that have formed the backbone of pharmaceutical practice, as well as attempts to preserve this heritage, appear in 2j—Equipment and Museology. What the pharmacist does has not always been portrayed in the most positive light. Histories of patent medicines and the mis-representation of the scientific processes and goals in preparing and marketing medicines fall into the last category of part 2: Patent Medicines and Quackery.

Finally, the "art" of pharmacy has been reflected in the art of the period. Whether you view the structures that house the work of the pharmacist (3a—Architecture and Interior Design), images of the pharmacist or pharmacies as viewed by the public (3b—Painting, Sculpture, Graphic Arts, and Photography), or presentations of the pharmacist's profession in creative literature or music (3c—Creative Literature and 3d—Music), you can see how the profession of pharmacy has taken its place in society.

Acknowledgments

Any study that covers such a broad chronological and disciplinary range must rely on the help of experts in the field to accomplish the task. This help comes in many forms. The authors wish to thank the following Associate Editors, who contributed bibliographic citations as well as abstracts in their field of expertise: David Cowen, Marvin Fischbaum, William H. Helfand, Ramunas Kondratas, John Parascandola, Ernst Stieb, John Swann, James Whorton, and James Harvey Young. For additional support and consultation, we would like to thank Alex Berman, J. Worth Estes, John Riddle, and Eunice Bardell. Robert Multhauf offered his editorial advice, and we could not have accomplished this task without the excellent resources available in the University of Wisconsin Library system, and the help in checking references from Rosemary Zurlo-Cuva, Craig Anderson, and Alisa Risse. Without the generous institutional support of the American Institute of the History of Pharmacy, located at the University of Wisconsin School of Pharmacy, our participation in this project would have been impossible.

The History of Pharmacy

Part One: Bibliographies and General Studies

1a—Bibliographies, Encyclopedias, Dictionaries

1. Andrews, Theodora. *Guide to the Literature of Pharmacy and the Pharmaceutical Sciences*. Littleton, CO: Libraries Unlimited, 1986. viii + 383 pp., index.

   A useful reference but limited in coverage.

2. Artelt, Walter, et al., eds. *Index zur Geschichte der Medizin, Naturwissenschaft und Technik*. Erster Band. Munich: Urban and Schwarzenberg, 1953. 398 pp.

   The period 1945-48 is covered; a section is devoted to pharmacy. [See Steudel, citation #63 for Vol. 2.]

3. Austin, Robert B. *Early American Medical Imprints: A Guide to Works Printed in the United States 1668-1820*. Washington: U. S. Department of Health, Education and Welfare, 1961. x + 240 pp., chronological index.

   An alphabetical list of 2106 imprints with bibliographic descriptions, annotations, and library holdings. The microform Austin Collection contains most of the bibliography's monographs. For addendum, see *Journal of the History of Medicine and Allied Sciences* 20(1965): 59 ff.

4. *Bibliography of the History of Medicine.* Issued annually by the National Library of Medicine since 1964 and in five-year accumulations, viz: 1964-69, 1970-74, 1975-79, 1980-84, 1985-89: National Library of Medicine, 1964-.

    A comprehensive, world-wide bibliography that gives complete coverage to pharmacy.

5. Blake, John B., comp. *A Short Title Catalogue of Eighteenth Century Printed Books in the National Library of Medicine.* Bethesda: National Library of Medicine, 1979. 501 pp.

    Bibliographic details on the NLM collections arranged alphabetically by author but with some subject headings, e.g., "Pharmacopoeia." Contains some annotation and cross references.

6. Blake, John B., and Charles Roos, eds. *Medical Reference Works 1679-1966; A Selected Bibliography.* Chicago: Medical Library Association, 1967. viii + 343 pp., index.

    Although there is no special rubric "Pharmacy," this is still a useful guide.

7. Bouvet, Maurice. *Les traveaux d'histoire locale de la pharmacie en France des origines à ce jour. Répertoire Bibliographique.* Paris: Société d'Histoire de la Pharmacie, 1957. 43 pp.

    A list by French place names, although many citations are of more than local interest.

8. Buerki, Robert A. *Bibliography of Papers Published by the American Pharmaceutical Association's Section on Historical Pharmacy, 1904-1967.* Madison, WI: American Institute of the History of Pharmacy, n.d. 27 pp.

    Updates George Griffenhagen's 1957 bibliography.

9. *Bulletin signaletique*. 522 Histoires des Sciences et des Techniques. Paris: Centre National de la Recherche Scientifique, 1947-.

Bibliography in the history of science and technology, published three times a year (since 1947), with an annual index. Pharmacy is classified under "Medicine, Surgery; Pharmacy & Therapeutics."

10. Callisen, Adolf Carl Peter. *Medicinisches Shriftsteller-Lexicon*. 33 vols. Copenhagen: Köngl. Taubstummen Institut zu Schleswig, 1830-45.

A seminal source for publications before 1845; includes bibliographic descriptions, some commentary, biographic information on authors and citations to reviews of books listed. Second edition (1962-65, 33 vols.) is an unchanged photomechanical reprint of the 1830-45 edition.

11. Cordasco, Francesco. *American Medical Imprints 1820-1910. A Checklist of Publications Illustrating the History and Progress of Medical Science, Medical Education, and the Healing Arts in the United States* . . . 2 vols. Totowa, NJ: Rowman and Littlefield, 1985. 1654 pp., index.

A list of American imprints arranged by decades and alphabetically by author within each decade. Library holdings are included.

12. Cowen, David L. *A Bibliography of the History of Colonial and Revolutionary Medicine and Pharmacy*. Madison: American Institute of the History of Pharmacy, 1975. 16 pp.

Medicine and pharmacy are treated separately for the colonial period and together for the Revolutionary period. Books, monographs, and articles are included.

13. *Current Work in the History of Medicine*. London: Wellcome Institute for the History of Medicine, Jan./March 1954-.

A list of journal literature issued quarterly since 1954, arranged by subject and followed by an index of authors, addresses of authors, and a list of new books.

14. Dann, Georg Edmund, and Gregory J. Higby. "Bibliography of the Publications of George Urdang on his Birth Centenary." *Pharmacy in History* 24 (1982): 106-14.

    A list originally compiled by Georg Dann and updated by Gregory Higby.

15. Dunglison, Robley. *Medical Lexicon: A Dictionary of Medical Science*. 14th ed., rev. Philadelphia: Blanchard and Lea, 1856. 927 pp.

    Strong historical orientation and ready availability of copies make this a handy source for brief, quick information.

16. Durling, Richard J., comp. *A Catalogue of Sixteenth Century Books in the National Library of Medicine*. Bethesda: National Library of Medicine, 1967. xii + 698 pp., indexes.

    A primary source for bibliographic information on sixteenth-century works. An alphabetical list, with some annotations and cross references.

17. Engelmann, W. *Bibliotheca medico-chirurgica et pharmaceutico-chemica, oder Verzeichniss . . . Bücher, welcher vom Jahre 1750 bis zur Mitte des Jahres 1837 in Deutschland erschienen sind*. 5th ed., Leipzig: 1838. index.

    Pages 495-541 are a detailed A-Z listing of German pharmacochemical publications.

18. Erlen, Jonathon. *The History of the Health Care Sciences and Health Care 1700-1980: A Selective Annotated Bibliography*. New York: Garland, 1984. xvi + 1028 pp., index.

A list of books and articles, topically arranged. Topics include pharmacy, pharmacology, pharmacognosy, and pharmacopoeia, and there are references to pertinent materials in other categories. A précis of each item is provided.

19. Ferguson, John. *Bibliotheca Chemica, A Catalogue of the Alchemical, Chemical and Pharmaceutical Books in the Collection of the late James Young of Kelly and Durris, Esq., LL. D., F. R. S., F. R. S. E.* 2 vols. Glasgow: Maclehose, 1906. xxi + 487; 598 pp.

    A very rich list, alphabetically arranged by author, with exceptional biobibliographic annotations.

20. Folch Jou, Guillermo, and Sagrario Muñoz Calvo. *Catalogo de los documentos conservados en el Archivo de la Real Academia de Farmacia*. Annales de la Real Academia de Farmacia, No. 2, 1978, pp. 199-351. Madrid: Real Academia de Farmacia, 1978. index.

    A catalogue describing 1,290 documents.

21. Folch Jou, Guillermo, Sagrario Muñoz Calvo, and Victoria Núñez Varela. *Catálogo de los documentos conservados en el Archivo del Departmento de Historia de la Farmacia y Legislacíon Farmacéutica de la Facultad de Farmacia de Madrid*. Madrid: Universidad Complutense Facultad de Farmacia, 1982. x + 356 pp., index.

    Over 700 documents are listed and briefly described.

22. Garrison and Morton.

    see Norman, citation #49.

23. Garrison, Fielding H. "The Medical and Scientific Periodicals of the 17th and 18th Centuries." *Bulletin of the Institute of the History of Medicine* 2 (1934): 285-343.

A classic list arranged topically and chronologically, with bibliographic descriptions. Cf., Kronick, citation #40.

24. Geissler, Ewald, and Josef Moeller. *Real-encyclopädie der gesammten Pharmacie: Handwörterbuch für Apotheker, Ärtze und Medicinalbeamte.* 10 vols. Vienna: Urban and Schwarzenberg, 1886.

   A detailed, comprehensive reference work for late nineteenth-century pharmacy.

25. Guerra, Francisco. *American Medical Bibliography 1639-1783.* Yale University Department of the History of Science and Medicine, Publ. no. 40. New York: Lathrop C. Harper, 1962. 885 pp., illus., indexes.

   A comprehensive chronologically arranged listing of American imprints, including books, pamphlets, broadsides, almanacs, magazines, and newspapers. Descriptions, collations, library locations, and copious annotations are included, as are lists of reprints, facsimile editions, European publications of American originals, publications by American printed abroad, and indexes.

26. Guitard, Eugène-Humbert (ed). *Index des travaux d'histoire de la pharmacie de 1913 à 1963.* Paris: Société d'Histoire de la Pharmacie, n.d. 80 + 103 pp., illus.

   Index of publications of the Société d'Histoire de la Pharmacie (1913-63) with a 72-page introduction on the evolution of pharmacy.

27. Guitard, Eugène Humbert. *Manuel d'histoire de la littérature pharmaceutique . . . et Biobibliographie pharmaceutique.* Paris: Librairie Caffin (Collection Occitania), 1942. 138 pp.

   Index of the general history of pharmacy literature printed before 1860 (international before A.D. 1600 and then French to 1860).

28. Hamarneh, Sami. *Bibliography on Medicine and Pharmacy in Medieval Islam.* Veröffentlichungen der Internationalen Gesellschaft für Geschichte der Pharmazie e.V., NF 25. Stuttgart: Wissenschaftliche Verlagsgesellschaft, 1964. 204 pp., index, illus.

Provides annotated lists of books on medicine and pharmacy, on the history of Islamic civilization, and on reference books and bibliographies (all arranged alphabetically by author), and a list of then-current periodicals.

29. Hedges, Henry T. *A Polyglot Index of All the Principal Articles in the Materia Medica, in Latin, English, French, German, Swedish and Norwegian-Danish, with separate indexes referring to all . . .* Chicago: 1884. 295 pp.

Common names as well as pharmaceutical names of drugs. Tables and glossaries in back.

30. Hirsch, Rudolf (ed). *A Catalogue of the Manuscripts and Archives of the Library of the College of Physicians of Philadelphia.* Philadelphia: University of Pennsylvania Press, Francis Clark Wood Institute, College of Physicians of Philadelphia, 1983. xx + 259 pp., index.

A descriptive listing; considerable material is of interest to the history of pharmacy.

31. Hügel, Herbert. *Die Veröffentlichungen der (Internationalen) Gesellschaft für Geschichte der Pharmazie 1927-1952: Eine Bibliographie.* Veröffentlichungen der Internationalen Gesellschaft für Geschichte der Pharmazie, NF 7. Eutin: Internationale Gesellschaft für Geschichte der Pharmazie, 1955. 40 pp., author and subject indexes.

A listing of publications, with bibliographic notations, issued under the auspices of the Gesellschaft für Geschichte der Pharmazie and its successor (in 1949), the Internationale Gesellschaft für Geschichte der Pharmazie.

32. Hügel, Herbert. *Die Veröffentlichungen der Internationalen Gesellschaft für Geschichte der Pharmazie 1953-1965: Eine Bibliographie*. Veröffentlichungen der Internationalen Gesellschaft für Geschichte der Pharmazie, NF 29: 1967. 75 pp., author and subject indexes.

   A listing of publications, with bibliographic notations, issued under the auspices of the Gesellschaft für Geschichte der Pharmazie and its successor (in 1949), the Internationale Gesellschaft für Geschichte der Pharmazie. The contents of each of the first 30 *Bände* of the new series (*Neue Folge*) of the *Veröffentlichungen* are detailed, followed by listings of the contents of *Zur Geschichte der Deutschen Apotheke* (1933-39), of *Zur Geschichte der Pharmazie* (1949-1965), and of special publications.

33. *Index Catalogue of the Library of the Surgeon-General's Office, United States Army*. Washington, DC: United States Government Printing Office, in four series beginning 1880, 1896, 1918, 1936.

   Most historico-medical journals that were published are indexed. For help in using the catalog, there is an authoritative article available: Claudius Francis Mayer, "The index-catalogue as a tool of research in medicine and history," in *Science, Medicine and History*, E. Ashworth Underwood, ed.(Cambridge: Oxford University Press, 1953),Vol. 2, pp. 482-93.

34. *Isis Current Bibliography of the History of Science and Its Cultural Influences*. Issued as part of *ISIS*, now annually compiled by John Neu, previously under variant titles.

   Pharmacy and related fields are included in this international index.

35. James, Robert. *A Medicinal Dictionary, including Physic, Surgery, Anatomy, Chymistry, and Botany, with a History of Drugs*. 3 vols. London: 1743-45. illus.

Bibliographies, Encyclopedias, Dictionaries 11

>Detailed entries (with short-form literature references); exceptionally useful. Rare.

36. Jayawardene, S. A. (comp.). *Reference Books for the Historian of Science: A Handlist*. London: Science Museum, 1982. xiv + 229 pp., index.

    The annotated list is presented in three categories: The History of Science and its Sources, History and Related Subjects, and General Reference.

37. Julien, Pierre. *Catalogue de la collection d'anciens ouvrages de pharmacopée français et étrangers*. Paris: Ordre national des pharmaciens, 1967. 95 pp., index, illus.

    Bibliographic descriptions are divided first into general works published in France in three historic periods, then into French local pharmacopeias, and then into pharmacopeias of twenty-three countries other than France.

38. Krivatsy, Peter (comp). *A Catalogue of Incunabula and Sixteenth Century Printed Books in the National Library of Medicine*. First Supplement. Bethesda: National Library of Medicine, 1971. v + 51 pp.

    This supplement lists 27 incunabula and 271 sixteenth-century books not listed in previous NLM catalogues. There is a geographic index and an index of printers and publishers.

39. Krivatsy, Peter (comp). *A Catalogue of Seventeenth Century Printed Books in the National Library of Medicine*. Bethesda: National Library of Medicine, 1989. 1315 pp.

    Alphabetical listing of approximately 13,000 books printed between 1601 and 1700; includes a large number of pharmacopeias.

40. Kronick, David A. "The Fielding H. Garrison List of Medical and Scientific Periodicals of the 17th and 18th centuries; Addenda et corrigenda." *Bulletin of the History of Medicine* 32 (1958): 456-74.

   An intensive and extensive updating of the Garrison list. Cf. Garrison, citation #23.

41. Ledermann, François. *Bibliographie des ouvrages suisses de pharmacopée.* Veröffentlichungen der Schweizerischen Gesellschaft für Geschichte der Pharmazie, Band 3. Zürich: Juris Druck + Verlag, 1984. 135 pp.

   A list of 184 pharmacopeial works published in Switzerland with full titles, library locations, and bibliographic notations.

42. Lloyd, John Uri, Theodor Just, and Corinne Miller Simons. *Catalogue of the Pharmacopoeias, Dispensatories, Formularies and Allied Publications (1493-1957) in Lloyd Library.* Cincinnati: Lloyd Library and Museum, 1957. 42 pp., index [Reprint from *Lloydia* Vol. 20, No. 1, March, 1957.].

   A large list geographically arranged.

43. Mann, Gunter (ed). *Internationale Bibliographie zur Geschichte der Medizin, 1875-1901.* Hildesheim: George Olms Verlag, 1970. ix + 597 pp.

   A reprint of five bibliographies issued by Julius Pagel from 1898 to 1902 and of one issued by Theodor Puschmann and Robert Ritter von Töply in 1898.

44. Meyer, Minnie. "The Pharmaceutical Journals of the United States." *Journal of the American Pharmaceutical Association* 22 (1933): 424-29.

   Listing of American journals, by states, including obscure and local journals.

45. Miller, Genevieve. *Bibliography of the History of Medicine of the United States and Canada, 1939-1960. With a Historical Introduction by W. B. McDaniel, 2nd.* Baltimore: The Johns Hopkins Press, 1964. xvi + 428 pp., list of journals, index.

   A comprehensive bibliography, topically arranged, including pharmacy.

46. Multhauf, Robert P. *The History of Chemical Technology: An Annotated Bibliography.* New York & London: Garland, 1984.

   Includes a section on pharmaceuticals and some pharmaceutical manufacturing companies.

47. National Library of Medicine. *History of Medicine: A Guide to Sources of Information in the Reference and General Collection.* Joy S. Richmond, comp. Bethesda: Reference Section, National Library of Medicine, 1984. iii + 29 pp., index.

   A highly selective list of reference materials available in the Reference Collection of the Main Reading Room of the National Library of Medicine.

48. Neu, John, ed. *Chemical, Medical and Pharmaceutical Books Printed Before 1800 in the Collections of the University of Wisconsin Libraries.* Madison, WI: University of Wisconsin Press, 1965. 280 pp.

   Bibliographic descriptions of 4442 items in the University of Wisconsin Libraries are provided, but more recent titles are absent.

49. Norman, Jeremy M., ed. *Morton's Medical Bibliography: An Annotated Check-List of Texts Illustrating the History of Medicine (Garrison and Morton).* 5th ed. Brookfield, VT: The Scholar Press, 1991. 1243 pp., index of personal names and subjects.

An indispensable reference tool, although pharmacy is not treated extensively.

50. Ordre National des Pharmaciens. *Catalogue de la collection d'anciens ouvrages de pharmacopée Français et étrangers.* Paris: 1967. 95 pp., illus. index.

    Catalog of 524 titles, from the collection of Edmond Leclair (historian of pharmacy). Not strictly limited to pharmacopeias; includes official pharmacopeias, regional or national ones, as well as general and special texts (i.e., hospital formularies), from the fourteenth to the twentieth century, international in scope.

51. Parascandola, John, and Elizabeth Keeney. *Sources in the History of American Pharmacology.* Madison, WI: American Institute of the History of Pharmacy, 1983. 59 pp.

    A bibliography that traces pharmacology's institutionalization in the major estates of science (and in individual institutions in the case of academe), its presence among societies and journals, and brief biographical sketches for about two dozen prominent pharmacologists--including biographical bibliographies for each-- in the nascent years of the discipline.

52. *Pharmaziegeschichtliche Rundschau. Beilage zur Pharmazeutische Zeitung.* Frankfurt/M: 1949-87.

    Issued frequently but irregularly since 1949, these supplements to the *Pharmazeutische Zeitung* list and briefly abstract publications by country. Included are dissertations in the history of pharmacy and lists of reprints.

53. Poggendorff, Johann Christian. *Biographisch-Literarisches Handwörterbuch zur Geschichte der Exacten Wissenschaften.* 7 vols. Leipzig: Barth, 1863-1904. [Supplements published thereafter, with variant titles, in several volumes by various publishers, and currently in segments.].

Bibliographies, Encyclopedias, Dictionaries 15

A seminal source; includes eminent scientists coming from pharmacy.

54. Quincy, John. *Lexicon Physico-Medicum or A New Physical Dictionary...* London: 1719. 462 pp.

    Based largely on famous medical dictionary in Latin that is still much valued: Bartolomeo Castelli, *Lexicon Medicum...*, 1st ed. 1598, et. seq.

55. Sarton, George. *Introduction to the History of Science.* Baltimore: For Carnegie Institution of Washington by Williams & Wilkins, Co., 1927-48. 3 vols. in 5.

    A monumental work of descriptive bibliography covering up to 1500.

56. Schullian, Dorothy M., and Francis E. Sommer. *A Catalogue of Incunabula and Manuscripts in the Army Medical Library.* New York: Henry Schuman, ca. 1948. xiii + 361 pp., illus. index.

    A catalogue that describes each item carefully and provides some references to pertinent literature.

57. Sivin, Nathan. "A Cornucopia of Reference Works for the History of Chinese Medicine." *Chinese Science* 9 (1989): 29-52.

    Chinese Science is a journal edited by Nathan Sivin. This article, as the title implies, describes the virtual avalanche of reference works that have appeared primarily over the last decade. This is an essential reference.

58. Sivin, Nathan. "Science and Medicine in Imperial China--The State of the Field." *Journal of Asian Studies* 47 (1988): 41-90.

    A "state-of-the-field" article written by an author with access to scholarship from all the major centers of research on the history of Chinese medicine and science. It contains an important annotated bibliography (pp. 73-90).

59. Smit, Pieter. *History of the Life Sciences: An Annotated Bibliography.* New York: Hafner, 1974. xiv + 1071 pp., index.

    Bibliographic information on, and succinct descriptions of, over 4000 items.

60. Sonnedecker, Glenn, and Alex Berman. *Some Bibliographic Aids for Historical Writers in Pharmacy.* Madison, WI: American Institute of the History of Pharmacy, 1958. 15 pp. mimeo.

    A very selective bibliography covering (1) historical method, (2) bibliographic aids in the history of pharmacy, (3) sources of biographical data, (4) bibliographic aids in the history of hospital pharmacy, (5) surveys in the history of pharmacy, and (6) publications of the American Pharmaceutical Association.

61. Sonnedecker, Glenn, and Gregory J. Higby. *Bibliography on the History of Dosage Forms.* Madison, WI: American Institute of the History of Pharmacy, n.d. (ca. 1983). 10 pp., mimeographed.

    A listing of the journal literature on dosage forms.

62. Sonnedecker, Glenn, and Gregory J. Higby. *Pharmacy in the Individual States: A Selective Historical Bibliography.* Madison, WI: American Institute of the History of Pharmacy, 1984. rev. 1991. 19 pp., mimeo.

    A list of books, journal articles, and archival sources, by state.

63. Steudel, Johannes, et al. *Index zur Geschichte der Medizin und Biologie.* Zweiter Band. Munich: Urban & Schwarzenberg, 1966. vii + 312 pp.

An international, topical, cross-referenced, listing of over 7000 items in the historical literature of 1949-1951/52, with an index of personal names. Also includes some biographies. Cf. Artelt, citation #2.

64. Styran, Roberta, and Andrew Watson. "Books of 'Materia Medica in Toronto Libraries: Herbals, Books of Simples and Compounds, Formularies, Pharmacopoeias, etc. 300 B.C. to 1800 A.D." *Renaissance and Reformation* 6, no. 2 (1969-70): 16-35.

Analytic, bibliographic historical information of works held in seven Toronto libraries is presented in a narrative fashion, organized by time period and subject matter.

65. Thoms, Hermann, and Josef Moeller. *Realenzyklopädie der gesamten Pharmazie: Handwörterbuch für Apotheker, Ärzte und Medizinalbeamte.* 2nd ed., 14 vols. Berlin: Urban & Schwarzenberg, 1904-1914.

See Geissler, E., citation #24. A detailed, comprehensive reference work for early twentieth-century pharmacy.

66. Urdang, George. "History, Ethics, and Literature of Pharmacy: A Select Bibliography." *American Journal of Pharmaceutical Education* 8 (1944): 491-503.

Includes many items not usually found listed in bibliographies.

67. Valverde, José Luis. *Bibliografía Española de historia de la farmacia.* Vol. 1 [all issued], Granada: Universidad de Granada, 1971. [ix] + 120 pp.

Bibliographic information is provided on 1500 items with no particular arrangement but augmented by full subject, author, and biographical indexes.

68. Valverde, José Luis. "Orientacion bibliografica basica para la historia de farmacia." *Ars Pharmacéutica* 17, no. 1 (1976): 117-48.

   Bibliographic essays on history, history of science, and history of medicine are followed by a substantial essay on the bibliography of the history of pharmacy world wide. There is also a listing of general histories of pharmacy and national histories of pharmacy arranged by country.

69. Valverde, José Luis, Teresa Bautista, and Ma Teresa Montaña. *Libros de interés histórico-médico-farmaceútico conservados en la Biblioteca de la Real Academia de Medicina de Sevilla.* [Granada]: Universidad Granada, 1980. xiii + 130 pp.

   Sixth in a series of monographs by the University of Granada about the pharmaceutical works in archives and libraries in Spain. Earlier volumes deal with other collections.

70. Valverde, José Luis, and Rafael Garcia Serrano. *Coleccion documental de interés histórico-farmacéutico conservada en el Archivo General de Navarra.* Granada: Universidad de Granada, 1979. 158 pp., index.

   Following a considerable historical discussion of pharmacy in Navarre, 822 documents are described.

71. Valverde, José Luis, and Del Carmen Vidal. *Coleccion documental historico-farmacéutica (1) Catálago de documentos de interés histórico-farmacéutico conservados en el Archivo del Palacio National de Madrid.* Granada: Universidad de Granada, 1971. xiv + 266 pp.

   Over 4000 documents are described and their identifying numbers given. [not seen].

72. Vester, Helmut. *Deutsche pharmaziehistorische Bibliographie.* Eutin: Vesters Archiv, 1956. xii + 474 pp.

Bibliographies, Encyclopedias, Dictionaries 19

Despite the date on the title page, the volume combines four issues (NF 9, 14, 17, 19) of the *Veröffentlichungen der Internationalen Gesellschaft für Geschichte der Pharmazie* that appeared between 1956 and 1961 under the title *Topographische Literatursammlung zur Geschichte der deutschen Apotheken*. The first, and major part of the volume is arranged by localities, the second by German lands and provinces, the third covers works pertaining to the German Empire.

73. Wankmüller, Armin. "Hinweise zur Literatur für die Pharmaziegeschichte." *Beiträge zur Geschichte der Pharmazie* (through 1989, thereafter the title is *Geschichte der Pharmazie*): 1. Germany, Bd. 31 Nr. 7 (1980): 55; 2. German serial publications, Bd. 31 Nr. 11 (1981):86; 3. Periodicals in German-speaking countries (1901-1975), Bd. 31 Nr. 14 (1982): 110-11; 4. Books on industrial products since 1900, Bd. 31 Nr. 15 (1982): 117-18; 5. U. S. A. 1940-1975 [with D. L. Cowen], Bd. 31 Nr. 20 (1983): 163-65; 6. Pharmacopoeias in German-speaking countries, 1801-1900, Bd. 31 No. 25 (1984): 218-20; 7. Norway [with Y. Torud], Bd. 31 Nr. 36/37 (1987): 315; 8. Pharmaceutical industry house organs(1850-1975), Jg. 41 Nr. 4 (1989): 38-40; 9. Doctoral dissertations in the history of pharmacy, in German, 1930-1980, Jg. 42 Nr. 1(1990):5-9.

Published in the supplement to *Deutsche Apotheker Zeitung*, this bibliography is scattered over the years, designed to give overviews of the literature in each category, occasionally with annotations.

74. Wankmüller, Armin. "Pharmazeutische Zeitschriften in der deutschen pharmazeutischen Zentralbibliotek." *Pharmazeutische Zeitung* 121, no. No. 10 (1976): 322-25.

An alphabetical list of the pharmaceutical journals in the German Pharmaceutical Library in the state library at Stuttgart.

75. Waring, Edward John. *Bibliotheca Therapeutica, or Bibliography of Therapeutics, chiefly in Reference to Articles of the Materia Medica, with Numerous Critical, Historical and Therapeutical Annotations, and an Appendix Containing the Bibliography of*

> *British Mineral Waters.* 2 vols. London: New Sydenham Society, 1878-79. xx + 933 pp., index.
>
> A comprehensive listing arranged topically (e.g., General Therapeutics; Preparation, Uses and Modus Operandi of Medicines) and a bibliography individually of 427 articles of the materia medica. Within each category, the arrangement is chronological. There are Indexes of Diseases and of Authors. Still an indispensable bibliography on therapeutics up to 1878.

76. Wittop Koning, Dirk A. "Farmaceutisch-historische bibliografie van Nederland." *Pharmaceutisch Weekblad* 91, September 22 (1956): 705-20.

    A list, almost entirely of journal articles, on the history of pharmacy in the Netherlands on the national level and then by locality.

1b—General Historical Literature and Historiography

77. Berendes, Julius. *Geschichte der Pharmazie.* Leipzig: E. Gunther, 1898. 80 pp.

    Limited to ancient Egyptian and Semitic cultures.

78. Berendes, Julius. *Die Pharmacie bei den alten Culturvölkern: historisch-kritische Studien . . .* 2 vols. in 1. Halle: Tausch & Grosse, 1891. 308 pp.; 220 pp. index.

    Well-documented and indexed. Includes material on trade. A broader time period was surveyed by Berendes in his *Das Apothekenwesen; seine Entstehung und geschichtliche Entwicklung bis zum XX Jahrhundert.* Stuttgart, 1907.

79. Berman, Alex. "The Problem of Science in Nineteenth-Century French Pharmaceutical Historiography." In *Actes du dixième*

Congress internationale d'histoire des sciences. pp. 891-94. Paris, 1964.

The give and take interaction between science and pharmacy in nineteenth-century France are discussed in this essay.

80. Berman, Alex, ed. *Pharmaceutical Historiography.* Madison: American Institute of the History of Pharmacy, 1967. 145 pp.

   Colloquium proceedings that include discussions of contributions to historiography of George Urdang and others and discussions of writing in the history of pharmacy in France, Great Britain, and the United States. Medieval Arabic pharmaceutical literature and aspects of medical historiography are also discussed.

81. Conci, Giulio. *Pagine di storia della farmacia.* Milan: 1934. 351 pp.

   Organized topically; documented, but with no bibliography or index.

82. Cowen, David L. "Pharmacy and Civilization." *American Journal of Pharmaceutical Education* 22 (1958): 70-76.

   Shows how the history of civilization can be understood via a history of pharmacy, which reflects cultural, scientific, and religious developments of a particular time and place.

83. Cowen, David L. "Pharmacy and Freedom." *Pharmacy in History* 26 (1984): 70-82.

   Looks at professional pharmaceutical standards throughout history, using the concept of freedom for individual pharmacists and for the profession.

84. Cowen, David L., and William H. Helfand. *Pharmacy: An Illustrated History*. New York: Harry N. Abrams, Inc., 1990. 272 pp., illus.

With 308 illustrations (half in color) drawn from sources ranging from archaeological artifacts to photographs of contemporary practices, including pharmacies, equipment, portraits, paintings, prints, postcards, caricatures and advertisements, along with a thorough text covering the major events in pharmaceutical history.

85. Debus, Allen G. "History with a Purpose: The Fate of Paracelsus." *Pharmacy in History* 26 (1984): 83-96.

Historiographic review of the changing views of Paracelsus and his role in the development of pharmacy.

86. Debus, Allen G. "The Pharmaceutical Revolution of the Renaissance." *Clio Medica* 11 (1976): 307-17.

The incorporation of chemistry into pharmacy during the sixteenth and seventeenth centuries is discussed. Article is a summary of the author's *The Chemical Philosophy*.

87. Debus, Allen G. "Quantification and Medical Motivation: Factors in the Interpretation of Early Modern Chemistry." *Pharmacy in History* 31 (1989): 3-11.

In his evaluation of early modern chemistry, Debus stresses the importance of medicinal chemistry over quantification.

88. Doyle, Paul A. *Readings in Pharmacy*. New York: John Wiley & Sons, Inc., 1962.

This textbook contains fifty readings for pharmacy students divided into eight parts: introduction, history, biographies, international pharmacy, drug discovery, education, issues in pharmacy, and pharmacy in the arts. Several of the readings are now quite dated, but some of them are excellent primary sources, such as John Uri Lloyd's memoirs of his apprenticeship and J. Edgar Hoover's provocatively titled, "The Druggist, Secret Agent of the FBI."

89. Earles, Melvin P. "Early Scientific Studies of Drugs and Poison." *Pharmaceutical Journal* 188 (1962): 47-51.

   Outlines the difficulties of evaluating drug action in the seventeenth century, based on the available scientific information and techniques. As a result, the materia medica remained largely unchanged, despite advances in other scientific areas.

90. Ganzinger, Kurt, ed. *Die Vorträge des International Pharmaziehistorischen Kongresses Innsbruck 1977*. Veröffentlichungen der Internationalen Gesellschaft für Geschichte der Pharmazie, e.V., Bd. 47. Stuttgart: Wissenschaftliche Verlagsgesellschaft, 1979. 213 pp.

   Historiography of the history of pharmacy in a number of countries as well as general discussion by various authors.

91. Gaude, Werner. *Alte Apotheke: Eine tausendjahrige Kulturgeschichte*. 2nd ed. Stuttgart: Deutscher Apotheker Verlag, 1986. 222 pp., illus., index.

   Well-illustrated general history of the profession of pharmacy, the pharmacy, and its contents. Primarily German.

92. Grier, James. *A History of Pharmacy*. London: Pharmaceutical Press, 1937. 274 pp., index.

   Designed as a textbook, this work covers the early history of pharmacy in a general way and spends more time on post-seventeenth-century history, with a focus on the development of the profession in England.

93. Matthews, Leslie G. *The Pepperers, Spicers and Apothecaries of London During the Thirteenth and Fourteenth Centuries.*

London: Society of Apothecaries of London, 1980. 63 pp., illus.

A booklet that examines the activities of the three trade groups from which English pharmacy would evolve as a separate profession (with the founding of The Worshipful Society of Apothecaries, in 1617).

94. Needham, Joseph, et al. *Science and Civilisation in China.* 7 volumes projected. Cambridge: Cambridge University Press, 1954-.

Joseph Needham, the patriarch of historians of Chinese medicine and science, now in his nineties, continues to be the driving force behind his self-styled "gigantic enterprise." This work, begun nearly forty years ago and originally intended to be contained in seven volumes, has grown into a mammoth fifteen fascicles so far and is still growing. The works of particular value to the history of pharmacy are volume five, which deals with all aspects of chemistry and volume six, which deals with biology. Volume six, subsection 45 (forthcoming) will deal with the history of pharmaceutics. All volumes contain extensive bibliographies of both Asian and Western sources.

95. Roeske, W. "Geschichte der Pharmaziehistorik in Polen." In *Vorträge des Internationalen Pharmaziehistorischen Kongresses Innsbruck 1977.* pp. 155-61. Stuttgart: Wissenschaftliche Verlagsgesellschaft, Bd. 47, 1979.

The author's earlier publication, "The Bibliography of the Polish Pharmaceutical Historiography (1861-1971)" [in Polish], 1973, contains a list of all the history of pharmacy literature in Poland. Here in this publication, he only outlines the main historical investigations.

96. Scarborough, John. "Texts and Sources in Ancient Pharmacy." *Pharmacy in History* 29 (1987): 81-84; 133-39.

Reviews recent literature dealing with ancient drug lore. Translations and editions of source material from the ancient

Near East and Greece, as well as poetic sources and fragments from the Hellenistic period are discussed in this extensive bibliographic essay.

97. Schelenz, Hermann. *Geschichte der Pharmazie*. Berlin: J. Springer, 1904. 935 pp., bibl., index.

    A monumental reference work; still widely useful. Covers antiquity to Middle Ages by culture areas and by centuries. Painstaking documentation; bibliography; detailed index.

98. Shryock, Richard Harrison. *The Development of Modern Medicine: An Interpretation of the Social and Scientific Factors Involved*. New York: Knopf, 1947; reprint, Madison: University of Wisconsin Press, 1979. 473 pp., index.

    Studies the many factors that contribute to the development of medicine from 1600 to the 1930s. Looks at American developments.

99. Sonnedecker, Glenn (revisor). *Kremers and Urdang's History of Pharmacy*. 4th ed. Philadelphia: Lippincott, 1976; repr. ed. Madison: American Institute of the History of Pharmacy, 1986. 556 pp. + index. illus.

    The most comprehensive reference work in English on the history of pharmacy. Fully documented with useful appendices, including a historical glossary, this work is an appropriate starting place for many inquires. The first half of the text covers the development of the pharmaceutical profession in Europe from its ancient and medieval antecedents. The second half charts the course of American pharmacy, using a topical structure that facilitates further reading and research. Published in 1976, the book is becoming somewhat dated.

100. Wootton, A. C. *Chronicles of Pharmacy*. London: Macmillan, 1910;Tuckahoe, NY: USV Pharmaceutical Corp., 1972. 2 vols.

A useful pot pourri; indexed. No documentation or bibliography except abbreviated citations in text.

1c—National Studies

101. Fehlmann, Hans-Rudolf, and Cora Hartmeier-Sutter (eds.). *Panorama der Pharmaziegeschichte: 13 Themen aus 12 Ländern.* Veröffentlichungen der Schweizerischen Gesellschaft für Geschichte der Pharmazie, Band 7. Zurich: Juris Druck & Verlag, 1987. 115 pp.

    Articles in several languages; includes information on South Africa, Netherlands, Moldavia, Egypt, Spain, Hungary, China, and New Guinea.

1c—National Studies: Africa

102. Carlson, D. G. "Drug Supply Systems in West Africa: A Historical Overview with Particular Reference to Nigeria." *Pharmacy in History* 24 (1982): 73-82.

    Covers British influence on pharmaceutical supply system in Africa and the subsequent effect of independence on the system.

1c—National Studies: Arabic

103. Ali, Mohammad, and J. S. Qadry. "Contributions of Arabs to Pharmacy." *Studies in the History of Medicine* 6 (1982): 43-53.

    Review of major contributors to Arabic pharmacy from the ninth through the twelfth centuries, as well as a description of Arabic contributions to pharmacy in general. Contains minimal documentation.

104. Hamarneh, Sami. "A History of Arabic Pharmacy." *Physis* 14 (1972): 5-54.

Describes development of pharmacy as a distinct profession, up to the twelfth century, focussing on the contributions to the literature and nature of the discipline.

1c—National Studies: Argentina

105. Cignoli, Francisco. *Historia de la farmacia argentina*. Rosario: Librería y Editorial Ruiz, 1953. 403 pp., index, appendices, bibl.

    Covers education, legal aspects of pharmacy, and literature. Brings the comprehensive history up to the twentieth century, with detailed notes.

1c—National Studies: Australia

106. Feehan, H. V., and G. N. Vaughan. "100 Years of 'Modern' Pharmacy in Australia, 1881-1981." *Pharmacy International* 2 (1981): 149-51.

    Emphasis is on early schools of pharmacy in Australia, with particular focus on the Victorian College of Pharmacy (celebrating its centennial).

107. Haines, Gregory. *Pharmacy in Australia: The National Experience*. Sydney: Australian Pharmaceutical Publishing Company for the Pharmaceutical Society of Australia, 1988. 433 pp., illus., bibl., index.

    Lively presentation of the history of pharmacy in Australia, from the early years to the period of developing national organization. Includes many photos, appendices with the code of ethics, and an editorial on improving pharmacy education.

108. Haines, Gregory. *"The Grains and Threepenn'worths of Pharmacy": Pharmacy in New South Wales, 1788-1976*. Kilmore, Victoria:

Pharmaceutical Society of New South Wales, 1976. 335 pp., illus., bibl., index.

Covers the legal, commercial, ethical, and political aspects of pharmacy in New South Wales, with a focus on the influence of British heritage as well as the life and circumstances of the colony on the developing profession.

109. Lloyd, Alistair. "Pharmacy in the Australian Colonies—The British Influence." *Pharmaceutical Historian* 18(4) and 19(1) (1988 and 1989): 7-8 and 6-8.

Very general; abstract of a paper presented at a conference. Demonstrates the influence of the United Kingdom on Australian pharmacy through two administrators of the late nineteenth-, early twentieth-century pharmacy organization. No notes.

1c—National Studies: Austria

110. Zekert, Otto, and Kurt Ganzinger. *Beiträge zur Geschichte der Pharmazie in Österreich.* Veröffentlichungen der Internationalen Gesellschaft für Geschichte der Pharmazie e.V., N.F. 18. Vienna: Oesterreichische Gesellschaft für Geschichte der Pharmazie, 1961. 125 pp., illus.

Ten articles covering topics on Austrian history of pharmacy, Austrian pharmacists, and pharmacies.

1c—National Studies: Belgium

111. Guislain, André. *Contribution à l'histoire de la pharmacie en Belgique sous le régime français (1794-1814).* Brussels: Impr. Dioncre, 1959. 174 pp., illus., index, bibl.

Examines history of pharmacy in Belgium during this era of French control. The changes that took place in pharmacy are viewed not as an aberration of the traditional order, but in terms

National Studies

of great changes in the profession where the imposition of laws unified the profession.

1c—National Studies: Brazil

112. Araujo, Carlos da Silva. *Figuras e factos na história da farmácia no Brasil português*. Lisbon: Editorial Império, 1954. 87 pp., bibl.

    Outlines the Portuguese influence on the pharmacy profession in Brazil, including their introduction of new plants, and pharmaceutical legislation.

113. Araujo, Carlos da Silva. *L'Influence française sur la culture brésilienne, sur la pharmacie et la médicine en particulier*. Rio de Janeiro: Grafico Olimpica Editora, 1973. 88 pp., illus., ports., bibl.

    Brief review of French influence on Brazilian pharmacy.

1c—National Studies: Britain

114. Bell, Jacob, and Theophilus Redwood. *Historical Sketch of the Progress of Pharmacy in Great Britain*. London: Butler & Tanner, Printed for the Pharmaceutical Society of Great Britain, 1880. 383 pp. + index.

    The first 143 pages written by Bell in 1842 was an introduction to the *Pharmaceutical Journal*, with the remaining pages composed by Redwood in 1880 to cover the years 1841 to 1868.

115. Cooper, Norman. "The Development of a Pharmaceutical Profession in Ireland." *Pharmacy in History* 29 (1987): 165-76.

    Condensed chronological outline of the growth of pharmacy as a profession in Ireland, covering the period from the seventeenth century to the early twentieth century.

116. Matthews, Leslie G. *History of Pharmacy in Britain.* Edinburgh: Livingstone, 1962. 427 pp., illus., bibl., index.

Comprehensive classic history covering the profession from Roman times to the modern world. Covers literature, biography, equipment and manufacturing, and education.

117. Trease, George Edward. *Pharmacy in History.* London: Ballière, Tindall and Cox, 1964. vii + 264 pp., illus., index.

The role of the purveyors of drugs in England is placed within a broader historical context. The book provides detailed coverage of the thirteenth through eighteenth centuries, with relatively summary treatment of more recent events.

1c—National Studies: Canada

118. McDougall, D. (ed). *History of Pharmacy in Manitoba, 1878-1953.* Winnipeg: Manitoba Pharmaceutical Association, 1954. 190 pp.

General history of pharmacy in this province, with material on educational history, the development of pharmacy in individual towns of rural Manitoba, and biographical sketches.

119. *One Hundred Years of Pharmacy in Canada (1867-1967).* Toronto: Canadian Academy of the History of Pharmacy, 1969. 38 pp.

Contains three articles to commemorate the centennial, with Glenn Sonnedecker covering "Education," Ernst W. Stieb on "Organization," and David R. Kennedy on "Legislation" for the period under consideration.

120. Raison, Arnold (ed). *A Brief History of Pharmacy in Canada.* Toronto, Canada: Canadian Pharmaceutical Association, [1969]. 113 pp.

National Studies 31

History of education in each of the provinces is dealt with in a section (pp. 30-90) that deals with the history of pharmacy across Canada. Undocumented and with names of original authors removed.

121. Stieb, Ernst W. "Some Branches of Canadian Pharmacy's Family Tree—How They Sprouted and Grew." *Canadian Pharmaceutical Journal* 115, no. 10 (1982): 374-79.

    A series of short histories, including some related to education, such as the Association of Faculties of Pharmacy of Canada, the Canadian Foundation for Pharmacy, the Pharmacy Examining Board of Canada, and the Canadian Association of Pharmacy Students and Interns.

122. Wilson, Eugene. "How Pharmacy Developed in the Shadow of Parliament Hill." *Canadian Pharmaceutical Journal* 115, no. 10 (1982): 369-73.

    Development of pharmacy in Ottawa. Includes biographical information from interviews.

1c—National Studies: China

123. Bretschneider, Emile V. "Botanicon Sinicum: Botanical Investigations into the Materia Medica of the Ancient Chinese." *Journal of the North China Branch, Royal Asiatic Society* NS29, no. 1-623 (1895):

    Dr. Bretschneider (1833-1901) was a polymath of the late nineteenth century who served as physician to the Russian Legation in Peking from 1866-1883. Joseph Needham claims "No one can do anything on the history of Chinese botany without a copy of his *Botanicon Sinicum* on one's desk...." See Needham, *Science and Civilisation in China* (citation #94), Vol. VI:1 for an extended bibliography of Bretschneider's work.

124. Unschuld, Paul U. *Medicine in China: A History of Pharmaceutics*. Comparative Studies of Health Systems and Medical Care 14. Berkeley: University of California Press, 1968.

This is a significant work on the pharmaceutical literature written by a prominent historian of Chinese pharmacy and medicine. Unschuld provides a wealth of information on the most important works of materia medica from earliest times to the present. This is a revised and expanded edition of *Pen-ts'ao. 2000 Jahre traditionelle pharmazeutische Literatur Chinas*, Munich, 1973. The German edition published by H. Moos contains some beautiful illustrations not reproduced in the American edition.

125. Unschuld, Paul U. "The Development of Medical-Pharmaceutical Thought in China." *Comparative Medicine East and West* 5, no. 2 (1977): 109-15; 5(1977):211-31.

Excerpt of a translation and adaptation of the *Pen-ts'ao—200 Years of Chinese Pharmaceutical Literature*. [not seen].

1c—National Studies: Cuba

126. García Hernández, Manuel, and Susana Martinez-Fortun y Foyo. *Apuntes históricos relativos a la farmacia en Cuba*. Cuadernos de Historia de la Salud Publica, 33. Havana: 1967. 71 pp.

Outline history of pharmacy in Cuba, in the context of public health. Includes important names and dates in Cuban pharmacy.

1c—National Studies: Egypt

127. El-Gammal, Samir Yahia. "Ancient Egyptian Pharmacy." *Veröffentlichungen der Schweizerischen Gesellschaft für Geschichte der Pharmazie* 7 (1987): 37-50.

Very general history with no documentation.

1c—National Studies: France

128. André-Pontier, L. *Histoire de la pharmacie: Origines, moyen age, temps modernes.* Paris: 1900. 729 pp., illus., index.

    Primarily a history of French pharmacy before 1900, covering individual regions of France as well as general history of the country. There is a section on foreign countries (pp. 565-645).

129. Bouvet, Maurice. *Histoire de la pharmacie en France des origines à nos jours.* Paris: Editions Occitania, 1937. 445 pp., illus., bibl., index.

    Considers various aspects of the history of pharmacy in France, including discussion of specific medications, development of the profession, commercial, and legal aspects of pharmacy. Some interesting illustrations and colored plates.

130. Debus, Allen G. "The Paracelsians in Eighteenth-Century France: A Renaissance Tradition in the Age of Enlightenment." *Ambix* 28 (1981): 35-54.

    Alchemy and Paracelsian medicine continued to have an influence in eighteenth-century chemistry. This understanding is useful as a background to nineteenth-century chemistry.

131. Dulieu, Louis. *La Pharmacie à Montpellier de ses origines à nos jours.* Avignon: Les Presses Universelles, 1973. 343 pp., illus., bibl., index.

    Extensively documented piece about pharmacy in Montpellier. This book includes biographical information on apothecaries and pharmacists from the Middle Ages to the twentieth century.

132. Fabre, R., and Georges Dillemann. *Histoire de la pharmacie.* Paris: Presses Universitaires de France, 1971. 126 pp., bibl.

A condensed general history of pharmacy that includes the history of French pharmacy organizations.

133. Laurent, Jean. *La Pharmacie en France: Etude de géographie economique*. Paris: 1959. 254 pp., illus., bibl.

    From a thesis about the pharmaceutical industry c.1957, and its demographics and statistics. Prices, specific drug products, and manufacturing are discussed. The third section deals with the pharmaceutical industry.

134. Liot, Andre. *Les apothicaires Dieppois du XVIe au XIX siècle*. Rouen: 1912. 88 pp.

    Professional organization of pharmacists.

135. Phillippe, A. *Histoire des apothicaires chez les principaux peuples du monde . . .* Paris: Publicité Médicale, 1853. 452 pp.

    The first full-length general history of pharmacy to be published in France. Deals mostly with French pharmacy. Still useful, but flawed.

136. Prevet, François. *Histoire de l'organisation sociale en pharmacie*. Paris: Recueil Sirey, 1940. 878 pp., bibl., index.

    A valuable source of information on the organizational and legal structure of pharmacy in France, especially relating to the numerous apothecary guilds of the Old Regime.

1c—National Studies: Germany

137. Adlung, Alfred, and George Urdang. *Grundriss der Geschichte der deutschen Pharmazie*. Berlin: J. Springer, 1935. 647 pp., tables.

This important history includes extensive tables summarizing and listing laws, taxes, and the different kinds of pharmaceutical literature in Germany from the twelfth century to the early twentieth century.

138. Dann, Georg Edmund. *Einführung in die Pharmaziegeschichte.* Stuttgart: Wissenschaftliche Verlagsgesellschaft, 1975. 127 pp., illus., bibl., index.

    The emphasis of this brief historical survey is on German pharmacy, especially sixteenth century to twentieth century. Includes chronology of pharmacy literature, including periodicals.

139. Hickel, Erika. *Apotheken, Arzneimittel, und Naturwissenschaften in Braunschweig, 1677-1977.* Braunschweig: Hagenmarkt-Apotheke, 1977. 81 pp., bibl.

    History interspersed with pictures and documents.

140. *Quellen und Studien zur Geschichte der Pharmazie.* 1960-.

    Monograph series published by the Wissenschaftliche Verlagsgesellschaft, usually dealing with the history of German pharmacy, although the general history of pharmacy is also included.

141. Telle, Joachim, ed. *Pharmazie und der gemeine Mann: Hausarznei und Apotheker in der frühen Neuzeit.* 1982. 154 pp., illus., index.

    Seven articles on different aspect of medical care and the common man (sixteenth and seventeenth century), including pharmacy. Also includes illustrations and catalog of publications and artifacts.

1c—National Studies: India

142. Srivastava, G. P. *History of Indian Pharmacy.* 2nd ed. Calcutta: Pindars, 1954. ports., bibl., index.

    With foreword by George Urdang. This volume only covers ancient and medieval pharmacy. Descriptions of pharmaceutical apparatus and preparations used in early pharmacies as well as background to pharmaceutical literature.

1c—National Studies: Indonesia

143. Tan, Sian Nio. *Zur Geschichte der Pharmazie in Niederländisch-Indien (Indonesien): 1602-1945.* Quellen und Studien zur Geschichte der Pharmazie, 15. Würzburg: Jal-Verlag, 1976. 274 pp., appendices, illus. notes, bibl., index.

    History of pharmacy during the Dutch colonial period. Includes names and dates of pharmacists in Indonesia in the nineteenth and twentieth centuries.

1c—National Studies: Italy

144. Palmer, R. "Medical Botany in Northern Italy in the Renaissance." *Journal of the Royal Society of Medicine* 78, no. 149-57 (1985):

    Botany was one of the most lively and fast-moving disciplines associated with sixteenth-century medicine. Its appeal extended to medicine, pharmacy, and others outside the profession.

145. Palmer, R. "Pharmacy in the Republic of Venice in the Sixteenth Century." In *The Medical Renaissance of the Sixteenth Century.* ed. A. Wear, R. K. French, and I. M. Lonie, pp. 100-117. Cambridge: Cambridge University Press, 1985.

    Examines the influence of botany and chemical medicine on pharmacy in Venice. He shows pharmacists' strong interest in botanical research, and the entrance of chemical medicine through the techniques employed.

146. Rubiola, Carlo. *La periode française du Piémont et son influence sur la pharmacie (1798-1814)*. Turin: Edizioni la Farmacia nuova, 1975. 108 pp., illus., bibl.

    Well-written and informative. Provides a valuable historical insight into Franco-Italian pharmacy.

1c—National Studies: Japan

147. Okazaki, Kanzo. *The Pharmaceutical History of Japan*. Tokyo: Naito Foundation, 1979. 85 pp.

    General overview of historical periods in Japan, the rise of Dutch science in Japan, and nineteenth- and twentieth-century influences. No documentation.

1c—National Studies: Latin America

148. Gicklhorn, Renée. *Missionsapotheker: Deutsche Pharmazeuten im Lateinamerika des 17. und 18. Jahrhunderts*. Veröffentlichungen der Internationalen Gesellschaft für Geschichte der Pharmazie e.V., N.F., Band 39. Stuttgart: Wissenschaftliche Verlagsgesellschaft, 1973. 111 pp., illus., bibl.

    Discusses German Jesuit "mission pharmacists" in South America, Mexico, and the Philippines. The nature of colonial pharmacy in the seventeenth and eighteenth centuries as well as individuals and the works are surveyed.

1c—National Studies: Malta

149. Cassar, Paul. "Impact of British Pharmacy in Malta." *Pharmaceutical Historian* 8, no. 1 (1978): 2-4.

Reviews the British influence on Maltese pharmacy (nineteenth and twentieth centuries), in terms of structure, literature, and professionalism.

1c—National Studies: Mexico

150. Elferink, Jan G. R. "Pharmacy and the Pharmaceutical Profession in the Aztec Culture." *Janus* 71 (1984): 41-62.

    Based on chroniclers' writings about Aztec culture, the author places pharmacists (as sellers of medicinal products as well as users and preparers of the products) in the context of their society and religion.

151. Perez, Valentin Islas, and Juan Francisco Sanchez Ruiz. *Breve historia de la farmacia en Mexico y en el mundo*. Mexico: Asociación Farmacéutica Mexicana, 1992. 188 pp., bibl., illus.

    Although lacking documentation (other than a five-page bibliography) this book fills a gap in knowledge about the meaning of "pharmacist" in Aztec culture as well as presenting a general history of pharmacy in Mexico.

1c—National Studies: New Zealand

152. Combes, Reg. *Pharmacy in New Zealand: Aspects and Reminiscences*. Auckland: Ray Richards, 1981. 249 pp., illus., bibl., index.

    Not intended as a definitive history, this collection of records from colonial times to 1980 gives a first-hand view of pharmacy in New Zealand.

1c—National Studies: Romania

153. Lipan, Visile I. *Geschichte der rumänischen Pharmazie in der Moldau und der Walachei bis zum Jahre 1921*. Braunschweiger Veröffentlichungen zur Geschichte der Pharmazie und der Naturwissenschaften, 28. Braunschweig: Deutschen Apotheker Verlag, 1985. 413 pp., notes, bibl.

   Comprehensive coverage of pharmaceutical development, influences, and laws up to 1921 in this region.

1c—National Studies: Russia

154. Appleby, John H. "Ivan the Terrible to Peter the Great: British Formative Influence on Russia's Medico-Apothecary System." *Medical History* 27 (1983): 289-304.

   Emphasizes close links between pharmacy and commerce in the sixteenth and seventeenth century, and the evolution of Russian medicine under British influence from 1581-1718.

155. Conroy, Mary Schaeffer. "Pharmacy in Pre-Soviet Russia." *Pharmacy in History* 27 (1985): 115-37.

   Excellent coverage of a subject generally neglected in English publications. Emphasis is on eighteenth through early twentieth centuries, with attention given to organization, education, professional literature, regulation, and economics.

1c—National Studies: Spain

156. Folch Jou, Guillermo. *Historia de la Farmacia*. 3rd ed. Madrid: 1951. 486 pp., illus., bibl., index.

   Includes development of the pharmacy profession, military pharmacy in Spain. The chronology is from earliest times to the twentieth century. It is international in scope but with an emphasis on Spain, with some special chapters devoted to Spanish pharmacy.

157. *Homenaje al Profesor Guillermo Folch Jou. Communicaciones presentadas a la reunión de la Sociedad Española de Historia de la Farmacia, celebrada en Madrid los días 4 y 5 de noviembre de 1982, con motivo de la concesión de la medalla Schelenz al doctor Guillermo Folch Jou.* Madrid: Sociedad Española de Historia de la Farmacia, 1982. 193 pp.

Papers dealing with various aspect of history of pharmacy in Spain, arranged in chronological categories, from the thirteenth to the twentieth century.

158. Vernia, Pedro. *Historia de la farmacia Valenciana, siglos XII al XVIII.* Valencia: De Cenia al Segura, 1990. 252 pp., illus., appendices.

Covers the many influences on pharmacy in Valencia, including historical, geographic, and cultural. Special emphasis on legal privileges accorded to pharmacy over this period.

1c—National Studies: Switzerland

159. Fehlmann, Hans-Rudolf. "Beziehungen zwischen Arzt und Apotheker im 16. bis 18. Jahrhundert in der Schweiz." *Gesnerus* 40 (1983): 67-74.

Relationship between doctors and pharmacists in Switzerland affected more by external influences (i.e., epidemics, politics) than by legal constraints in this period.

1c—National Studies: United States

160. Bender, George A., and John Parascandola (eds.). *American Pharmacy in the Colonial and Revolutionary Periods: A Bicentennial Symposium Sponsored by the American Institute*

of the History of Pharmacy with the Co-Sponsorship of the American Pharmaceutical Association and the American Society of Hospital Pharmacists, New Orleans, April 5, 1976. Madison, WI: American Institute of the History of Pharmacy, 1977. 49 pp., illus., bibls.

Contents: G. E. Osborne, "Pharmacy in British Colonial America," J. Duffy, "Pharmacy in Franco-Spanish Louisiana," G. B. Griffenhagen, "Medicines in the American Revolution," R. Schmitz, "The Medical and Pharmaceutial Care of the Hessian Troops in the American Revolution."

161. Cowen, David L. *The Colonial and Revolutionary Heritage of Pharmacy in America.* Trenton and Madison, WI: New Jersey Pharmaceutical Association and American Institute of the History of Pharmacy, 1976. 24 pp., illus.

Series of essays with listing of general sources that cover this historical period.

162. "Golden Jubilee Issue." *Druggists Circular* 51, no. 1 (1907): 1-196.

Contains a wealth of information on pharmacy in the United States between 1857 and 1907, in the form of biographical sketches, recollections, essays on schools and associations, etc.

163. Griffenhagen, George. "Bartholomew Browne, Pharmaceutical-Chemist of Salem, Massachusetts, 1698-1704." *Essex Institute Historical Collections* (Jan. 1961): 19-30.

Through the records of Browne, the author gives an unusual look at pharmacy practice in seventeenth-century America.

164. King, Nydia. *A Selection of Primary Sources for the History of Pharmacy in the United States. Books and Trade Catalogs from the Colonial Period to 1940.* Madison, WI: American Institute of the History of Pharmacy, 1987. xv + 123 pp.

A copiously annotated catalog topically arranged, followed by a chronological listing and an alphabetical list of authors. A library location is given for each item. Facsimiles of eighty-five of the eighty-nine out-of-print books are indicated as available as a microfiche collection or as selected individual soft bound volumes from University Microfilms International. These eighty-nine volumes were selected to represent the core of pharmaceutical literature during this period. Brief biographical information about the authors and characterization of the content of the books follow each entry.

165. LaWall, Charles H. *Four Thousand Years of Pharmacy: An Outline History of Pharmacy and the Allied Sciences.* Philadelphia: Lippincott, 1927. 665 pp., illus., index.

A lively and pioneering history in American literature, but now outmoded. Bibliography mainly from works in authors' personal library. Undocumented. A corrected edition has not been issued. Reprinted as *The Curious Lore of Drugs and Medicines* (NY: Garden City Publ. Co., 1936).

166. Sonnedecker, Glenn. "Pharmacy in the United States." In *Kremers and Urdang's History of Pharmacy.* ed. Glenn Sonnedecker, pp. 145-335. 4th ed. Madison, WI: American Institute of the History of Pharmacy, 1976.

The first place to look for overview of American pharmacy and sources on its history. Well-documented.

167. Urdang, George. "Pharmacy in Colonial North America." *The Merck Report* (April 1947): 4-8.

This review of pharmacy in the early history of the United States was reprinted along with a second article by Urdang ("Pharmacy in the United States Prior to the Civil War" *The Merck Report,* July 1947) in a booklet distributed by the American Institute of the History of Pharmacy entitled: *Pharmacy in the United States: In Colonial North America; Prior to the Civil War,* 1976.

1c—National Studies: Yugoslavia

168. Tartaglia, Hrvoje. *l'Histoire de la pharmacie en Yougoslavia et sa situation actuelle.* Zagreb: Societé pharmaceutique de Croatie, Institut d'histoire de la pharmacie, 1959. 178 pp., illus., index.

    Doctoral thesis, Paris, 1956, with monographs on individual cities, rules governing the profession, and biographies. Takes on a difficult task, since no general study of this question has been done.

1d—Company Histories

169. Boussel, Patrice, Henri Bonnemain, and Frank J. Bové. *History of Pharmacy and the Pharmaceutical Industry.* Transl. by Desmond Newell and Frank J. Bové. Paris: Asklepios Press, 1983. 285 pp., bibl., illus.

    Includes brief company histories, with illustrations, for the following companies: Abbott (pp. 212-16), Bayer (pp. 217-21), Boehringer Ingelheim (pp. 223-25), Ciba-Geigy (pp. 227-32), Eli Lilly & Co. (pp. 233-37), Glaxo (pp. 239-40), Hoffmann-La Roche (pp. 241-48), Merck (pp. 249-250), Sandoz (pp. 251-56), Schering AG (pp. 257-61), Searle (pp. 262-63), Squibb (pp. 264-70), Upjohn (pp. 271-72), Wyeth (p. 273), Wellcome Foundation Ltd. (pp. 275-77).

170. Florey, K. "Edward Robinson Squibb—The Man and His Company." *Pharmaceutical Historian* 19, no. 3 (1989): 2-9.

    Script from a lecture that gives an overview of Squibb's life but places most emphasis on subsequent development of the company.

171. Haynes, William. *American Chemical Industry.* 6 vols. N.Y.: D. Van Nostrand, 1945-54. illus., bibl., index.

The first five volumes cover from colonial America to the beginning of World War II; volume 6 is devoted to company histories (includes: Abbott; Burroughs Wellcome & Co.; CIBA; Frizsche Bros.; Heyden; Hoffmann-La Roche; Hynson, Wescott & Dunning; Eli Lilly; Mellon Institute; Merck & Co.; Miles Laboratories; Norwich Pharmacal; Parke, Davis & Co.; S. B. Penick & Co.; Charles Pfizer & Co.; Pharma Chemical Co.; Rexall Drug Co.; Rohm & Haas Co.; Sandoz Chemical Works; G. D. Searle & Co.; Sharp & Dohme; E. R. Squibb & Sons; Sterling Drugs, Inc.; Takamine Labaoratory, Inc.; The Tilden Co.; Upjohn Co.; William R. Warner & Co.). Haynes includes some attention to the pharmaceutical industry. This is a definitive history of the chemical industry, and the author's proximity to the industry, according to one of the leading historians of chemistry, make the copious data in Haynes's many tables perhaps even more reliable than government statistics.

172. Jack, D. B., and N. P. Mason. "The Pharmaceutical Industry in the USSR." *Journal of Clinical Pharmacy and Therapeutics* 12 (1987): 401-407.

Describes modern (1960s-on) industry in the USSR, showing the various stages in drug development.

173. Laar, J., et al. "Beiträge zur Geschichte der pharmazeutischen Industrie in Deutschland." *Forschung. Praxis. Fortbildung* 17 (1966): 558-60.

Brief histories of 24 German firms. [not seen].

174. Mahoney, Tom. *The Merchants of Life: An Account of the American Pharmaceutical Industry.* NY: Harper & Bros., 1959. 278 pp., index.

Good general work.

175. Nelson, Gary L., ed. *Pharmaceutical Company Histories.* Vol. 1. Bismark, ND: Woodbine, 1983. 180 pp., illus., index.

Includes chapters discussing the following companies: Ayerst Laboratories, Burroughs Wellcome, Central Pharmaceutical, Hoechst-Roussel Pharmaceuticals, Eli Lilly, Merck Sharp & Dohme, Miles Laboratories, Norwich Eaton Pharmaceuticals, Reed & Carnick Pharmaceutical, A. H. Robins, Schering-Plough, SmithKline Beckman, Walker Corp & Co. Not definitive histories at all, but the chapters generally include information about the early years of the company and highlights in pharmaceutical developments related to the company. Useful for understanding some of the name changes and mergers within the industry. Only volume 1 is published.

176. *The Pharmaceutical Era* Dec. (1896): 910-1012.

   Pictures and text on the pharmaceutical industry of the period, divided into a section on "American Laboratories": Schieffelin & Co.; N. Y. Quinine & Chemical works; E. R. Squibb & Sons; John Wyeth & Brother; Sharp & Dohme; Keasbey & Mattison; Fraser Tablet Triturate Manufacturing Co.; Frederick Stearns & Co.; Wm. R. Warner & Co.; Johnson & Johnson Laboratories; Upjohn Bill & Granule Co.; Billings, Clapp & Co. A section on "Wholesale Drug Houses": McKesson & Robbins; Smith, Kline & French Co.; Meyer Bros. Drug Company; Morrison, Plummer & Co.; Lehn & Fink; Charles N. Crittenton Co.; and paragraphs on other small drug houses. There is also a section entitled "Manufacturing Industries of the Drug Trade": Fairchild Bros. & Foster; Schering & Glatz; California Fig Syrup Co.; Merck & Co.; Pabst Brewing Co.; Merz Capsule Company; Plantan's American Medical Capsulary.

1d—Company Histories: Abbott

177. Kogan, Herman. *The Long White Line: The Story of Abbott Laboratories*. New York: Random House, 1963. x + 310 pp., illus., bibl., index.

   For the general reader, this book covers the first seventy-five years of the firm.

178. Pratt, William D. *The Abbott Almanac: 100 Years of Commitment to Quality Health Care 1888-1988*. Elmsford, NY: Benjamin, 1988. 224 pp., illus., index.

A synopsis of the major events of each of the first 100 years of the company, with illustrations.

179. Vliet, Elmer B. "The Abbott Laboratories." *Journal of Industrial and Engineering Chemistry* 24 (1932): 588-90.

Brief review of the early developments in this company.

1d—Company Histories: Allen & Hanburys

180. Chapman-Huston, Desmond, and Ernest C. Cripps. *Through a City Archway: The Story of Allen and Hanburys 1715-1954*. London: John Murray, 1954. 326 pp., illus., appendices, index, bibliography.

A narrative account of Plough Court pharmacy, describing the historical and political context of the growing industry.

181. Tweedale, Geoffrey. *At the Sign of the Plough: 275 Years of Allen & Hanburys and the British Pharmaceutical Industry 1715-1990*. London: John Murray, 1990. 264 pp., illus., index.

Not designed as a comprehensive history but as a concise account of the growing industry, taking into account earlier histories of the company. The goal was to bring the history up to date and add more information on business developments. Well-illustrated.

1d—Company Histories: Bayer

182. Verg, Erik, Gottfried Plumpe, and Heinz Schultheis. *Milestones: The Bayer Story 1863-1988*. Leverkusen: Bayer AG, 1988. 623 pp., subject index, photo index.

Covering the many components that go into the development of a multi-national industry, this book delves into social history, environmental issues, and legal concerns, as well as the basic scientific components of research and development. The pharmaceutical side of Bayer is only one of the topics covered in this very readable and well-illustrated history.

1d—Company Histories: CIBA

183. CIBA. *The Story of Chemical Industry in Basel*. Olten and Lausanne: Urs Graf, 1959. 233 pp., illus.

    General text, starts with late Middle Ages, and includes chapter on pharmaceuticals.

1d—Company Histories: CIBA-Geigy

184. Erni, Paul. *The Basel Marriage: History of the CIBA-Geigy Merger (adapted from German original by Stanley Hubbard)*. Basel: 1979.

    The business history of this merger is related, based on an insider's view.

1d—Company Histories: Dodge & Olcott

185. *The Story of a Unique Institution: Dodge & Olcott, Inc., 1798-1948*. New York: Dodge & Olcott, 1948. 95 pp., illus.

    Commemorating 150 years of business in manufacturing essential oils, vanilla derivatives, flavor bases, etc.—serving the drug industry. The company grew from a drug importing business.

1d—Company Histories: Geigy

186. Bürgin, Alfred. *Geschichte des Geigy Unternehmens von 1758 bis 1939*. Basel: Geigy, 1958. 325 pp., illus.

    One of the best histories of a firm, fully documented, especially on Geigy's specialty as a dye company.

1d—Company Histories: Glaxo

187. Davenport-Hines, R. P. T., and Judy Slinn. *Glaxo: A History to 1962*. Cambridge: Cambridge University Press, 1992. 406 pp., illus., bibl., index.

    From the early days in New Zealand to a leading pharmaceutical company in Britain. A good history of Glaxo, where the authors had access to extensive company records as they traced the business and scientific developments of the company.

1d—Company Histories: Lehn & Fink

188. [Lehn & Fink]. *Fifty Years. Commemorating the Fiftieth Anniversary of the Founding of Lehn & Fink*. NY: 1924. 47 pp., illus.

    Good photographs of the labs and manufacturing areas of the company.

1d—Company Histories: Lilly

189. Eli Lilly & Co. *The Lilly Laboratories*. Indianapolis: Eli Lilly & Co., 1931.

    Primarily illustrations of the laboratories, showing the manufacturing process.

190. Kahn, Ely Jacques, Jr. *All in a Century: The First Hundred Years of Eli Lilly & Co.* Indianapolis: Eli Lilly, ca. 1976.

Lively narrative that focusses on people.

191. *Lilly Research Laboratories: Dedication.* Indianapolis: [Lilly], 1934. 128 pp.

Includes addresses presented at the opening of the Lilly Research Laboratories, with presentations by J. K. Lilly, Irving Langmuir, Frederick Banting, and Henry Dale on various aspects of research and manufacturing. Includes illustrations of the labs.

1d—Company Histories: Merck

192. Galambos, Louis, Michael S. Brown, Joseph L. Goldstein, and P. Roy Vagelos. *Values & Visions: A Merck Century.* n.p.: Merck, [1991]. 192 pp., index.

Through short biographical sketches, this history of Merck calls attention to the individuals behind the company, beginning with the founding of Merck & Co. in New York in 1891. The research component is also revealed through individuals and their impact on the company. Many elegant photos and company data at the end complement the text.

193. Merck & Co. *E. Merck Chemisches Fabrik Darmstadt.* Darmstadt: 1927. 127 pp., illus.

History of the firm that includes manufacturing pictures and some discusses of the scientific basis of manufacturing. Has some lab illustrations.

194. Merck AG, E. *From Merck's "Angel Pharmacy" to the World-Wide Merck Group.* Darmstadt: E. Merck, ca. 1968.

Public relations work, mostly pictures.

1d—Company Histories: Meyer Bros.

195. Meyer, A. C. *The Early Years of the Drug and Allied Trades in the Mississippi Valley.* St. Louis: 1948. 164 pp., illus., index.

    History of Meyer Bros. as well as a general history of wholesaling in the late nineteenth century.

196. Meyer Bros. Drug Co. *Seventy-Five Years of Service.* 1927.

    A series of articles and pages from *The Meyer Druggist* that gives a practical picture of the American drug trade and the wholesale business.

1d—Company Histories: Michigan Drug Co.

197. [Michigan Drug Co.]. *One Hundred Years.* Detroit: 1919. 42 pp., illus.

    Chronology of the company that served retail merchants for 100 years.

1d—Company Histories: Miles

198. Cray, William C. *Miles 1884-1984—A Centennial History.* Englewood Cliffs, NJ: Prentice-Hall, 1984. 277 pp., illus., index.

    An interesting history of many of the well-known Miles products and their role in the company's development. This history takes into account personalities and the marketing aspects of drug development as well as the scientific considerations.

1d—Company Histories: Mulford

199. Stewart, Francis. "Mulford Growth Shows Great Achievement." *Northwestern Druggist* 30 (December 1922): 14-19.

    Inspirational review of the company's history—undocumented.

1d—Company Histories: Parke, Davis

200. Parke, Davis and Company. *The Saga of Parke, Davis and Company.* Detroit: 1942.

    An anniversary booklet by the company.

201. Taylor, Frank O. "Forty-Five Years of Manufacturing Pharmacy." *Journal of the American Pharmaceutical Association* 4 (April, 1915): 468-81.

    Brief history of Parke, Davis with account of their advances in pharmacy and medicine. Includes a chronological list of drugs introduced by Parke, Davis. Good review.

202. Taylor, Frank O. "Parke, Davis and Company." *Industrial and Engineering Chemistry* 19, no. 10 (October, 1927): 1202-1205.

    Under the guiding principle of growth for the future, Parke, Davis developed a research and manufacturing program as outlined in this article.

1d—Company Histories: Pfizer

203. Mines, Samuel. *Pfizer: An Informal History.* New York: Pfizer, 1978. 248 pp.

    Narrative history, partly based on interviews, presented as a drama for the general reader.

204. Pratt, Edmund. *Pfizer: Bringing Science to Life*. NY: Newcomen Society of U. S., 1985. 24 pp., illus.

Taken from a speech, with illustrations.

1d—Company Histories: Sandoz

205. *Sandoz, 1886-1961: 75 Years of Research and Enterprise*. Basel: Sandoz, 1961. 139 pp., illus.

The various departments of Sandoz present their history. The pharmaceutical department, founded in 1917, describes the development of techniques to isolate the active principles of medicinal plants.

1d—Company Histories: Schieffelin

206. *One Hundred Years of Business Life, 1794-1894, W. H. Schieffelin & Co.* NY: [1894].

Reveals the history of this firm through biographical information about the Schieffelin family.

207. Schieffelin & Co. *150 Years of Service to American Health*. New York: Schieffelin & Co., 1944. 73 pp., illus.

Traces the history of the self-proclaimed "oldest Drug House in America." Includes a family history and presents the development of this company as an example of the growth and expansion of the American economy.

208. Schieffelin & Company. *One Hundred Years of Business Life— 1794-1894*. New York: Schieffelin, 1894. 56 pp., illus.

General history from the period of Lawrence & Schieffelin (1794) on. Appendix has illustration of material from their archives and an essay, "One Hundred Years of Chemistry and Pharmacy."

1d—Company Histories: SmithKline

209. Marion, John Francis. *The Fine Old House*. Philadelphia: SmithKline Corporation, 1980. 256 pp., illus., index.

    A brief historical dialogue about SmithKline Company, interspersed with colorful illustrations.

1d—Company Histories: Squibb

210. Peck, F. H. "Squibb and the House He Founded." *Northwestern Druggist* 30 (1922): 19-21. illus.

    One of a number of brief inspirational articles about leaders in American pharmacy in this journal. With the basic theme expressed by the introduction: "From drug store apprentice to a leader with influence."

1d—Company Histories: Upjohn

211. Armstrong, James W. "Dr. Upjohn's Company." *Michigan History* 70, no. 3 (1986): 24-31.

    Covers early years under W. E. Upjohn, discussing changes in manufacturing, advertising, and business practices. Based partly on sources in Upjohn's historical archives.

212. Carlisle, Robert D. B. *A Century of Caring: The Upjohn Story*. Elmsford, NY: The Benjamin Company, 1987. 256 pp., illus., index.

A history presented through biographical information about critical individuals in the company's development.

213. Engel, Leonard. *Medicine Makers of Kalamazoo*. New York: McGraw-Hill, 1961. viii + 261 pp., illus., index.

    Upjohn history without notes, references, or bibliography.

214. "The Upjohn Company." In *American Chemical Industry*. William Haynes, pp. 455-57. New York: Van Nostrand.

    Concise review of the history of the company.

1e—Biographies

215. Blockstein, William L., and C. Boyd Granberg (eds.). *Remarkable Pharmacists*. West Des Moines, IA: Rob Lee Hill Publ. Co., 1973. 163 pp., illus.

    Careers of modern pharmacists, with brief introduction for each, followed by an autobiographical sketch. Includes Charles F. Dahl, Joseph A. Oddis, Varro E. Tyler, Charles R. Walgreen, Jr., Sir Hugh Linstead, Lorraine E. Bribbons, Larry R. Pilot, George F. Slavin, Jr., George Bender, William Rumford, and Hubert Humphrey. Some still living.

216. Ferchl, Fritz. *Chemisch-pharmazeutisches Bio- und Bibliographikon*. Mittenwald: 1937. 603 pp.

    Cites literature (at the end of each brief biographical sketch, a-z) published in the period between about 1500 and the mid-nineteenth century.

217. "Fifty Distinguished [American] Pharmacists." *Druggists Circular* 51 (1907): 81-95.

50th anniversary issue. Brief biographical sketches for each individual, including a small portrait, and covering the second half of the nineteenth century.

218. *Figures pharmaceutiques française. Notes historiques et portraits, 1803-1953.* Paris: Masson, 1953. 276 pp., illus.

Biographies and portraits of 38 important French pharmacists whose lives reflect the development of pharmacy in France during this 50-year period.

219. Ganzinger, Kurt. "Apotheker-Biographien (3)." *OAZ, Osterreichische Apotheker-Zeitung (Vienna)* 42, no. 7 (1988): 122-28.

Focus on the important names in the history of pharmacy in Austria. Reviews various references for biography in German-speaking countries.

220. Gillispie, Charles Coulston, ed. *Dictionary of Scientific Biography.* New York: Scribner, 1970. 18 vols.

Multivolume work that contains biographies of scientists through history, written by major historians of science. Most biographies also contain references for further reading as well as bibliographies of the subject's work. Includes significant pharmacists and pharmaceutical scientists.

221. Häfliger, Josef Anton. "Biographikon." In *Handbuch der Pharmakognosie.* Alexander Tschirch, pp. 1008-1151. 2nd ed. Leipzig, 1932.

Includes references to works by or about biographees. [not seen].

222. Hein, Wolfgang-Hagen, and Holm-Dietmar Schwarz (eds.). *Deutsche Apotheker-Biographie.* Veröffentlichungen der Internationalen Gesellschaft für Geschichte der Pharmazie e.V.,

Neue Folge, 43 and 46. Stuttgart: Wissenschaftliche Verlagsgesellschaft, 1975 and 1978.

Volumes 1 (A-L) and 2 (M-Z) include the life and accomplishments of German pharmacists from the Middle Ages to the modern period, who died before 1950. The Supplement volume (Bd. 55 of Veröffentlichung) (see citation #223) contains pharmacists who died between 1950 and 1970. Criteria for inclusion also requires that subjects belonged to pharmacy profession, and had significant accomplishments (in pharmaceutical and other spheres). In terms of geography, they consider the German cultural and language areas as one entity, which means Austria and German-speaking Switzerland are included. Also includes pharmacists born near Germany who later moved away and those foreign-born pharmacists as long as a substantial part of their life was in Germany. Important works by the pharmacist are listed as well as biographical sources in which they are listed.

223. Hein, Wolfgang-Hagen, and Holm-Dietmar Schwarz (eds.). *Deutsche Apotheker-Biographie Ergänzungsband.* Veröffentlichungen der Internationalen Gesellschaft für Geschichte der Pharmazie e.V., Bd. 55. Stuttgart: Wissenschaftliche Verlagsgesellschaft MBH, 1986. vii + 466 pp.

This completes the set of biographies of German pharmacists begun in 1975 with Band 43 of the Veröffentlichung. This supplement included those pharmacists who died between 1950 and 1970, as well as those that were missed in the two earlier volumes of the set. (See citation #222.)

224. Kremers Reference Files. University of Wisconsin School of Pharmacy Library. University of Wisconsin-Madison.

The "A2" classification in this extensive manuscript file contains biographical information about pharmacists, past and present. Focus is on history of American pharmacy.

225. Roldan y Guerrero, Rafael. *Diccionario biográfico y bibliografico de autores farmacéuticos españoles*. 4 vols. Madrid: Real Academia de Farmacia, 1958-1976. Also published as supplements to *An. real Acad. Farm*.

2468 biographies that record the publications of individuals as well as biographical details.

226. Slocum, Robert B., ed. *Biographical Dictionaries and Related Works: An International Bibliography of Approximately 16,000 Collective Biographies*. 2nd ed. Detroit: Gale Research Co., ca. 1986. 2 vols.

Includes materials publications from the sixteenth century to the present. Unique 1,079 page international bibliography encompasses collective biographies, bio-bibliographies, bibliographies of individual and collective biographies, and selected portrait catalogs.

227. Youngken, Heber W. "Eminent American Pharmacognosists of the Nineteenth Century." *Journal of the American Pharmaceutical Association* 24 (1935): 148-52, 215-19.

Professional biographies, with portraits, of: John Maisch, Edson Bastin, Julius Schlotterbeck, Albert Schnedier, Henry Kraemer, Lucius Sayre, Otto Wall.

228. Zekert, Otto. *Berühmte Apotheker*. Stuttgart: Deutscher Apotheker Verlag, 1955. 2 vol. (160 pp., 95 pp.), ports., index.

Well-known apothecaries from German-speaking areas. Portraits accompany brief biography and literature review. Vol. 1 covers fifteenth-eighteenth centuries. Although vol. 2 purports to cover multiple nations (nineteenth-twentieth centuries), the coverage is still mostly German, with some French and English individuals.

1e—Biographies: Abel, John Jacob (1857-1938)

229. Marshall, E. K. "An Exhibit at the Centennial Celebration of John Jacob Abel's Birth." *Bulletin History of Medicine* 32 (1958): 356-65.

    Includes illustrations of the exhibit materials, including photographs of Abel at various stages in his life.

230. Parascandola, John. "John J. Abel and the Early Development of Pharmacology at the Johns Hopkins University." *Bulletin of the History of Medicine* 56 (1982): 512-27.

    Abel's career is closely tied to the establishment of the profession of pharmacology in America.

1e—Biographies: Albert-Buisson, François (1881-1961)

231. Bonnemain, Henri. "Albert-Buisson, pharmacien, membre de l'Académie française (1881-1961)." *Revue d'histoire de la pharmacie* 251 (1981): 255-59.

    Portrait and outline of his life and work.

1e—Biographies: Allen, William (1770-1843)

232. Cripps, Ernest C. *Plough Court: The Story of a Notable Pharmacy, 1715-1927.* London: Allen & Hanburys Ltd., 1927. 227 pp., illus.

    Discusses William Allen, English pharmacist who became a well-known chemist.

1e—Biographies: Arny, Henry V. (1868-1943)

233. Millman, Morton M. "Dr. Henry Vincome Arny." *New York State Pharmacist* 10 (Deca.1936): 9, 24, 38.

    Presents Henry V. Arny as editor, author, professor and Dean at New York College of Pharmacy; includes his views on the state of pharmacy at that time.

1e—Biographies: Attfield, John (1835-1911)

234. Mrtek, Marsha B. "The Professional Legacy of John Attfield." *Pharmacy in History* 29 (1987): 55-59.

    Describes his contributions to the field of pharmacy.

235. Remington, Joseph P. "John Attfield." *Journal of the American Pharmaceutical Association* 1 (1912): 490-93.

    Brief review of Attfield's career, in memorium.

236. Smith, F. A. Upsher. "Professor John Attfield, F. R. S." *American Journal of Pharmacy* 78 (1906): 103-13.

    Overview of the professional life of John Attfield, English pharmacist, professor at Pharmacy School of the Pharmaceutical Society of Great Britain, and author of a textbook widely used in the U.S. and England.

1e—Biographies: Avicenna (980-1037)

237. Gohlman, William E., ed. and transl. *The Life of Ibn Sina: A Critical Edition and Annotated Translation*. Albany: State University of New York Press, 1974. 163 pp., bibl., index.

    Translation of Avicenna's autobiography.

1e—Biographies: Bache, Franklin (1792-1864)

238. LaWall, Charles H. "Dr. Franklin Bache, Chairman of the U.S.P. Revision Committee." *Journal of the American Pharmaceutical Association* 20 (1931): 478-79.

    Includes portrait. Very brief biography.

1e—Biographies: Balard Antoine Jérome (1802-1876)

239. "Antoine J. Balard (1802-1876)." *Revue d'histoire de la pharmacie* 24, no. 232 special (1977): 1-96.

    Issue entirely devoted to Balard's life and times, chronology, applications of discovery of bromine, includes descriptive catalog of Balard exposition at Montpelier on centennial of his death.

240. Jeanjean, Jean-Félix. "Antoine-Jérôme Balard. Sa vie—son oeuvre." *Monspeliensis Hippocrates* 12 (Spring 1969): 21-28.

    Reprint of a 1926 study of Balard, with illustrations, covering his years at Montpellier.

241. Julien, Pierre, and Louis Marquet. "Essai de bibliographie des publications sur A.-J. Balard et sur son oeuvre." *Revue d'histoire de la pharmacie* n.s.24 (1977): 203-17.

    Annotated bibliography, indicating location of portraits.

1e—Biographies: Banting, Frederick Grant (1891-1941)

242. Bliss, Michael. *Banting: A Biography.* Toronto: McClelland and Stewart, 1984. 336 pp., illus., index.

Reveals a portrait of the man, not so much the scientist. The author had access to more documents than available to earlier biographers.

1e—Biographies: Barton, Benjamin Smith (1776-1815)

243. Bell, W. J. "Benajamin Smith Barton, MD (Kiel)." *Journal of the History of Medicine and Allied Sciences* 26 (1971): 197-203.

    Corrects view of Barton's education and raises questions about the sort of man he was.

1e—Biographies: Bartram, Moses (1732-1809)

244. Kremers, Edward. "Two Invoices of 1785." *Journal of the American Pharmaceutical Association* 20 (1931): 682-95.

    Moses Bartram, son of famous botanist (John) and pharmacist in Philadelphia. Pages 191-92 give brief details of his heritage.

1e—Biographies: Baumé, Antoine (1728-1804)

245. Davy, René. *L'apothicaire Baumé (1728-1804), les origines de la droguerie pharmacaeutique et de l'industrie du sel ammoniac en France*. Cahors: A. Coucslant, 1955. 147 pp.

    A doctoral thesis at the Faculté de Pharmacie de Strasbourg. This biography emphasizes Baumé's contributions to chemistry and analyzes his major writings. The thesis lacks complete documentation.

246. Julien, Pierre. "Antoine Baumé, la vie et l'homme." *Revue d'histoire de la pharmacie* 26 (1979): 11-22.

Review of his life and professional career, stressing his attachment to pharmacy. Color portrait and bibliography. This issue contains other articles about Baumé.

247. Julien, Pierre. "Baumé . . . ce n'est pas que l'areometre, ni les gouttes amères . . ." *Bulletin de l'Ordre National des Pharmaciens* 177 (April 1975): 498-509.

Life and works.

1e—Biographies: Beecham, Thomas (1820-1907)

248. Francis, Anne. *A Guinea a Box. A Biography*. London: Hale, 1968. 191 pp., illus., index.

Colorful personal story of Thomas Beecham and the development of his company. Focuses on his personality and the historical and social context of his career.

1e—Biographies: Bliven, Charles W. (1911-   )

249. Gibson, Melvin R. "President Charles W. Bliven: A Biographical Sketch." *American Journal of Pharmaceutical Education* 23 (1959): 499-502.

Outlines achievements and affiliations of Charles A. Bliven, first full-time Exec. Sec. of AACP (1961-74).

1e—Biographies: Bobst, Elmer Holmes (1884-)

250. Bobst, Elmer Holmes. *Bobst: The Autobiography of a Pharmaceutical Pioneer*. New York: David McKay, 1973. vii + 360 pp., illus.

Biographies

A candid memoir by the man who headed the American branch of Hoffmann La Roche, and then became chief executive officer of Warner Lambert.

1e—Biographies: Brockedon, William (1787-1854)

251. Wilkinson, Lisa. "William Brockedon, F. R. S. (1787-1854)." *Notes and Records of the Royal Society of London* 26 (June 1971): 65-72.

    Biography of this inventor who devised a tablet and lozenge compressor.

1e—Biographies: Buchheim, Rudolf (1920-1879)

252. Bruppacher-Cellier, Marianne. *Rudolf Buchheim (1820-1879) und die Entwicklung einer experimentellen Pharmakologie*. Zürcher medizingeschichtliche Abhandlungen, N.R. 88. Zurich: Juris-Verlag, 1971. 73 pp., bibl.

    Biographical details about Buchheim as well as his scientific work with documentation.

253. Habermann, Ernst R. "Rudolf Buchheim and the Beginning of Pharmacology as a Science." *Annual Review of Pharmacology* 14 (1974): 1-8.

    Sketch of his life and contributions to pharmacology.

1e—Biographies: Carson, Joseph (1808-1876)

254. LaWall, Charles H. "Dr. Joseph Carson, Chairman of the USP Revision Committee, 1870." *Journal of the American Pharmaceutical Association* 20 (1931): 480-81.

    Review of his education, teaching, and other work.

1e—Biographies: Caventou, Joseph Bienaimé (1795-1877)

255. Berman, Alex. "Joseph Bienaimé Caventou." In *Dictionary of Scientific Biography*. ed. Charles C. Gillispie, New York: Charles Scribner's Sons, 1970-90.

    French pharmacist who investigated alkaloids. He discovered strychnine, brucine, veratrine (with Meissner), quinine, and cinchonine (after Gomes). He also named chlorophyll and wrote a textbook on pharmacy.

1e—Biographies: Cordus, Valerius (1515-1544)

256. Dann, Georg Edmund. "Der Familienkreis [des] Valerius Cordus." *Farmaceutiski Glasnik* 23 (1967): 391-98.

    Covers what details of his life and family are known, with references and illustrations.

1e—Biographies: Cushny, Arthur Robertson (1866-1926)

257. MacGillivray, Helen. "A Personal Biography of Arthur Robertson Cushny, 1866-1926." *Annual Review of Pharmacology* 8 (1968): 1-24.

    Reminiscence done by his daughter, with portrait.

1e—Biographies: Domagk, Gerhard (1895-1964)

258. Colebrook, L. "Gerhard Domagk, 1895-1964." *Biogr. Mem. Fellows Roy. Soc.* 10 (1964): 39-50.

    General biography emphasizing scientific achievements. Portrait.

1e—Biographies: Dorvault, François-Laurent (1815-1879)

259. Boussel, Patrice. *Dorvault: Sa vie et son oeuvre.* Editions de la Porte Verte, [1979]. 304 pp., illus. bibl.

   Biography focusing on the career of François-Laurent Dorvault.

1e—Biographies: Dyott, Thomas W. (1771-1861)

260. McKearin, Helen. *Bottles, Flasks, and Dr. Dyott.* NY: Crown Publishers, 1970. 160 pp., illus., index.

   Study of Dyott the merchant and business man, with many illustrations of his glass containers.

1e—Biographies: Ehrlich, Paul (1854-1915)

261. Bäumler, Ernst. *Paul Ehrlich: Scientist for Life.* transl. Grant Edwards. New York: Holmes & Meier, 1984. 288 pp., illus., bibl., index.

   The development of his scientific ideas and career. Extensively documented.

1e—Biographies: Florey, Howard Walter (1898-1968)

262. MacFarlane, Gwyn. *Howard Florey: The Making of a Great Scientist.* Oxford: Oxford University Press, 1979. 396 pp., illus., index.

   Focuses on Florey's development as a scientist, with the climax of his work on penicillin.

263. Williams, Trevor I. *Howard Florey: Penicillin and After.* Oxford and New York: Oxford University Press, 1984. 404 pp., illus., index.

> Devotes most of the book to Florey's life after his appointment to the Chair of Pathology at Oxford, 1935. Complements McFarlane's biography (see citation #262).

1e—Biographies: Flückiger, Friedrich August (1824-1894)

264. Haug, Thomas. *Friedrich August Flückiger (1828-1894): Leben und Werk.* Quellen und Studien zur Geschichte der Pharmazie, 32. Stuttgart: Deutscher Apotheker Verlag, 1985. 405 pp., illus., bibl., index.

> An extensive biography supported by Flückiger correspondence. Covers his life and career.

265. Kremers, Edward. "Flueckigeriana. V. Flueckiger letters to Power 1882-1890." *Journal of the American Pharmaceutical Association* 19 (1930): 879-82, 1131-32; 20(1931): 252-53, 462-63.

> Reveals Flückiger's American connections, with notations.

1e—Biographies: Fourcroy, Antoine François (1755-1809)

266. Julien, Pierre. "Un chimiste, conventionnel et conseiller d'État, pharmacien d'adoption: A. F. de Fourcroy (1755-1809)." *Bulletin de l'Ordre National des Pharmaciens* 179 (June) (1975): 871-87.

> Briefly covers life and career, with one section focusing on his interest in pharmacy.

267. Kersaint, G. "Antoine-François de Fourcroy (1755-1809), sa vie et son oeuvre." *Revue d'histoire de la pharmacie* 18 (Dec 67): 589-96.

Reviews the life of Fourcroy as presented in the author's thesis ("Antoine François de Fourcroy, 1755-1809, sa vie et son oeuvre," *Mémoires du Muséum d'histoire naturelle. Nouv. sér. d: Sciences physico-chimiques,* t.2, fasc. unique. Paris, 1966, 296 pp.).

1e—Biographies: Fourneau, Ernest (1872-1949)

268. Fourneau, Jean-Pierre. "Ernest Fourneau, fondateur de la chemie thérapeutique française: feuillets d'album." *Revue d'histoire de la pharmacie* 34 (1987): 335-55.

Fourneau's training, career, family life, and personality are described by his son, with lots of photographs and bibliography.

1e—Biographies: Geiger, Philipp Lorenz (1785-1836)

269. Thomas, Ulrike. *Die Pharmazie im Spannungsfeld der Neuorientierung. Philipp Lorenz Geiger (1785-1836): Leben, Werk und Wirken—eine Biographie.* Quellen un Studien zur Geschichte der Pharmazie, 36. Stuttgart: Deutsche Apotheker Verlag, 1985. 652 pp., illus., bibl., index.

Extensively documented biography of both private and professional life.

1e—Biographies: Gmelin, Johann Friedrich (1784-1804)

270. Raubenheimer, Otto. "Gmelin, A German Family of Pharmacists, Chemists and Botanists." *Journal of the American Pharmaceutical Association* 19 (1930): 259-65.

Genealogy of Gmelin family dating from the seventeenth century.

1e—Biographies: Göttling, Johann Friedrich August (1755-1809)

271. Möller, Rudolf. "Chemiker und Pharmazeut der Goethezeit: Eine Skizze des Lebens und Schaffens Johann Friedrich August Göttlings." *Pharmazie* 17 (1962): 624-34.

    Documented sketch of Göttling's life and his connection with Goethe, with illustrations.

1e—Biographies: Hallberg, Carl Svante N. (1856-1910)

272. "Carl S. N. Hallberg, 1856-1910." *Bulletin of the American Pharmaceutical Association* 5 (1910): 532-35.

    Obituary and comment. More material in succeeding issues. Portrait facing p. 531.

1e—Biographies: Hébert, Louis (1580-1627)

273. Bradley, Theodore J. "The First Pharmacist in North America [Louis Hébert]." *Journal of the American Pharmaceutical Association* 25 (1936): 625-28.

    General biography, although not much personal data is available. Links are made with the history of the period.

1e—Biographies: Helmont, Jean Baptiste van (1577-1644)

274. Mepham, J. "Johann van Helmont, 1579-1644." In *Early Seventeenth-Century Scientists*. ed. R. Harré, pp. 129-57. Oxford, New York: Pergamon Press, 1965.

    Only a general review of his theories.

Biographies

275. Pagel, Walter. *Joan Baptista van Helmont: Reformer of Science and Medicine*. Cambridge Monographs in the History of Medicine. Cambridge: Cambridge University Press, 1982. 219 pp.

   Aspects of van Helmont's life are covered as they reveal the context for his philosophy and writings.

1e—Biographies: Hildegard of Bingen (1098-1170)

276. Flanagan, Sabina. *Hildegard of Bingen, 1098-1178: A Visionary Life*. Routledge, 1989. 230 pp., illus.

   This biography of Hildegard deals with the broad scope of her life, although chapter 5 (of the ten in the book) examines her writings on simple and compound remedies. This book is documented and includes a short bibliography.

1e—Biographies: Hoffmann, Frederick (1832-1904)

277. Memorial tribute. "[Memorial Tribute to Frederick Hoffmann]." *Pharmaceutical Review* 23 (1905): 1-3.

   Portrait.

278. Schütze, Sabine Knoll. "European Influence on American Pharmacy: Frederick Hoffmann (1832-1904)." *Pharmacy in History* 33 (1991): 118-22.

   Describes Hoffmann's important influence on the development of American pharmacy, includes some early biographical information.

1e—Biographies: Humboldt, Alexander von (1769-1859)

279. Hein, Wolfgang-Hagen, ed. *Alexander von Humboldt: Leben und Werk*. Frankfurt am Main: Weisbecker Verlag, 1985. 334 pp., illus., notes, index.

    Beautifully produced book covering the diverse aspects of his career and life. Chapter devoted to pharmacy.

280. Hein, Wolfgang-Hagen. *Alexander von Humboldt und die Pharmazie*. Veröffentlichungen der Internationalen Gesellschaft für Geschichte der Pharmazie, Bd. 56. Stuttgart: Wissenschaftliche Verlagsgesellschaft, 1988. 130 pp., illus., index.

    Describes the influences and contacts in pharmacy, from his early education, throughout his expeditions, and in later years.

1e—Biographies: King, John (1813-1893)

281. Felter, Harvey Wickes. *Biographies of John King, M.D., Andrew Jackson Howe, A.B., M. D., and John Milton Scudder*. Lloyd Library and Museum Bulletin, Pharmacy Series No. 5 (Cincinnati: Lloyd Library, 1912).

    Describes the life and goals of the author of *American Dispensatory*, with attention to the influence of Eclectic medicine. With illustrations.

1e—Biographies: Kipp, Petrus Johannes (1808-1864)

282. Snelders, H. A. M. "De Delftse Apotheker en Chemicus Petrus Johannes Kipp (1808-1864)." *Scientiarum Historia* 12 (1970): 79-92.

    "Kipp is still known as the inventor of a compact and simple gas generator, which bears his name (1844)... In this article a survey is given of the life and work of Kipp. In addition the trade in scientific instruments and the academic education in Delft are summarized." From the English summary.

1e—Biographies: Klaproth, Martin Heinrich (1743-1817)

283. Dann, Georg Edmund. *Martin Heinrich Klaproth (1743-1817). Ein deutscher Apotheker und Chemiker sein Weg und seine Leistung.* Berlin: Akademie-Verlag, 1958. 171 pp., illus., index.

    A detailed biography of Klaproth, including pharmacy, with a bibliography of Klaproth's works, and a literature review of works about Klaproth.

284. Urdang, George. "Birth Bicentennial of Famed Pharmacist: M. H. Klaproth." *Journal of the American Pharmaceutical Association, Practical Pharmacy Edition* 4 (1943): 358-61.

    Presents a brief sketch of his training in pharmacy, with an emphasis on his scientific contributions.

1e—Biographies: Krayer, Otto (1899-1982)

285. Goldstein, Avram. "Otto Krayer: October 22, 1899-March 18, 1982." *Biographical Memoires of the National Academy of Science* 57 (1987): 151-225.

    Personal history and scientific achievements in cardiovascular pharmacology.

1e—Biographies: Kremers, Edward (1865-1941)

286. Urdang, George. "Edward Kremers (1865-1941): Reformer of American Pharmaceutical Education." *American Journal of Pharmaceutical Education* 11 (1947): 631-58.

This is a broad biographical sketch, intent less on detail than noting influences and contributions.

1e—Biographies: Laubert, Charles-Jean (1762-1834)

287. Peumery, Jean-Jacques. "Charles-Jean Laubert (1762-1834) pharmacologiste, membre de l'Académie royale de médicine." *Histoire des Sciences Medicales* 15 (1981): 91-97.

    Chief pharmacist of the French army during this period.

1e—Biographies: Lawrence, Henry C. (1820-1862)

288. McCormick, G. E. "Henry C. Lawrence, 1820-1862, Mentor of Eli Lilly." *Pharmacy in History* 16 (1974): 89-96.

    Pulls together available information on Lawrence, in whose store Eli Lilly served as apprentice.

1e—Biographies: Leake, Chauncey D. (1896-1978)

289. Leake, Chauncey D. "How I am." *Annual Review of Pharmacology and Toxicology* 16 (1976): 1-14.

    Autobiographical note revealing the progression of co-workers, mentors, and educational settings for his work and philosophy.

290. "Leake, Chauncey Dewpew (1896-1978): An Appreciation [by] Thomas E. Keys." *Journal of the History of Medicine and Allied Sciences* 33 (1978): 428-31.

    Review of the main points in Leake's career. Not documented.

1e—Biographies: Li, Shih-chên (1518-1593)

291. Sivin, Nathan. "Li Shih-chên." In *Dictionary of Scientific Biography*. ed. Charles C. Gillispie, pp. 390-98, vol. 8. New York: Charles Scribner's Sons, 1970-90.

    Li Shih-chên (1518-1593) was China's greatest naturalist. His most famous work, *Pen-ts'ao kang mu (Systematized Materia Medica)* (1596), is a vast storehouse of historical material.

1e—Biographies: Lilly, Eli (1885-1977)

292. Madison, James H. *Eli Lilly: A Life, 1885-1977*. Indianapolis: Indiana Historical Society, 1989. 342 pp., notes, illus., index.

    Includes a detailed study of scientific management methods at one of the major drug companies in America. A unique contribution to the literature.

1e—Biographies: Limousin, Stanislas (1831-1887)

293. Goris, Albert. *Stanislas Limousin*. Supplement to *Pharmacie Française*, March-April, 1939. 20 pp.

    Commemorative booklet devoted to life and work of Limousin; in French. Brief discussion of his invention of ampuls.

1e—Biographies: Lloyd, John Uri (1849-1936)

294. Cook, Roy Bird. "John Uri Lloyd, Pharmacist, Philosopher, Author, Man." *Journal of the American Pharmaceutical Association, Practical Pharmacy Edition* 10 (1949): 538-44.

    Compilation of anecdotes about Lloyd.

295. Simons, Corinne Miller. *John Uri Lloyd. His Life and His Works, 1849-1936, With a History of the Lloyd Library.* Cincinnati: 1972. 337 pp., illus.

   A chronicle based on papers and letters of Lloyd, to preserve the facts of his life.

296. Tyler, V. E., and V. M. Tyler. "John Uri Lloyd, 1849-1936." *Journal of Natural Products* 50 (1987): 1-8.

   Overview of Lloyd's influence.

1e—Biographies: Long, Crawford (1815-1878)

297. Young, Hugh. "Crawford W. Long: The Pioneer in Ether Anesthesia." *Bulletin of the History of Medicine* 12 (1942): 191-225.

   Personal documents of Crawford are used to describe Long's role in ether anesthesia. Presented in commemoration of the 100th anniversary of the first application of ether anesthesia.

1e—Biographies: Lukasiewicz, Ignacy (1822-1882)

298. Roeske, Wojciech. *Ignacy Lukasiewicz: Pharmacist-Inventor-Social Worker, 1822-1882.* Warsaw: Polish Medical Publisher, 1976. 32 pp.

   Biographical review in English.

1e—Biographies: Lyman, Rufus A. (1875-1957)

299. Burt, Joseph B. "Rufus Lyman, A Biographical Sketch." *American Journal of Pharmaceutical Education* 20 (1956): 1-7, port.

Lyman (1875-1957) was founding editor (1937-1955) of the *American Journal of Pharmaceutical Education*, dean of two schools of pharmacy, and influential within the American Association of Colleges of Pharmacy and pharmaceutical education generally in the USA.

300. Tom, J. "Rufus Ashley Lyman, Pioneer in Pharmacy." *Pharmacy in History* 14 (1972): 91-94; 111.

    Reflections of his personal philosophy that influenced his work in the profession of pharmacy.

1e—Biographies: Magendie, François (1783-1855)

301. Olmsted, J. M. D. *François Magendie: Pioneer in Experimental Physiology and Scientific Medicine in Nineteenth Century France. With a Preface by John F. Fulton.* NY: Schuman's, 1944.

    Documented biography that examines views of Magendie's experimental science by his contemporaries.

1e—Biographies: Maisch, John Michael (1831-1893)

302. "Professor John Michael Maisch." *Proceedings of the American Pharmaceutical Association* 41 (1893): frontispiccc, i-vi.

    Excellent portrait and biographical sketch.

1e—Biographies: Markoe, George F. H. (1840-1896)

303. Scoville, Wilbur L. "Professor George F. H. Markoe." *American Journal of Pharmacy* 68 (1896): 593-96.

    Biographical information about the "father" of the Massachusetts College of Pharmacy.

1e—Biographies: Marshall, Charles (1744-1825)

304. Parrish, Dillwyn. "Biographical Sketch of Charles Marshall." *American Journal of Pharmacy* 37 (1865): 241-44.

    First President of the Philadelphia College of Pharmacy, and son of Christopher Marshall.

1e—Biographies: Martius, E. Wilhelm (1756-1849)

305. Martius, E. Wilhelm. *Erinnerungen aus meinem 90 jährigen Leben*. Leipzig: 1847; republ. by Gesellschaft für Gesch. der Pharm., 1932,

    Perhaps the oldest known pharmacist autobiography.

1e—Biographies: Mattioli, Pietro Andrea (1501-1577)

306. Stannard, Jerry. "P. A. Mattioli: Sixteenth Century Commentator on Dioscorides." *Bibliographic Contributions University of Kansas Libraries* 1 (1969): 59-81.

    Some biographical information included with the history of Mattioli's work on Dioscorides.

1e—Biographies: Mésué, Johann, Sr. (777-857)

307. Sournia, J. C., and G. Troupeau. "Médicine arabe: biographies critiques de Jean Mésué (VIIIe siècle) et du prétendu "Mésué le Jeune (Xe siècle)." *Clio Medica* 3, no. May (1968): 109-17.

    The authors sort out the biographical details of Jean Mésué, who died in 857, as the only one known in the medical literature of the High Middle Ages, whose therapeutics exerted considerable influence through the end of the Renaissance.

1e—Biographies: Meyers, Christian F. G. (1830-1905)

308. "Christian F. G. Meyers (obituary)." *Canadian Pharmaceutical Journal* 39 (1905): 36.

   Founder and head of Meyers Bros. Drug Co., St. Louis. [not seen].

1e—Biographies: Milhau, John (1795-1874)

309. Sonnedecker, Glenn. "A Franco-American Pharmacist: John T. G. F. De Milhau (1795-1874)." In *Die Vorträge der Hauptversammlung in Paris*. pp. 141-52. Veröffentlichungen der Internationalen Gesellschaft für Geschichte der Pharmazie e.V., N.F. Bd. 42. Stuttgart: Wissenschaftliche Verlagsgesellschaft, 1975.

   Considers his role in the U.S. Pharmacopoeia and the development of the profession in the nineteenth century.

1e—Biographies: Mitchill, Samuel Latham (1764-1831)

310. Francis, John W. *Reminiscences of Samuel Latham Mitchill, M. D., LL. D. Enlarged from Valentine's City Manual*. NY: J. F. Trow, 1859. 32 pp.

   This pen portrait by a friend, almost 30 years after his death, concentrates on his natural history work. Nothing is mentioned regarding the U. S. Pharmacopoeia.

311. Hall, Courtney Robert. *A Scientist in the Early Republic, Samuel Latham Mitchill, 1764-1831*. New York: Columbia University Press, 1934. 162 pp., port., bibl., index.

Only a brief discussion of his work on the Pharmacopeia.

312. Kebler, Lyman F. "The President of the First Convention Called to Formulate the United States Pharmacopeia: Samuel Latham Mitchill, August 20, 1764-September 7, 1831; Physician, Chemist, Author, Senator, Representative, and Promoter of the Sciences." *Journal of the American Pharmaceutical Association* 26 (1937): 908-18.

Portrait. Excellent summary of Mitchill's life and involvement with the U. S. Pharmacopeia.

1e—Biographies: Mohr, Friedrich (1806-1879)

313. Figurovskii, N. A., and V. I. Zaharans. "Friedrich Mohr (1806-1897)." *NTM* 14, no. 2 (1977): 37-54.

His innovation in instrumentation and his contribution to a classic text in pharmacy are covered in this annotated biography. Illustrations.

1e—Biographies: Moissan, Louis (1885-1914)

314. Viel, Claude. "Louis Moissan, un pharmacien trop tôt disparu." *Revue d'histoire de la pharmacie* 34, no. 272 (1987): 36-39.

Bare outline of the facts of his short life. Portrait and bibliography.

1e—Biographies: Monardes, Nicolas (c.1493-1588)

315. Boxer, C. R. *Two Pioneers of Tropical Medicine: Garcia d'Orta and Nicolás Monardes*. London: 1963. 36 pp.

Shows the many parallels and influences in the lives of Garcia d'Orta and Monardes.

316. Guerra, Francisco. *Nicolas Bautista Monardes: Su vida y su obra (c. 1493-1588).* Yale University. Department of History of Medicine, publ. #41. Mexico D.F.: Compania Fundidora de Fierro y Acero de Monterrey, S. A., 1961. 226 pp., bibl., illus.

Discusses Monardes' life, financial ventures, medical theories, scientific contributions, and writings. On the basis of new evidence, corrects some previous biographical errors.

1e—Biographies: Morton, William T. G.

317. Woodward, Grace Steele. *The Man Who Conquered Pain: A Biography of William Thomas Green Morton.* Boston: Beacon Press, 1962. 175 pp., bibl., index.

Not as much a biography as a history of his work on anesthesia.

1e—Biographies: Neumann, Caspar (1683-1737)

318. Stechl, Peter. "Caspar Neumann: An Early Teacher of Pharmaceutical Chemistry." *Pharmacy in History* 12 (1970): 51-56.

Author suggests reasons why Neumann's contribution to eighteenth-century pharmacy is recognized but not his work as a pharmaceutical chemist.

1e—Biographies: Niemann, Albert (1834-1861)

319. Zaunick, Rudolf. "Albert Niemann, der Entdecker des Kokains." *Die Pharmazie* 4 (1949): 475-78.

He began in practical pharmacy and continued with scientific studies, most notably under Wöhler. Fills in and connects what sketchy information is available on Niemann.

1e—Biographies: Orta, Garcia de (16th c.)

320. Boxer, C. R. *Two Pioneers of Tropical Medicine: Garcia d'Orta and Nicolás Monardes*. London: 1963. 36 pp.

    Shows the many parallels and influences in the lives of Garcia d'Orta and Monardes.

321. Pelner, Louis. "Garcia Da Orta." *Journal of the American Medical Association* 197 (1966): 996-98.

    Brief recounting of the general points of his life and contributions to pharmacognosy.

1e—Biographies: Paracelsus, Theophrast von Hohenheim (ca.1493-1541)

322. Kerner, Dieter. *Paracelsus, Leben und Werk*. Stuttgart: Schattauer, 1965. 160 pp., illus.

    General presentation of the life of Paracelsus based partly on autobiographical elements in Paracelsus's work.

323. Pagel, Walter. *Paracelsus: An Introduction to Philosophical Medicine in the Era of the Renaissance*. 2nd rev. ed. Basel: Karger, 1982. 399 pp., illus., index.

    A thorough analysis of the details known of Paracelsus's life as well as his philosophy, influence, and sources. The revised edition's addenda corrects many misstatements of facts about Paracelsus that have been uncovered since the first edition (1958). A well-documented source that provides good context for Paracelsian ideas.

1e—Biographies: Pelletier, Pierre Joseph (1788-1842)

324. Dillemann, Georges. "La vie de Joseph Pelletier." *Revue d'histoire de la pharmacie* 36, no. 281-82 (1989): 128-34.

> Pelletier's work in pharmacy, his personal life, and university career are reviewed. Bibliography.

1e—Biographies: Perkin, William Henry (1838-1907)

325. "Sir William Henry Perkin." *Ciba Review* 10, no. 115 (1956): 2-49.

> His career touches on the major developments in the history of nineteenth-century chemistry, including the birth of the pharmaceutical industry. Illustrations.

1e—Biographies: Pinkham, Lydia

326. Washburn, Robert Collyer. *The Life and Times of Lydia E. Pinkham.* 1931; repr. Arno Press, 1976. 221 pp., illus.

> Personal life and links to her business are described.

1e—Biographies: Power, Frederick B. (1853-1927)

327. Griffith, Ivor. "A Half Century of Research in Plant Chemistry: A Chronological Record of the Scientific Contributions of Frederick Belding Power." *American Journal of Pharmacy* 96 (1924): 601-14.

> The biographical sketch here is reprinted from *The First Century of the Philadelphia College of Pharmacy.* Lists his publications and awards.

328. Phillips, Max. "Frederick Belding Power, Most Distinguished American Phytochemist." *Journal of Chemical Education* 31 (1954): 258-61.

   Covers the main periods of Powers' career, with brief summary of some of his most well-known work.

1e—Biographies: Procter, William, Jr. (1817-1874)

329. Higby, Gregory J. *In Service to American Pharmacy: The Professional Life of William Procter, Jr.* Tuscaloosa, Alabama: University of Alabama Press, 1992.

   A landmark in the historiography of American pharmacy, this well-documented biography covers his personal and professional history. Procter was an indefatigable worker in pharmacy, striving to elevate pharmacy from a trade to a profession and deserving of the sobriquet "Father of American Pharmacy."

1e—Biographies: Reber, Burkhard (1848-1926)

330. Röthlisberger, Paul. "Burkhard Reber, Genf (1848-1926), und sein Beitrag zur Geschichte der Medizin und Pharmazie." *Gesnerus* 34 (1977): 213-31.

   Review of the career of the chief pharmacist at the cantonal hospital in Geneva, who was also a prolific collector and writer in the history of pharmacy. With bibliography.

William Procter, Jr., editor of the first American textbook of pharmacy, Practical Pharmacy (1849).

1e—Biographies: Redwood, Theophilus (1806-1892)

331. Bett, W. R. "Theophilus Redwood (1806-1892)." *Pharmaceutical Journal* 177 (1956): 480.

    Outlines Redwood's career in teaching, editing, and writing pharmacy.

332. Ince, Joseph. "Obituary." *Pharmaceutical Journal and Transactions* 93rd series, 22, 5 (1891-92): 763-66.

    Detailed note on Redwood.

333. Thomas, P. H. "Professor Theophilus Redwood (1806-1892)." *Pharmaceutical Historian* 13 (1983): 9-12.

    Portrait. Fairly detailed early biographical information, with a discussion of the changing nature of the profession during this period.

1e—Biographies: Rice, Charles (1841-1901)

334. Wolfe, H. George. "Charles Rice (1841-1901), An Immigrant in Pharmacy." *American Journal of Pharmaceutical Education* 14 (1950): 285-305.

    The best biographical treatment of the most enigmatic character in American pharmacy. Rice was head of the largest hospital pharmacy operation in North America, centered at New York's Bellevue. He led the reform of the United States Pharmacopeia in 1880, as well as the revision of 1890. For all his achievements, almost nothing is known about his background or personal life. In contrast to other sketches, this article is fully documented.

1e—Biographies: Richards, Alfred Newton (1876-1966)

335. Schmidt, C. F. "Alfred Newton Richards: 1876-1966." *Biogr. Mem. Fellows Roy. Soc.* 13 (1967): 327-42.

    Describes his career, especially his teaching and laboratory work, with a list of his publications.

336. Starr, Isaac, et al. "Alfred Newton Richards, Scientist and Man." *Annals of Internal Medicine* 71, Suppl. 8 (Nov 69): 1-88.

    This memorial volume brings together reminiscences and articles about his life and work, which covers a number of important topics in the history of pharmacology.

1e—Biographies: Rusby, Henry Hurd (1855-1940)

337. Bender, George A. "Henry Hurd Rusby—Scientific Explorer, Societal Crusader, Scholastic Innovator." *Pharmacy in History* 23 (1981): 71-85.

    A colorful review of Rusby's life and work.

1e—Biographies: Scheele, Carl Wilhelm (1742-1786)

338. Nordenskiöld, A. E. *Carl Wilhelm Scheele. Nachgelassene Briefe und Aufzeichnungen.* Stockholm: 1892. 491 pp.

    Pioneering work on Scheele, using a comprehensive selection of Scheele's papers.

339. Urdang, George. *The Apothecary Chemist Carl Wilhelm Scheele: A Pictorial Biography.* 2nd ed. Madison, WI: American Institute of the History of Pharmacy, 1958. 66 pp., illus.

Photographs complement the biographical sketch of the apothecary-chemist Scheele, filling a need for an English text on Scheele.

340. Zekert, Otto. *Carl Wilhelm Scheele: Apotheker—Chemiker—Entdecker*. Grosse Naturforscher, Band 27. Stuttgart: Wissenschaftliche Verlagsgesellschaft, 1963. 149 pp., illus., bibl., index.

Reveals his personal life and the important role pharmacy had in his scientific development. Major text for biography of Scheele.

1e—Biographies: Sertürner, Friedrich Wilhelm Adam (1783-1807)

341. Krömeke, Franz. *Friedrich Wilhelm Sertürner der Entdecker des Morphiums. Lebensbild und Neudruck der Original-Morphiumarbeiten*. Jena: 1925. 93 pp., illus.

Covers his life and the discovery of morphine, using excerpts from journal articles.

342. Schmitz, Rudolf. "Friedrich Wilhelm Sertürner and the Discovery of Morphine." *Pharmacy in History* 27 (1985): 61-74.

Translation from a German article. Includes a bibliography and references to biographical information on Sertürner.

1e—Biographies: Spalding, Lyman (1775-1821)

343. Lord, R. A. "Lyman Spalding and the U. S. Pharmacopoeia . . ." *Pharmacy in History* 17 (1975): 21-23.

The text of a previously unpublished letter by Spalding is featured in this short note.

344. Spalding, James Alfred. *Dr. Lyman Spalding; The Originator of the U. S. Pharmacopoeia.* Boston: Leonard, 1916. 380 pp., index.

Chronicle style of biography with limited use. Primarily valuable because of transcribed letters to Spalding.

1e—Biographies: Squibb, Edward R. (1819-1900)

345. Blochman, Lawrence. *Doctor Squibb: The Life and Times of a Rugged Idealist.* New York: Simon and Schuster, 1958. 371 pp., index.

Using the many volumes of Squibb's personal diaries, the author describes Squibb in his role as a crusader for pure food and drugs, and a manufacturing pharmacist, as well as Squibb's personal goals and ambitions.

1e—Biographies: Stahl, Georg Ernst (1660-1734)

346. Strube, Irene. *Georg Ernst Stahl.* Biographien hervorragender Naturwissenschaftler, Techniker und Mediziner, 76. Leipzig: Teubner, 1984. 82 pp., illus.

His life and chemical work are summarized.

1e—Biographies: Stearns, Frederick (1831-1907)

347. Lakey, Roland T. "Frederick Stearns, Pharmacist." *Journal of the American Pharmaceutical Association, Practical Pharmacy Edition* 9 (1948): 486-89.

Reviews Stearns' early career and his problems with the American Pharmaceutical Association.

1e—Biographies: Thomson, Samuel (1769-1843)

348. Lloyd, John Uri. "Life and Medical Discoveries of Samuel Thomson and a History of the Thomsonian Materia Medica." *Bulletin of the Lloyd Library* 11 (1909): 1-140.

    Reproduces his "New Guide to Health" and other texts to present the life of Thomson to readers. Not expressly biographical. Portrait.

1e—Biographies: Trommsdorff, Johannes Bartholomaeus (1770-1837)

349. Götz, Wolfgang. "250 Jahre Trommsdorff und die Pharmazie." *Beiträge zur Geschichte der Pharmazie* 31, no. nr. 26/27 (1985): 12-15 (Beilage zur Deutschen Apotheker Zeitung); nr. 28, pp. 17-19; nr. 29, pp. 28-30.

    Excellent 3-part series that details the significant interaction between Trommsdorff and the development of chemistry and pharmacy.

350. "Johann Bartholomäus Trommsdorff (1770-1837) und die Begründung der modernen Pharmazie." *Beiträge zur Geschichte der Universität Erfurt* 16 (1971-72): 11-295.

    A monograph with 9 articles about Trommsdorff and his contributions to pharmacy and chemistry, as well as biographical information.

351. Wimmer, Curt P. "Johann Bartholomaus Trommsdorff: Pharmacist, Teacher, Scientist." *Journal of the American Pharmaceutical Association* 27 (1938): 56-57.

    Testimonial (on the 100th anniversary of his death), emphasizing his influence in putting pharmacy on a scientific basis.

1e—Biographies: Tschirch, Alexander (1856-1939)

352. Raubenheimer, Otto. "Tschirch, Master of Pharmacognosy." *Journal of the American Pharmaceutical Association* 15 (1926): 886-92.

    Outline review of his achievements, honors, and list of students.

353. Steinegger, E. "Alexander Tschirch und die Pharmakognosie." *Schweizerische Apotheker-Zeitung* 94 (1956): 925-30.

    On the 100th anniversary of Tschirch's birth, a review of his life and career.

1e—Biographies: Urdang, George (1882-1960)

354. Sonnedecker, Glenn. "George Urdang, 1882-1960." *Isis* 51 (1960): 562-64.

    Biography and character sketch of this major figure in the history of pharmacy.

355. Wolfe, H. George. "George Urdang, 1882-1960: The Man and His Work." *Pharmacy in History* 5 (1960): 33-42.

    Tribute to Urdang from a long-time friend and colleague. Especially valuable for Urdang's life before he came to America. Other memorial vignettes also appear in this volume.

1e—Biographies: Virey, Julien Joseph (1755-1846)

356. Berman, Alex. "Romantic Hygeia: J. J. Virey (1775-1846), Pharmacist and Philosopher of Nature." *Bulletin of the History of Medicine* 39 (1965): 134-42.

Places Virey within the utilitarian and scientific context of French pharmacy. Virey saw pharmacists as exercising a public health function.

1e—Biographies: Wiegleb, Johann Christian (1732-1800)

357. Moeller, R. "Ein Apotheker und Chemiker der Aufklärung. Beiträge zur Biographie Johann Christian Wieglebs." *Pharmazie* 20 (1965): 230-39.

    One of the last of the "phlogiston" school of chemistry in Germany. Well-documented.

1e—Biographies: Wilbert, Martin Inventius (1865-1916)

358. Burkholder, D. F. "Martin Inventius Wilbert (1865-1916), Hospital Pharmacist, Historian, and Scientist." *American Journal of Hospital Pharmacy* 25 (1968): 330-43.

    The biographical details included in this article are rather scanty, but it does contain a full bibliography of Wilbert's writings. Describes his career at the German Hospital in Philadelphia.

1e—Biographies: Wilder, Hans M. (1831-1901)

359. *Druggists Circular* 51 (1907): 94.

    Short biography of Hans Wilder is one of fifty in this issue (pp. 81-94), highlighting distinguished pharmacists of the previous fifty years. Portrait.

1e—Biographies: Wiley, Harvey W. (1844-1930)

360. Björkman, Edwin. "Our Debt to Dr. Wiley." *World's Work* 19 (1909-10): 12443-48.

Biographies 91

>Gives an interesting, convincing character analysis by a contemporary.

361. Wiley, Harvey W. *Harvey W. Wiley—An Autobiography*. Indianapolis: Bobbs-Merrill Co., 1930. 339 pp.

    Although slanted for a defense of Wiley's life and work, this autobiography presents a colorful personal view of his battles.

1e—Biographies: Wood, Horatio C. (1841-1920)

362. Hale, Hobart Amory. "Horatio C. Wood, the Pioneer in American Pharmacology." *Therapeutic Gazette* 44 (1920): 322-24.

    Reveals Wood's personality.

363. Roth, George B. "An Early American Pharmacologist: Horatio C. Wood (1841-1920)." *Isis* 30 (1939): 38-45.

    Outlines Wood's importance in the development of pharmacology and a general history of his professional life.

1e—Biographies: Wyeth, John

364. "Pharmaceutical Company Founders: Meet Mr. Wyeth." *American Professional Pharmacist* 24 (1958): 323-27; 334.

    Illustrations. Colorful summary of Wyeth and early years of the company.

Part Two:
Special Subjects

2a—Practice of Pharmacy

365. Alderson, Wroe, and W. H. Meserole. *Drug Store Arrangement.* Domestic Commerce Series, #57. Washington, DC: U.S. Government Printing Office, 1932. 126 pp.

    This well-illustrated guide, part of the National Drug Store Survey, contains several case studies of remodeled stores. Several different floor plans are compared and contrasted. This booklet is full of tips and hints, especially about usually ignored subjects such as fixtures and storage.

366. Alpers, William C. *The Pharmacist at Work.* Philadelphia: J. B. Lippincott, 1898. 326 pp.

    This dialogue between a pharmacy owner, "Proprietor," and his young apprentice, "the Junior," considers several practice challenges confronting pharmacists at the end of the nineteenth century. Modern readers should read this book with caution, however, since it represents an ideal level of practice (with all preparations made in-house rather than bought ready-made) that existed in only the most prestigious pharmacies.

367. Berridge, Virginia. "Opium Over the Counter in Nineteenth-Century England." *Pharmacy in History* 20 (1978): 91-100.

    This well-documented article describes a side of over-the-counter practice usually ignored by historians.

368. Brockbank, William. *Ancient Therapeutic Arts*. London: William Heinemann, 1954. 161 pp., bibliography.

The "therapeutic arts" covered by Brockbank are enemas, cupping and leeching, counter-irritation, and intravenous injection. Although limited in scope, Brockbank provides a great amount of information in a readable text. The short book is well illustrated.

369. Bromell, John R. *Merchandising in Country Drug Stores*. Domestic Commerce Series, #65. Washington, DC: U. S. Government Printing Office, 1932. 32 pp., tables, maps.

In the early 1930s, the country drug trade was quite different from that of the city. Because orders to wholesalers were larger and less frequent, country store owners had problems balancing credit and cash flow. This booklet, part of the National Drug Store Survey, reports on areas such as store location, soda fountains, show windows, cleanliness, rent, advertising, sales, and wholesaler relations. (Compare with Edward J. Carroll, *Merchandising in City Drug Stores*, Domestic Series #70.).

370. [Brown, William]. "The Lititz Pharmacopoeia." *Badger Pharmacist*, no. #22-25 (1938): 1-70.

In 1778, a small hospital formulary written by William Brown was published in Philadelphia for use by the revolutionary army. The "Lititz Pharmacopoeia" as it is called is provided here in facsimile (in Latin) with a translation on facing pages and explanatory notes by Edward Kremers. The ingredients and a few manipulations are also analyzed by Kremers.

371. Buerki, Robert A. "Caleb Taylor, Philadelphia Druggist, 1812-1820: A Preliminary Analysis." *Pharmacy in History* 30 (1988): 81-88.

The contents of a collection of letters connected with Caleb Taylor's business as a wholesaler are analyzed in brief. The article's greatest value is its list of over three hundred "drugs, chemicals, dyestuffs, equipment and sundries" sold by Taylor during the covered period.

372. Buerki, Robert A., and Gregory J. Higby. "History of Dosage Forms and Basic Preparations." In *Encyclopedia of Pharmaceutical Technology*. ed. James Swarbrick, and James C. Boylan, pp. 299-339. New York: Marcel Dekker, 1992.

   This chapter consists of a glossary of dosage forms and preparations with many of the entries containing historical information. Each entry is referenced to a primary or secondary work.

373. Carroll, Edward J. *Merchandising in City Drug Stores*. Domestic Commerce Series, #70. Washington, DC: U. S. Government Printing Office, 1932. 18 pp.

   This report, part of the National Drug Store Survey, is similar to that of Bromell on country drugstores, except it is lacking the volume of detail. As with Bromell, Carroll asked 250 store owners about location, customer entrances, soda fountains, show windows, rent, advertising, sales, and so forth.

374. Carroll, Edward J. *Wholesale Druggists' Operation, A Case Study*. Domestic Commerce Series, #86. Washington, DC: U. S. Government Printing Office, 1934. 110 pp.

   In contrast with the rest of the National Drug Store Survey, this study looks at a single, unnamed business. Data on the stocking and sales of many different goods are described in 75 tables. Unfortunately, the basics of wholesaling are not discussed, so the reader must go elsewhere to discover the utility of these "middlemen."

375. Caspari, Charles Jr. *A Treatise on Pharmacy for Students and Pharmacists*. 2nd ed. Philadelphia: Lea Brothers and Co., 1901. 747 pp., index, 301 illustrations.

This work is divided into three sections: Part I on General Pharmacy (basic apparatus and techniques), Part II on Practical Pharmacy (dosage forms), and Part III on Pharmaceutical Chemistry (synthesis and analysis). What distinguishes this primary source is its excellent illustrations, often showing apparatus in use.

376. Charters, W. W., A. B. Lemon, and Leon M. Monell. *Basic Material for a Pharmaceutical Curriculum.* New York: McGraw-Hill, 1927. 358 pp., index.

The approach of Charters to educational planning was direct — study how people practice pharmacy and design curricula to meet those practice needs. The resulting work contains information such as tabulated inventories from 27 stores and a chart for personality trait analysis by pharmacists. Unfortunately, this work helped to fossilize pharmaceutical education for a generation.

377. Cook, E. Fullerton, and Charles H. LaWall. *Remington's Practice of Pharmacy.* Philadelphia: Lippincott, 1936. 8th edition, 2020 pp., index, illus.

First published in 1885 as *Practice of Pharmacy* under the pen of Joseph Remington, this textbook has remained the "bible" of American pharmacy practice up through its most recent edition (1990). The eighth edition is the last that bridged the character of the old "Remingtons" with modern developments. For example, chapter 17 covers the classification of biologicals, while chapter 124 describes homeopathic pharmacy.

378. Cook, Roy Bird. *The Annals of Pharmacy in West Virginia.* Charleston, West Virginia: West Virginia Pharmaceutical Association, 1946. 84 pp.

Most of this book contains details pertaining only to organized pharmacy in West Virginia, but the first 30 pages contains colorful (and enlightening) anecdotes concerning pharmacy practice.

379. Cowen, David L., Louis King, and Nicholas Lordi. "Nineteenth Century Drug Therapy: Computer Analysis of the 1854 Prescription File of a Burlington [New Jersey] Pharmacy." *Journal of the Medical Society of New Jersey* 78 (1981): 758-761.

Although mainly concerned with the drugs used in therapy, this article does touch as well on prescribing and dispensing practices. Unfortunately, this groundbreaking approach has not been duplicated widely.

380. Crellin, John K., and J. O'Mara. *"A Store Mixt, Various, Universal" Community Pharmacy Past and Present*. St. John's, Newfoundland: n.p., 1990. 50 pp.

This short booklet contains a mixture of primary material on pharmacy practice and historical commentary. Although it has a definite Newfoundland flavor, the booklet sheds some light on community pharmacy practice in North America and provides a few provocative interpretations.

381. Delgado, Frank A., and Arthur A. Kimball. *Prescription Department Sales Analysis in Selected Drug Stores*. Domestic Commerce Series, #59. Washington, DC: U. S. Government Printing Office, 1932. 37 pp.

This is a study of the prescriptions from 13 stores in the St. Louis area, as part of the National Drug Store Survey. Careful analysis is done of several aspects of prescription practice including legibility of writing, extent of doctor dispensing, frequency of ingredients, and the number of liquor prescriptions. Most of the information is provided in tabular form.

382. Delgado, Frank A., and Arthur A. Kimball. "The Professional Pharmacy: An Analysis of Prescription Department Activities." *Journal of the American Pharmaceutical Association* 22 (1933): 671-693; 764-782; 883-901; 983-1004.

By "professional pharmacy" the authors meant stores "in which the majority of the business is in prescriptions, and in which only the professional phase is promoted." Of the estimated 60,000 drug stores in the USA in 1933, only about 400 met these criteria. These were not "pure pharmacies," however, and several had cigar counters, soda fountains, and other "conveniences." Although descriptive of the elite of American pharmacies, this four-part series is full of pithy analysis of prescription pricing and hints about pharmacy management.

383. Dowling, Harry F. *Medicines for Man: The Development, Regulation, and Use of Prescription Drugs.* New York: Alfred A. Knopf, 1971. 347 pp., index.

Although a bit dated, this book is still a good introduction to the subject, with some documentation and an index.

384. *The Druggist's Manual. Being a Price Current of Drugs, Medicines, Paints, Dye-Stuffs, Glass, Patent Medicines, etc.* Philadelphia: Philadelphia College of Pharmacy, 1826. 119 pp.

This rare volume contains a brief history of the founding of PCP, its by-laws, and similar internal information. About half the manual is dedicated to a listing of drugs and other items stocked in shop with columns for prices by the pound, quarter pound, ounce, and drachm. Lists of Latin and English synonyms are followed by French, Spanish, and German indices. The book concludes with about 40 pages of tables dealing with weights and measures, specific gravity, incompatibilities, and abbreviations. A table of doses is included, which reminds us that the pharmacist's role as prescriber and prescription checker is an old one.

385. Fantus, Bernard. *A Textbook on Prescription-Writing and Pharmacy* . . . Chicago: Chicago Medical Book Company, 1913, 2nd edition. 375 pp., index.

In this book Fantus approaches the physician-pharmacist interface, that is, the prescription, and thereby sheds light on the practical interactions between the professions. Fantus also discusses some of the nitty-gritty practical issues surrounding the parts of the prescription and incompatibility issues from the physician's perspective.

386. Francke, Donald E., Clifton J. Latiolais, Gloria N. Francke, and Norman F. H. Ho. *Mirror to Hospital Pharmacy*. Washington, DC.: American Society of Hospital Pharmacists, 1964. 234 pp., index, tables.

This is the summary report of a national audit of pharmaceutical services in hospitals, directed by Don Francke. With a multitude of tables and graphs, *Mirror* describes the status of hospital pharmacy in America and puts forward new directions just before the era of "clinical pharmacy" began.

387. Freedley, Edwin T. *A Treatise on the Principal Trades and Manufactures of the United States*. Philadelphia: Edward Young, 1856.

Chapter five of this book contains an early description of the historical development of the American drug trade. The chapter also contains sketches of several pharmaceutical manufacturers, wholesalers, and retailers of the mid-nineteenth century, especially in the Philadelphia area.

388. Gathercoal, E. N., ed. *The Prescription Ingredient Survey*. n.p.: American Pharmaceutical Association, 1933. 163 pp.

As chairman of the National Formulary Revision Committee, Gathercoal collated seven prescription surveys done between 1885 and 1932, with the purpose of aiding the revision of the NF and the U. S. Pharmacopoeia. The data from the five most detailed surveys is tabulated together alphabetically by proprietary or official title. All told, over 500,000 prescriptions were analyzed.

389. Ginzburg, Isaiah. "A Pharmacist in Tsarist Russia: A Reminiscence, 1892-1909." *Pharmacy in History* 27 (1985): 139-159.

This version of Ginzburg's reminiscences, edited by Cleo Sonnedecker, touches on several aspects of Russian pharmaceutical life and practice. It contains details about daily pharmacy work that could be compared profitably with practices in other nations.

390. Griffenhagen, George. "The Pharmacy in History." *Journal of the International College of Surgeons* 29 (1958): 789-803.

An illustrated introduction to the form and function of the pharmacy from ancient times up to the early twentieth century.

391. Haffner, Gerald O., and William E. Wilson. "The Medical Inventory of a Pioneer Doctor." *Indiana Magazine of History* 46 (March 1960): 37-63.

In 1833 Dr. Andrew Rodgers of Charlestown, Indiana, died, and an inventory of his shop was taken. The inventory includes his personal belongings (horses, furniture, and so forth) as well. There is limited discussion about most of the medicinal items listed.

392. Helfand, William H., and David L. Cowen. "Evolution of Pharmaceutical Oral Dosage Forms." *Pharmacy in History* 25 (1983): 3-18.

This short review includes descriptions of the materials and techniques used in pill and tablet coating as well as capsule filling by pharmacists in the nineteenth and early twentieth centuries. Most of the article, however, deals with more modern manufacturing developments. The authors focus on timed-release dosage forms: Unna's enteric coating with Karatin in 1884, Smith Kline and French's Spansule system of 1952, and contributions of Theeuwes and Higuchi to the recent development of the Gastro-Intestinal Therapeutic System.

393. Kalman, Samuel H., and John F. Schlegel. "Standards of Practice for the Profession of Pharmacy." *American Pharmacy* 19 (1979): pp. 133-146.

Provides in outline form the basic responsibilities and tasks of American pharmacists of the late twentieth century. The standards are concrete and direct, advocating a high level of practice but short of an ideal level.

394. Kilmer, F. B., and Charles D. Deshler. "Drug Clerks One Hundred Years Ago." *Journal of the American Pharmaceutical Association* 18 (1929): 711-722.

Before becoming a writer, Charles Deshler worked as a drug clerk (employed pharmacist). His reminiscences of his experiences came into the hands of Kilmer, who edited them for publication. Although heavy on anecdotes, Deshler provides valuable details about day-to-day practice in the 1830s in New Jersey.

395. Lyman, Rufus A., ed. *American Pharmacy*. Philadelphia: J. B. Lippincott, 1945.

Pharmacist-historian George Urdang served as the technical editor of this overview of American pharmacy practice. Much of the work covers the preparation of dosage forms, and some of the authors included historical background on their subjects.

396. MacEwan, Peter. *The Art of Dispensing*. London: Chemist and Druggist, 1900. 6th edition, 473 pp., index, illustrated.

This compact manual covers the essential aspects of English pharmaceutical practices ca. 1900. Its chatty style is in contrast to the stiff prose of American manuals.

397. National Association of Retail Druggists. *The Independent Druggist (Report Number One)*. n.p.: Curtis Publishing, 1945. 112 pp., tables.

The study was based on survey replies from 1,723 independent store owners in 1944. It provides a snapshot of the "average" drugstore of the period. For example, of the stores surveyed, 9.4% had marble floors, 73% extended credit to customers, and 75% had soda fountains. With peace at hand, about 50% planned on remodeling their stores.

398. Noel, H. S., ed. *The Modern Apothecary*. Indianapolis: Eli Lilly & Company, 1941. 225 pp., illus.

   This book contains 26 essays on modernizing pharmacies covering topics as diverse as location, personnel, promotion, and lighting. The second part of the work deals with pharmacy interiors, exteriors, and displays, including floor plans and several illustrations of contemporary stores. It is a mixture of ideal elegant pharmacies and the traditional corner drugstores.

399. Parrish, Edward. *An Introduction to Practical Pharmacy* . . . Philadelphia: Blanchard and Lea, 1856. 525 pp., index, illus.

   In contrast to Procter's edition of Mohr and Redwood's *Practical Pharmacy*, Parrish's *Introduction* is truly illustrative of American pharmaceutical practice at mid-century. Parrish had been teaching pharmacy to physicians for several years and his book reflects the reality of a nation where most prescriptions were not compounded by pharmacists.

400. Porter, Glenn, and Harold Livesay. *Merchants and Manufacturers*. Baltimore: Johns Hopkins Press, 1971. 248 pp., index, bibl.

   In this general study of American manufacturing and distribution, the authors include a short case study of Troth and Company, a Philadelphia drug wholesaler. Although just a small part of the book, the treatment is excellent and insightful.

401. Shannon, Michael C. "The First National Organization for Employee-Pharmacists, 1910-1934." *Pharmacy in History* 17 (1975): 58-68.

Although focused mainly on the history of the organization, this article does portray the differences in hours, practice, and pay between owners and employee pharmacists in the early twentieth century.

402. Smith, George Winston. *Medicines for the Union Army: The United States Army Laboratories During the Civil War.* Madison, Wisconsin: American Institute of the History of Pharmacy, 1962. 119 pp., index, illus.

This small book not only describes the practice of military pharmacy in the mid-nineteenth century, it also touches upon general practices as well. The main context of the book deals with the manufacturing efforts of E. R. Squibb, John Maisch, and others. Full documentation is included as well as a copy of the U. S. Army's drug supply table.

403. Soubeiran, E[ugene]. *Nouveau traité de pharmacie théorique et pratique.* 2nd ed. Paris: Crochard et Cie, 1840.

The theoretical and practical sides of French pharmacy at its height are described by Soubeiran. Emulated by Procter in the USA, Soubeiran had great influence on American practice through Procter's Syllabus of Study. There are only a few illustrations in these two volumes, so Mohr is much more valuable for information about mid-nineteenth century apparatus.

404. Sprowls, Joseph B. "An Introduction to Dosage Forms." In *American Pharmacy*. ed. Joseph B. Sprowls, and Harold M. Beal, pp. 1-26. 6th ed. Philadelphia: J. B. Lippincott, 1966. 415 pp., index.

In his introductory essay, Sprowls pulled together much of the historical material scattered throughout previous editions of *American Pharmacy*. His comments on the ancient world should be used cautiously, but his later analysis appears more sound.

405. Steele, I. K., ed. *Atlantic Merchant-Apothecary: Letters of Joseph Cruttenden, 1710-1717.* Toronto: University of Toronto Press, 1977. 124 pp., index.

An edited and annotated set of 122 letters from Joseph Cruttenden, a London druggist, to his overseas customers during the years 1710-1717. Sprinkled among the letters (mainly to Boston, New York, and Barbados) are many references to drugs and their prices. The historical information about the drugs given by the editor is scanty and should be verified by the reader. Above all else, the letters document the difficulties of cross-Atlantic trade in the early eighteenth century.

406. Strickland, W. A. "Quinine Pills Manufactured on the Missouri Frontier (1832-1862)." *Pharmacy in History* 25 (1983): 61-68.

Dr. John Sappington's Anti-Fever Pills are the focus of this piece. The author compares surviving samples of the Pills with replicas he made using the original formula.

407. Wertheimer, Albert I., and Mickey Smith (eds.). *Pharmacy Practice: Social and Behavioral Aspects.* 3rd edition. Baltimore: Williams and Wilkins, 1989. 441 pp., index.

This textbook is a mixture of original essays and classic articles on various aspects of pharmacy practice from a social science perspective. Several of the contributions to the book analyze practice issues historically. Full references are provided for all articles.

2b—Basic Pharmaceutical Disciplines

408. Albert, Adrien. "Relations Between Molecular Structure and Biological Activity: Stages in the Evolution of Current Concepts." *Annual Review of Pharmacology* 11 (1971): 13-36.

Much more technical than other historical articles on this subject but useful because the coverage extends to the mid-twentieth century.

409. Autian, J., and G. Wood. "The Role of Toxicology in the Pharmacy Curriculum." *American Journal of Pharmaceutical Education* 40 (1976): 378-82.

For the most part, this concentrates on contemporary teaching of toxicology, but it also has a brief discussion on the growth (or absence) of this discipline in pharmacy schools, and the reasons why.

410. Bachmann, C., and Marcel H. Bickel. "History of Drug Metabolism: The First Half of the 20th Century." *Drug Metabolism Reviews* 16 (1985-86): 185-253.

A sequel to the article by A. Conti and M. H. Bickel on drug metabolism in the nineteenth century (citation #418). The introduction cites several histories of the field besides Conti and Bickel. It covers conjugation reactions, the mechanisms of which awaited elucidation until the twentieth century; metabolism of selected compounds (e.g., barbiturates, morphine, and sulfonamides) that received considerable attention; and the physiological role of drug metabolism reactions. The authors have several useful tables with chronologies, publication output from different institutions, and principal workers in the field, and they cite over 260 primary sources.

411. Bearman, David, and John T. Edsall (eds.). *Archival Sources for the History of Biochemistry and Molecular Biology: A Reference Guide and Report*. Boston: American Academy of Arts and Sciences; Philadelphia: American Philosophical Society, 1980. xii + 338 pp., indices, accompanying microfiche.

Useful research resource, principally on nineteenth- and twentieth-century Europe and America. This is a guide to manuscript collections that has much on scientists, institutions, and subjects (each category is indexed) relevant to pharmaceutical sciences. For example, it includes citations to papers of Carl Voegtlin, Robert Robinson, A. N. Richards, and Vincent DuVigneaud.

412. Bernsmann, W. "Arzneimittelforschung und -Entwicklung in Deutschland in der zweiten Hälfte des 19. Jahrhunderts." *Pharmazeutische Industrie* 29(1967): 448-49, 525-29, 669-73, 745-48, 834-36, 963-66, 1032-35; 30(1968): 58-59, 131-32, 199, 342-44, 408-9, 471-73

Useful source of information on the pre-1900 German pharmaceutical industry. It has a dozen tables, including a list of human and veterinary drug manufacturers and their date of establishment. Also included in the tables are manufacturer, therapeutic use, and date of introduction of analgesics and antipyretics, anesthetics and hypnotics, antiseptics and disinfectants, diuretics and antiarthritics, purgatives and vermifuges, tonics, alkaloids, and biologicals.

413. Brewer, William A. "Reminiscences of an Old Pharmacist." *Pharmaceutical Record* 4 (1884): 210-211, 232-233, 255-256, 282-283, 304-305, 326-327, 348-349, 410-411, 424-425, 442-443, 460-461, 475, 494; 5 (1885): 6-7, 23, 38, 54-55, 71-72, 89-90, 105-106, 122-123, 138, 169-170.

This series of 23 short articles was written by a septuagenarian pharmacist looking back over his years of practice. Mixed among various "old yarns" are details about pharmacy design, in-shop manufacturing techniques, relations with physicians, and general practices not available elsewhere.

414. Butler, T. C. "Some Historical Reflections on Drug Metabolism." *Annals of the New York Academy of Sciences* 179 (1971): 502-507.

A brief article that emphasizes drug metabolism work in the nineteenth century by Buchheim, von Mering, and Schmiedeberg. It mentions the slow recognition of the importance of drug distribution and the kinetics of drug elimination, due to limited progress in analytical chemistry. On the other hand, author cites the work on sulfas and antimalarials in the 1930s and 1940s as trailblazing with respect to distribution and elimination kinetics.

415. "Célébration du bicentenaire de la naissance de Joseph Pelletier (1788-1842), 26 November 1988." *Revue d'histoire de la pharmacie* 36 (1989): 117-242.

   A special number of the *Revue* devoted to this key figure in the early history of pharmaceutical chemistry. This issue has several articles and appendices of note, including P. Rossignol on Pelletier's work on alkaloids (pp. 135-52), and a guide to a Pelletier exhibit in honor of the event at the Faculté de Pharmacie de Paris (pp. 233-40).

416. Chen, K. K., ed. *The American Society for Pharmacology and Experimental Therapeutics, Incorporated: The First Sixty Years, 1908-1969.* [Bethesda, MD: American Society for Pharmacology and Experimental Therapeutics], 1969. viii + 225 pp., illus., index.

   Useful reference source on the institutionalization of pharmacology in America; includes biographical information about notable pharmacologists.

417. Connors, Kenneth A., ed. *Pharmaceutical Science: Its Past and Its Future.* Madison, WI: [available through the American Institute of the History of Pharmacy, 425 N. Charter St., Madison, WI 53706], Proceedings of a Centennial Symposium. The School of Pharmacy, University of Wisconsin-Madison (1883-1983), October 2-4, 1983.

   Includes presentation (and reactor panels) by L. W. Busse on the history of pharmaceutical research; B. J. Poulsen on research vs. development in industry; S. T. Crooke, K. C. Kwan, and J. A. Mollica on drug delivery systems; and T. Higuchi and G. Levy on educating the pharmaceutical scientist in industry and pharmacy schools.

418. Conti, A., and Marcel H. Bickel. "History of Drug Metabolism: Discoveries of the Major Pathways in the 19th Century." *Drug Metabolism Reviews* 6 (1977): 1-50.

With the preceding work by Bachmann and Bickel (citation #410), the most comprehensive study of the subject. It is arranged by major pathways (oxidation, glycine conjugation, etc.). While quite technical, this article includes a useful section on "General Comments," a chronology of developments, and nearly 150 references to the primary literature.

419. Cowen, David L. "The History of the Science of Pharmacy." *Pharmacy in History* 7 (1962): 17-20.

    A brief but useful examination of the historiography of science as a component of the history of pharmacy. He attributes the lack of much attention to science in the history of pharmacy to George Urdang's vision that history of pharmacy be established as an independent discipline. The author advocates the addition of pharmaceutical science to the study of history of pharmacy.

420. Cowen, David L. "Materia Medica and Pharmacology." In *The Education of American Physicians: Historical Essays*. ed. Ronald L. Numbers, pp. 95-121. Berkeley: University of California Press, 1980.

    Excellent treatment of the transition from materia medica to pharmacology in American medical education, eighteenth century to the present. He conveys the character of how each discipline was presented, how and why the teaching changed, and he relates some of the principals involved, including John Morgan, John Jacob Abel, and Arthur Cushny.

421. Cowen, David L. "Pharmaceutical Scientists and Pharmacokinetics." *Veröffentlichungen der Internationalen Gesellschaft für Geschichte der Pharmazie, e.V.* NF 57 (1989): 53-60.

    Overview of the contributions of American pharmaceutical scientists to the development of pharmacokinetics, from the 1950s forward. Included are Sidney Riegelman, Joseph Swintosky, Edward Garrett, John Wagner, and Gerhard Levy.

422. Debus, Allen G. *The English Paracelsians*. London: Oldbourne, 1965. 222 pp., bibl., index.

   The theory and practice of iatrochemistry in the sixteenth and seventeenth centuries, including the impact of Paracelsus on England.

423. Debus, Allen G. *The Chemical Philosophy: Paracelsian Science and Medicine in the Sixteenth and Seventeenth Centuries*. 2 vols. New York: Science History Publications, 1977. 606 pp., illus., bibl., index.

   Although quite broad in scope, this has much on the ideology of drug preparation and administration.

424. Delépine, M. "Joseph Pelletier and Joseph Caventou (transl. by Ralph Oesper)." *Journal of Chemical Education* 28 (1951): 454-61.

   Some biographical information on these two leading figures in the history of pharmaceutical chemistry. This article describes their methodology in isolating the many alkaloids on which they collaborated.

425. Earles, Melvin P. "Early Theories of the Mode of Action of Drugs and Poisons." *Annals of Science* 17 (1961): 97-110.

   Examination of theories and supporting experiments of drug action along nerves vs. blood transport, from the seventeenth to the mid-nineteenth centuries. This draws on the work of John Jones and others to represent the neural route, and Felice Fontana, François Magendie, and James Blake to suggest drug action via blood circulation. The neural route was not fully discredited until the second half of the nineteenth century.

426. Earles, Melvin P. "Pharmacy and Its Relation to Scientific Education in Nineteenth-Century Britain." *Pharmacy in History* 11 (1969): 43-49.

Discusses the efforts of the nascent Pharmaceutical Society to institute systematic scientific training for pharmacists in 1840s Britain.

427. Earles, Melvin P. "Studies in the Development of Experimental Pharmacology in the Eighteenth and Early Nineteenth Centuries." (Ph.D. diss., University College, London, 1961.)

Compares the ballooned materia medica of the early eighteenth century with the subsequent relational approach to therapeutics, relying on animal experimentation to demonstrate the effects of poisons and drugs. He follows with a discussion of the increasing attention to route of administration and posology vis-à-vis debates over neural versus vascular drug distribution in the body. Finally, he discusses the impact of the isolation of active ingredients from crude drugs.

428. Estes, J. Worth. *Dictionary of Protopharmacology: Therapeutic Practices, 1700-1850.* Canton, Mass.: Science History Publications, 1990. 215 pp., illus.

The 3,000 entries in this extended glossary describe drug materials used before the first academic pharmacology laboratory was established in 1849 and the physiological rationales for their use.

429. Estes, J. Worth. *Hall Jackson and the Purple Foxglove: Medical Practice and Research in Revolutionary America 1760-1820.* Hanover, N.H.: University Press of New England, 1979. xvi + 291 pp., illus., index.

Emphasizes the data used by Withering and early nineteenth-century investigators in assessing the efficacy and safety of digitalis. Especially chapters 4-7.

430. Estes, J. Worth. "Naval Medicine in the Age of Sail: The Voyage of the *New York*, 1802-1803." *Bulletin of the History of Medicine* 56 (1982): 238-53.

This paper uses a naval surgeon's unusually detailed patient record to show how and why drugs were given in various sequences in conventional eighteenth-century medicine.

431. Estes, J. Worth. "Quantitative Observations of Fever and Its Treatment before the Advent of Short Clinical Thermometers." *Medical History* 35 (1991): 189-216.

    The author uses graphs and table to show how and why drugs were used in the treatment of fevers, the most prevalent of all illnesses, before 1870.

432. Estes, J. Worth. "The Shakers and Their Proprietary Medicines." *Bulletin of the History of Medicine* 65 (1991): 162-84.

    Outlines the Shakers' entry into pharmaceutical manufacturing and the grey area between their enviable reputation for high quality drugs and the several commercial distributors who exploited them.

433. Estes, J. Worth, and Laverne Kuhnke. "French Observations of Disease and Drug Use in Late Eighteenth-Century Cairo." *Journal of the History of Medicine and Allied Sciences* 39 (1984): 121-52.

    At the end of the eighteenth century, the French pharmacist Pierre-Charles Rouyer traveled to Egypt and documented the drugs found in Cairo shops. The authors analyze and tabulate Rouyer's findings in this unusual article.

434. Estes, J. Worth, and Paul Dudley White. "William Withering and the Purple Foxglove." *Scientific American* 212, no. No. 6, June (1965): 110-19.

    Presents data Withering used in making his conclusions.

435. Farber, Eduard. *The Evolution of Chemistry: A History of Its Ideas, Methods, and Materials.* New York: Ronald Press, 1952. 349 pp., index.

   Good general history.

436. Friedrich, C., and H. J. Seidlein. "Die Bedeutung der Entdeckung des Morphins für die Entwicklung der Pharmazeutischen Wissenschaft." *Pharmazie* 39 (1984): 340-45.

   Part of an ongoing series, "Beitrage zur Geschichte der Pharmazeutischen Wissenschaft." This installment covers the significance of Sertürner's discovery of morphine in alkaloid chemistry.

437. Fruton, Joseph S. *Molecules and Life: Historical Essays on the Interplay of Chemistry and Biology.* New York: Wiley-Interscience, 1972. x + 579 pp., bibl., index.

   Useful intellectual context for the more chemically oriented pharmaceutical sciences.

438. Goodman, Louis, and Alfred Gilman. *The Pharmacological Basis of Therapeutics.* New York: Macmillan, 1941; 2nd ed., 1955; 3rd ed., 1965; 4th ed., 1970; 5th ed., 1975; 6th ed. 1980; 7th ed. 1985; 8th ed., 1990.

   Now in its 8th ed. (1990), "Goodman and Gilman" is a historically conscious source that addresses the evolution of pharmacological and clinical knowledge of drugs or drug groups of current therapeutic interest. On the development of this source, see Henry Swain, "G & G: The textbook which structured American pharmacology," *The Pharmacologist* 26 (1984): 41-44. Historical backgrounds are given for most major drugs and drug classes, but they tend to become shorter over successive editions, and are not updated even in the face of important new research. The material presented in the successive editions over fifty years is itself a major primary source for the history of pharmacology.

439. Helfand, William H., and David L. Cowen. "Evolution of Pharmaceutical Oral Dosage Forms." *Pharmacy in History* 25 (1983): 3-18.

Survey of developments since the nineteenth century, beginning with pill coatings and pill encapsulations. The authors focus on timed-release dosage forms: Unna's enteric coating with Karatin in 1884, Smith Kline and French's Spansule system of 1952, and contributions of Theeuwes and Higuchi to the recent development of the Gastro-Intestinal Therapeutic System.

440. Hickel, Erika. *Arzneimittel-Standardisierung im 19. Jahrhundert in den Pharmakopoen Deutschlands, Frankreichs, Grossbritanniens, und der Vereinigten Staaten von Amerika.* Stuttgart: Wissenschaftliche Verlagsgesellschaft, 1973. vii + 293 pp., index.

Covers drug standards in these four countries, comparing the different scientific, social, and political contexts for their development.

441. Hoch, J. Hampton. "Bibliographic Materials in English Relating to the History of Pharmacognosy." *American Journal of Pharmaceutical Education* 23 (1959): 154-60.

Cites a number of histories, with a brief annotation of each source. He mentions several works that do not appear in this bibliography—although many of his citations are far broader than pharmacognosy alone.

442. Holmstedt, Bo, and G. Liljestrand. *Readings in Pharmacology.* New York: Macmillan, 1963. Repr. New York: Raven Press, 1981. x + 395 pp., illus., index.

Extracts from important works in the history of pharmacology and toxicology, chronologically arranged. The emphasis is on contributions of the nineteenth and early twentieth centuries, with extensive discussion and biographical information preceding excerpts from crucial sources. *Readings* is a valuable tool.

443. Keys, Thomas E. *The History of Surgical Anesthesia.* 1945; rprt. ed., Huntington, N.Y.: Robert E. Krieger Publishing Co., 1978.

    Probably the best overall survey of the subject in print, although from time to time new details of the story have appeared.

444. Koch-Weser, Jan, and Paul Schecheter. "Schmiedeberg in Strassburg, 1872-1918: The Making of Modern Pharmacology." *Life Sciences* 22 (1978): 1361-72.

    Traces Schmiedeberg's arrival at Strassburg, prejudices against pharmacology by clinicians at the time, Schmiedeberg's role in establishing pharmacology as a discipline, and most useful of all, details on Schmiedeberg's view of the function of pharmacology, especially with respect to therapeutics.

445. Kohler, Robert E. *From Medical Chemistry to Biochemistry: The Making of a Biomedical Discipline.* Cambridge: Cambridge University Press, 1982. ix + 399 pp., index.

    Essential institutional background (there is purposely no discussion of biochemical science per se) for evolution of pharmacology and some of the other basic pharmaceutical sciences, ca. 1850-1950.

446. Kraemer, Henry. "Rise and Development of Pharmacognosy." *Pharmaceutical Era* 45 (1912): 633-36, 697-700, 763-67.

    First two parts focus (almost filiopietistically) on the great men in the history of pharmacognosy, such as Flückiger, Tschirch, Maisch, and others. The last part takes a more topical approach, examining the role of chemistry and crystallography and drug standardization methodology.

447. Kuschinsky, Gustav. "The Influence of Dorpat on the Emergence of Pharmacology as a Distinct Discipline." *Journal of the History of Medicine and Allied Sciences* 23 (1968): 258-71.

Begins with the contributions of Rudolf Buchheim, who set up the first real institute of pharmacology in 1847 at the University of Dorpat and published one of the earliest texts devoted to pharmacology two years later (*Beiträge zur Arzneimittellehre*). He mentions the resistance to pharmacology by some of the established medical faculty in Germany. Finally, he covers the furtherance of pharmacology as a discipline under his successor at Dorpat in 1869, Oswald Schmiedeberg.

448. Leake, Chauncey D. *An Historical Account of Pharmacology to the Twentieth Century*. Springfield, IL: Charles C. Thomas, 1975.

This is the only narrative history of pharmacology yet published. It contains several errors, and only short bibliographic citations are given in the text.

449. Leake, Chauncey D. "The Status of Pharmacology as a Science." *American Journal of Pharmaceutical Education* 23 (1959): 173-96.

Looks at some specific themes in pharmacology, such as the relationship between dose and therapeutic effect, drug absorption, and the mechanism of drug action (each of which are covered in far greater detail in later articles by others). Includes a useful bibliography on classic works, current texts, and periodicals.

450. Leicester, Henry M. *Development of Biochemical Concepts from Ancient to Modern Times*. Cambridge, Mass.: Harvard University Press, 1974.

Good general history.

451. Lesch, John. "Conceptual Change in an Empirical Science: The Discovery of the First Alkaloids." *Historical Studies in the Physical and Biological Sciences* 11 (1981): 305-28.

Puts Sertürner's discovery of morphine in the context of chemical theories of acids and bases of the day and explains why French chemists exploited this discovery. This was a crucial period in the history of pharmaceutical chemistry, involving the recognition of a new class of chemical compounds, the plant alkalis, as a result of the isolation of morphine and its identification as a salifiable base.

452. Lynn, E. V. "A Century of Research in Pharmaceutical Chemistry in Schools of Pharmacy in the United States." *American Journal of Pharmaceutical Education* 17 (1953): 183-93.

A discussion not so much of the research itself as where the research was coming from; little research was actually being done at this time. This addresses APHA's query system as a means of stimulating research in the nineteenth century and mentions several of the leaders in research by the late nineteenth century. Finally, the article discusses the disappointment with productivity from pharmacy schools and how this might be alleviated. Undocumented.

453. *Natural Product Reports* 4, no. 4 (1987): 1-75.

This issue is devoted to the centennial of the birth of Robert Robinson, a twentieth-century giant in the synthesis of numerous therapeutically significant substances of natural origin. Several articles discuss his life and work.

454. Parascandola, John. *The Development of American Pharmacology: John J. Abel and the Shaping of a Discipline*. Baltimore: Johns Hopkins University Press, 1992. 212 pp., notes, bibl. essay, index, illus.

Describes Abel's role in establishing pharmacology as a discipline in the United States. He identifies several elements that constitute discipline formation in this field, including creation of a national society and expansion of the workforce into government and industry. The coverage is from the nineteenth century to about World War II.

455. Parascandola, John. "The Beginning of Pharmacology in the Federal Government." *Pharmacy in History* 30 (1988): 179-87.

The personnel and character of the work, c. 1900 to World War I, of the Division of Pharmacology of the Hygienic Laboratory, the United States Public Health Service, and the Bureaus of Chemistry, of Plant Industry, and of Animal Industry in the United States Department of Agriculture.

456. Parascandola, John. "Carl Voegtlin and the 'Arsenic Receptor' in Chemotherapy." *Journal of the History of Medicine and Allied Sciences* 32 (1977): 151-71.

Contrasts Voegtlin's views about the mechanism of action of organic arsenicals with those of Ehrlich. Both concluded that arsenicals worked by combining with sulfhydryl groups of the pathogen molecule, but Voegtlin's conclusion came from a series of premises that explicitly criticized Ehrlich's assumptions.

457. Parascandola, John. "The Controversy over Structure-Activity Relationships in the Early Twentieth Century." *Pharmacy in History* 16 (1974): 54-63.

Discusses arguments by those who championed physical properties (surface tension, osmotic pressure, etc.) as an explanation for drug activity as opposed to chemical composition and structure. A. R. Cushny, H. H. Meyer, C. E. Overton, and even the early Ehrlich illustrate the former group. He concludes that both sides were right to some degree, and the debate facilitated a broader view of drug action.

458. Parascandola, John. "Structure-Activity Relationships: The Early Mirage." *Pharmacy in History* 13 (1971): 3-10.

Examines the increasingly sophisticated efforts of James Blake, Benjamin Ward Richardson, Alexander Crum Brown, and Thomas R. Fraser in the nineteenth century to experiment with inorganic and, later, organic compounds, from which they tried to draw generalizations or even laws about the relationship between chemical constitution and expected therapeutic action. But neither general rules nor rational therapeutic applications could be derived from their work.

459. Parascandola, John. "The Theoretical Basis of Paul Ehrlich's Chemotherapy." *Journal of the History of Medicine and Allied Sciences* 36 (1981): 19-43.

   Definitive treatment of the intellectual foundation of chemotherapy. This discusses the evolution of Ehrlich's ideas about selective affinity, the side-chain theory of immunity and why he was at first reluctant to apply this drug action, the application of his theories to produce Salvarsan, modification of the side-chain theory to explain chemotherapy, and his principal therapeutic tactics stemming from his theories of chemotherapy.

460. Parascandola, John, and Ronald Jasensky. "Origins of the Receptor Theory of Drug Action." *Bulletin of the History of Medicine* 48 (1974): 199-220.

   A lucid account of the pioneering contributions of Paul Ehrlich and John Newport Langley to the development of receptor theory. Addresses the development of Ehrlich's side-chain theory of immunity, his reluctance to extend this to drug action, and how J. N. Langley's own work on receptors as an explanation of drug action, together with Ehrlich's studies on drug resistance, eventually led Ehrlich to postulate his receptor theory of drug action.

461. Parascandola, John, and John P. Swann. "Development of Pharmacology in American Schools of Pharmacy." *Pharmacy in History* 25 (1983): 95-115.

   Examines the nineteenth-century resistance to introducing pharmacology in pharmacy schools, the pioneering role of the

University of Michigan and especially Rufus Lyman at the University of Nebraska in the late nineteenth and early twentieth centuries, the slow acceptance of the discipline in pharmacy schools between the World Wars, and the role of *The Pharmaceutical Curriculum* in establishing pharmacology after World War II.

462. Parnham, M. J., and J. Bruinvels (eds.). *Discoveries in Pharmacology*. 3 vols. Amsterdam: Elsevier, 1983-1986. xii + 507 pp. (vol. 1), xviii + 708 pp. (vol. 2), xviii + 404 pp. (vol. 3), illus., bibl., index.

Volumes are devoted to psycho- and neuropharmacology (vol. 1), hemodynamics, hormones, and inflammation (vol. 2), and pharmacological methods, receptors, and chemotherapy (vol. 3). Each volume has up to a dozen essays, each essay followed by a bibliography. Most essays examine a drug or drug group, with the evolution of pharmacological and clinical understanding of the drug or drugs.

463. Rosenberg, Charles E. "Martin Arrowsmith: The Scientist as Hero." In *No Other Gods: On Science and American Social Thought*. Charles E. Rosenberg, pp. 123-31. Baltimore: Johns Hopkins University Press, 1976.

A succinct study of the culture of the biomedical researcher, including the image of industrial pharmaceutical research, at the time of publication of Sinclair Lewis's *Arrowsmith* in 1925.

464. Rosenberg, Charles E. "The Therapeutic Revolution: Medicine, Meaning, and Social Change in Nineteenth-Century America." *Perspectives in Biology and Medicine* 20 (1977): 485-506.

This essay is essential for understanding the shift in public and professional acceptability of drugs in the later nineteenth century.

465. Schneider, Wolfgang. *Geschichte der Pharmazeutischen Chemie.* Weinheim/Bergstr.: Verlag Chemie, 1972. 376 pp., illus., index.

The most comprehensive source on the subject; coverage from antiquity to the mid-twentieth century.

466. Schneider, Wolfgang. "A Bibliographical Review of the History of Pharmaceutical Chemistry." *American Journal of Pharmaceutical Education* 23 (1959): 161-72.

Very useful discussion of problems in defining "pharmaceutical chemistry." His emphasis is on the German literature; it is especially useful in identifying segments of broader works (not included in this bibliography) that address this subject.

467. Sheehan, John C. *The Enchanted Ring: The Untold Story of Penicillin.* Cambridge, MA: MIT Press, 1982. 224 pp., illus., bibl., index.

Despite its focus on a single drug group, an excellent source on an important episode in the history of medicinal chemistry—structural elucidation and synthesis of penicillin, and elaborations of this knowledge. A first-hand account of the unraveling of penicillin's structure, its first use in patients, and the difficulties of getting it into production.

468. Shryock, Richard Harrison. *American Medical Research: Past and Present.* New York: Commonwealth Fund, 1947. Repr. Salem, NH: Ayer, 1980. xv + 350 pp., index.

The only work of its kind. Nothing is as literate and as broad (chronologically and topically). It emphasizes a social and institutional approach over an internalist, discipline-by-discipline study. It is desperately in need of updating, but it is still required reading for historians or anyone else interested in biomedical research.

469. Smith, Dale C. "Quinine and Fever: The Development of the Effective Dosage." *Journal of the History of Medicine and Allied Sciences* 31 (1976): 343-67.

Discusses posology as a function of assumed drug action in the case of quinine in the nineteenth century.

470. Stechl, Peter. "Biological Standardization of Drugs Before 1928." (Ph. D. diss., University of Wisconsin, 1969. vii + 317 pp., illus., bibl.)

The only book-length history of bioassay. It examines the need to standardize drugs, chemical efforts to meet this need and their shortcomings, the usefulness of bioassay in selected drugs, differences between the chemical and biological camps, gradual acceptance of bioassay, and international efforts to unify biological standards for insulin.

471. Stieb, Ernst W., with the collaboration of Glenn Sonnedecker. *Drug Adulteration: Detection and Control in Nineteenth-Century Britain*. Madison: University of Wisconsin Press, 1966. 335 pp., illus., index.

Includes much on the evolution of drug analysis from antiquity to the nineteenth century.

472. Swann, John P. *Academic Scientists and the Pharmaceutical Industry: Cooperative Research in Twentieth-Century America*. Baltimore: Johns Hopkins University Press, 1988. xiv + 249 pp.

On the significance of different institutional settings for drug research. This looks at different typologies of research interaction between two estates of science and the impact of this collaboration on each side.

473. Swazey, Judith P. *Chlorpromazine in Psychiatry: A Study of Therapeutic Innovation*. Cambridge: MIT Press, 1974. xvi + 340 pp., illus.

Probably the best account in print of the introduction and impact of any single drug.

474. Swintosky, Joseph V. "Personal Adventures in Biopharmaceutical Research During the 1953-1984 Years." *Drug Intelligence and Clinical Pharmacy* 19 (1985): 265-76.

   On the early history of physical concerns—in academe (the University of Wisconsin School of Pharmacy) and industry (Smith Kline and French). Despite the title, this article deals only with the 1940s and 1950s.

475. Talalay, Paul, ed. *Drugs in Our Society*. Baltimore: Johns Hopkins Press, 1964.

   This book includes several chapters on important determinants of the emergence of scientific pharmacology and of the economics of the drug industry, especially in the twentieth century.

476. Tschirch, Alexander. *Handbuch der Pharmakognosie*. 3 vols. in 6. Leipzig: C. H. Tauchnitz, 1909-1925. 2d ed., 1 vol. in 3. Leipzig: B. Tauchnitz, 1930-1933. illus., bibl., index,

   A definitive source, according to J. Hampton Hoch. The first edition was issued in 64 parts. It gives considerable attention to history and has literally hundreds of photos of specimen collection.

477. Vandam, Leroy D. "On the Origins of Intrathecal Anesthesia." *International Anesthesiology Clinics* 27 (1989): 2-7.

   Review of the development of spinal anesthesia up to 1900, when the basic techniques (as well as an understanding of the risks) were established.

478. Vandam, Leroy D. "Some Aspects of the History of Local Anesthesia." In *Handbook of Experimental Pharmacology*. ed. G. R. Strichartz, pp. 1-19. Berlin: Springer-Verlag, 1987.

Describes the advances in developing local anesthetics as well as the developments in understanding physiology that clarified their mode of action.

479. Wagner, John G. "History of Pharmacokinetics." *Pharmacology and Therapeutics* 12 (1981): 537-62.

A literature review of who discovered what in this field, mostly covering the 1950s, 1960s, and 1970s. There is no attempt to set these various discoveries in any context or tie them together in a rational way. Still, this has an extensive bibliography and the benefit of a principal player's perspective in identifying significant discoveries in pharmacokinetics.

480. Warner, John Harley. *The Therapeutic Perspective: Medical Practice, Knowledge, and Identity in America, 1820-1885.* Cambridge: Harvard University Press, 1986. x + 367 pp., illus.

The central section of this book ("The Process of Change") provides many innovatively collated raw data that help explain the new emphasis given to many old drugs in the late nineteenth century.

481. Young, L. "The Metabolism of Foreign Compounds—History and Development." In *Drug Metabolism, from Microbe to Man: A Symposium in Honour of Richard Tecwyn Williams*. ed. D. V. Parke, and R. L. Smith, pp. 1-11. London: Taylor and Francis, 1977.

Begins by summarizing the earliest work on the metabolism of drugs and other products in the nineteenth century. Next he addresses the evolution and problems with the term "detoxication mechanisms." Finally, there is mention of twentieth-century concerns in this field, especially about efforts to identify metabolites, and the discovery of different factors affecting metabolism of foreign compounds. A bibliography is included.

2c—Materia Medica (Drugs) and Drug Therapy

General

482. Ackerknecht, Erwin H. *Therapeutics from the Primitives to the 20th Century.* New York: Hafner Press, 1973. x + 194 pp., bibl., index.

   A translation of the author's *Therapie von den Primitiven bis zum 20. Jahrhundert* (1970). A useful and well-written overview of the history of therapeutics, with an appendix on the history of dietetics. The work is too brief, however, to cover the subject in sufficient depth, particularly for the period since 1800. The absence of footnotes and the relatively cursory bibliography also limit the value of this book for the serious scholar.

483. Ackerknecht, Erwin H. "Aspects of the History of Therapeutics." *Bulletin of the History of Medicine* 36 (1962): 389-419.

   Traces major trends in therapeutics, from ancient Greece to nineteenth-century Europe.

484. Cowen, David L., and A. B. Segelman eds. *Antibiotics in Historical Perspective.* Rahway, NJ: Merck, 1981. 225 + 17 pp., illus., bibl.

   Using modern concepts and techniques as well as historical illustrations, the history of antibiotics is put into perspective. The very lucid narrative examines both the causes of disease and the search for cures in the historical first part of the book, and the second half deals with specific antibiotics.

485. Dannenfeldt, Karl H. "Ambergris: The Search for Its Origin." *Isis* 73 (1982): 382-97.

This study of the search for the origin of ambergris contains significant information on the medicinal uses of this substance over the ages.

486. Debus, Allen G. *The Chemical Philosophy: Paracelsian Science and Medicine in the Sixteenth and Seventeenth Centuries.* 2 vols. New York: Science History Publications, 1977. 606 pp., illus., bibl., index.

    A detailed study of Paracelsian science and medicine and its influence in the sixteenth and seventeenth centuries. Of most interest to historians of pharmacy are the sections dealing with the chemical medicines of the Paracelsians and the debates over their entry into the pharmacopeias.

487. Debus, Allen G. "Chemistry, Pharmacy and Cosmology: A Renaissance Union." *Pharmacy in History* 20 (1978): 127-37.

    Sets the chemically prepared medicines of the Paracelsians within the broader framework of the Paracelsian chemical philosophy.

488. Dymock, William, C. J. H. Warden, and David Hooper. *Pharmacographia Indica: A History of the Principal Drugs of Vegetable Origin, Met with in British India.* 3 vols. + Index and Appendix volume. London: Kegan Paul, Trench, Trübner and Company, 1890-1893.

    Still useful as a reference tool on the history of the major plant drugs of India.

489. Efron, Daniel H., Bo Holmstedt, and Nathan S. Kline. *Ethnopharmacologic Search for Psychoactive Drugs.* Second Printing. New York: Raven Press, 1979. xviii + 468 pp.

    The proceedings of a symposium held in San Francisco in 1967. The "Historical Survey" by Bo Holmstedt is particularly useful to historians, but many of the papers contain historical information on the therapeutic and other uses of psychoactive botanical drugs.

490. Estes, J. Worth. "Making Therapeutic Decisions with Protopharmacologic Evidence." *Transactions and Studies of the College of Physicians of Philadelphia* NS 1 (1979): 116-37.

A discussion of the factors on which physicians based their conclusions about the safety and efficacy of drugs in the period before the development of modern pharmacology.

491. Foust, Clifford M. *Rhubarb: The Wondrous Drug*. Princeton, NJ: Princeton University Press, 1992. xxi + 371 pp., illus.

A detailed and well-researched study of the botanical, commercial, and medicinal use of rhubarb, with emphasis on the period since 1600. Includes an extensive bibliography.

492. Guerra, Francisco. *Historia de la Materia Medica Hispano-Americana y Filipina en la Epoca Colonial: Inventario Critico y Bibliografico de Manuscritos*. Madrid: Afrodisio Aguado, 1973. 218 pp., illus., index.

Although a catalog of manuscripts, this volume includes a bibliography of 438 references to printed works on the history of the materia medica of Latin America and the Philippines in the colonial era.

493. Guerra, Francisco. *Bibliografia de la materia medica Mexicana*. Mexico: La Prensa Medica Mexicana, 1950. 423 pp., illus., index.

A bibliography of over 5,000 primary and secondary sources on the history of Mexican materia medica.

494. Haller, John S., Jr. "A Drug for All Seasons. Medical and Pharmacological History of Aloe." *Bulletin of the New York Academy of Medicine* 66 (1990): 647-59.

A brief overview of the botanical drug aloe from antiquity to the twentieth century.

495. Hamarneh, Sami. "Sources and Development of Arabic Medical Therapy and Pharmacology." *Sudhoffs Archiv* 54 (1970): 30-48.

   Identifies and briefly discusses some of the key works on drug therapy from medieval Islam, including Moorish Spain.

496. Hartwell, Jonathan L. *Plants Used Against Cancer*. Lawrence, MA: Quarterman Publications, 1982. vii + 710 pp.

   A collection of eleven articles, originally published in *Lloydia* between 1967 and 1971, surveying folk remedies used against cancer over the ages. Contains extensive tables and literature citations.

497. Hein, Wolfgang-Hagen, ed. *Botanical Drugs of the Americas in the Old and New Worlds: Invitational Symposium at the Washington-Congress 1983. Veröffentlichungen der Internationalen Gesellschaft für Geschichte der Pharmazie e. V.*, vol. 53. Stuttgart: Wissenschaftliche Verlagsgesellschaft, 1984. 131 pp., illus.

   Five papers, in both English and German versions, on the Aztec herbal of 1552, the European reception of American plant drugs, curare research, North American Indian materia medica, and traditional medicine in Southern Appalachia.

498. Hickel, Erika, and Gerald Schröder (eds.). *Neue Beiträge zur Arzneimittelgeschichte. Festschrift für Wolfgang Schneider zum 70. Geburtstag*. Veröffentlichungen der Internationalen Gesellschaft für Geschichte der Pharmazie e. V., vol. 51. Stuttgart: Wissenschaftliche Verlagsgesellschaft, 1982.

   Twenty papers, the majority in German, on a wide variety of topics in the history of materia medica. Three papers in English address the prescribing of drugs in the mid-nineteenth century,

Materia Medica and Drug Therapy 127

      research on curare, and the search for the active oxytocic principle of ergot.

499. Higby, Gregory J. "Gold in Medicine: A Review of Its Use in the West Before 1900." *Gold Bulletin* 15 (1982): 130-40.

      An overview of the medicinal use of gold from antiquity up to the twentieth century, including a discussion of the efforts of Dr. Leslie Keeley in the late nineteenth century to cure alcoholism with the double chloride of gold.

500. Hu, Shiu-ying. *An Enumeration of Chinese Materia Medica*. Hong Kong: The Chinese University Press, 1980. vii + 287 pp., index.

      Hu Shiu-ying is a botanist trained in China and at Harvard University. She worked for more than thirty years at the Arnold Arboretum at Harvard. This reference work contains the identification of nearly 2,000 drugs used in Chinese medicine. It also supplies an English pharmaceutical name for each entry, which is quite useful.

501. Hughes, R. Elwyn. "The Rise and Fall of the 'Antiscorbutics': Some Notes on the Traditional Cures for 'Land Scurvy'." *Medical History* 34 (1990): 52-64.

      Discusses the use of several herb preparations used against "land scurvy." Analysis of the vitamin C content of these herbs indicates that they would have been ineffective against true scurvy and supports the belief that the term "scurvy" was widely used for a variety of conditions unrelated to lack of vitamin C.

502. Kawakita, Yosio, Shizu Sakai, and Yasuo Otsuka (eds.). *History of Therapy (Proceedings of the 10th International Symposium on the Comparative History of Medicine—East and West)*. Tokyo: EuroAmerica, Inc., 1990. xviii + 288 pp., illus.

      This volume contains ten papers on various topics in the history of therapeutics. Half of the papers deal with China and Japan, and the other half with Europe and the United States. The gamut of history is covered from therapeutics in ancient China and the Roman Empire to the history of antibiotics. [not seen]

503. Lloyd, John Uri. *Origin and History of All the Pharmacopeial Vegetable Drugs, Chemicals and Preparations, With Bibliography*. Volume 1, *Vegetable Drugs*. Cincinnati: Caxton Press, 1921.

   A useful reference work containing brief essays on the history of the plant drugs covered in the eighth and ninth decennial revisions of the *United States Pharmacopeia*. The bibliography includes 707 citations. A planned second volume on "Chemicals and Preparations" was never published.

504. Lucia, Salvatore P. *A History of Wine as Therapy*. Philadelphia: J. B. Lippincott, 1963. 234 pp., illus., index.

   A chronicle of the use of wine as a medicine from antiquity to the twentieth century. Includes a chronology and extensive literature references.

505. MacGregor, Alasdair B. "The Search for a Chemical Cure for Cancer." *Medical History* 10 (1966): 374-85.

   A brief overview (largely a chronology) of the use of chemical substances against cancer, with emphasis on the nineteenth and twentieth centuries.

506. Martin, Richard T. "The Role of Coca in History, Religion, and Medicine of South American Indians." *Economic Botany* 24 (1970): 422-38.

   A useful overview of the use (including medicinal) of coca by South American Indians. Includes a bibliography.

507. Multhauf, Robert. "Medical Chemistry and "the Paracelsians"." *Bulletin of the History of Medicine* 28 (1954): 101-26.

Discusses the use of chemical drugs by the Paracelsians, with particular emphasis on Oswald Croll's *Basilica Chymia*.

508. O'Hara-May, Jane. "Foods or Medicines? A Study in the Relationship Between Foodstuffs and Materia Medica from the Sixteenth to the Nineteenth Century." *Transactions of the British Society for the History of Pharmacy* 1 (1971): 62-97.

Using examples from the sixteenth, eighteenth, and nineteenth centuries, O'Hara-May attempts to illustrate some of the changes in the relationship between foodstuffs and drugs, largely by examining alterations in the criteria used for assessing the function and value of foods in the preservation of health.

509. Ortiz de Montello, Bernard R. *Aztec Medicine, Health, and Nutrition*. New Brunswick, NJ: Rutgers University Press, 1990. xvi + 308 pp., illus., bibl.

A broad overview of Aztec medicine and nutrition (includes the interaction with Spanish medicine) that contains significant information on the Aztec materia medica. Especially useful in this regard is the appendix entitled "Empirical Evaluation of Aztec Medicinal Herbs."

510. Parnham, M. J., and J. Bruinvels (eds.). *Discoveries in Pharmacology*. 3 vols. Amsterdam: Elsevier, 1983-1986. xii + 507 pp. (vol. 1), xviii + 708 pp., (vol. 2), xviii + 404 pp., illus., bibl., index.

This multi-authored work includes many articles on the history of individual drugs or therapeutic classes of drugs as well as articles on the history of pharmacological techniques and theories.

511. Phillips, Joel L. *A Cocaine Bibliography: Nonannotated*. DHEW Publications, Number ADM 75-203, Research Issues Series, Number 8. Rockville, MD: National Institute on Drug Abuse, 1975. v + 131 pp.

Contains over 1800 references from the scientific and popular literature on cocaine and coca (including medical use) from 1585 to the 1970s.

512. Read, Bernard E. [Li Yu-t'ien, and Yu Ching-mei]. *Chinese Materia Medica.* 6 vols. Peking: Peking Natural History Bulletin, 1931-41.

    Bernard E. Read was a pharmacologist working at Peking Union Medical College in the early decades of the twentieth century. Together with his Chinese and Korean collaborators he produced many works on Chinese materia medica. This one is reprinted from the *Peking Natural History Bulletin.* Basically an encyclopedia of traditional Chinese drugs, based extensively on the *Pen ts'ao kang mu* of Li Shih-chen (1597). Each volume contains a bibliography.

513. Read, Bernard E. [and Liu Ju-ch'iang]. *Chinese Medicinal Plants from the Pen Ts'ao Kang Mu . . .* Peiping: Peking Natural History Bulletin, 1936.

    Along with 2 other works (citation #512,#514), these references comprise summarized translations of chapters 8-37 and 39-51 of Li Shih-chen's (1518-1593) *Pen-ts'ao kang mu (Systematized Materia Medica)* (1596) as well as the identification of the drugs contained in those chapters. [not seen].

514. Read, Bernard E., and C. Pak. *A Compendium of Minerals and Stones Used in Chinese Medicine from the Pen Ts'ao Kang Mu.* 2nd ed. Peiping: Peking Natural History Bulletin, 1936. 98 pp.

    Along with 2 other works (citation #512, #513), these references comprise summarized translations of chapters 8-37 and 39-51 of Li Shih-chen's (1518-1593) *Pen-ts'ao kang mu (Systematized Materia Medica)* (1596) as well as the identification of the drugs contained in those chapters.

515. Rivier, L., ed. "Coca and Cocaine 1981." *Journal of Ethnopharmacology, Special Issue* 3 (1981): 105-379.

Contains fifteen papers on various aspects of coca and cocaine, three of which are specifically historical. Several other papers also contain significant historical information.

516. Scarborough, John, ed. *Folklore and Folk Medicines.* Madison, WI: American Institute of the History of Pharmacy, 1987. v + 122 pp.

Seven papers presented at a symposium on folk medicines held in San Francisco in 1986. The time periods covered by the papers range from ancient and medieval times to the twentieth century.

517. Schneider, Wolfgang. *Lexicon zur Arzneimittelgeschichte: Sachwörterbuch zur Geschichte der pharmazeutischen Botanik, Chemie, Mineralogie, Pharmakologie, Zoologie.* 7 vols., illus. Frankfurt: Govi-Verlag, 1968-1975.

This multi-volume encyclopedia is an indispensable reference tool on the history of drugs. It includes many useful references to the primary and secondary literature.

518. Schwamm, Brigitte. *Atropa Belladonna: Eine antike Helpflanze in modernen Arzneischatz. Historische Betrachtung aus botanischer, chemischer, toxikoligischer, pharmakologischer und medizinischer Sicht unter besonderer Berücksichtigung des synthetischen Atropins.* Quellen und Studien zur Geschichte der Pharmazie, vol. 49. Stuttgart: Deutscher Apotheker Verlag, 1988. xviii + 416 pp., illus., bibl.

A broad overview of the botanical, toxicological, medicinal, etc. history of belladonna. Includes an extensive bibliography.

519. Simon, James E., Alena F. Chadwick, and Lyle E. Craker. *Herbs, An Indexed Bibliography, 1971-1980: The Scientific Literature on Selected Herbs, and Aromatic and Medicinal Plants of the*

Temperate Zone. Hamden, CT: Archon Books, 1984. xviii + 770 pp.

Although mainly concerned with modern scientific literature, this volume is of interest to historians because it includes a substantial general bibliography of books on herbs, bibliographies on herbs, and reports, symposia, and conferences on herbs.

520. Stewart, Grace G. "A History of the Medicinal Use of Tobacco 1492-1860." *Medical History* 11 (1967): 228-68.

   A detailed account of the subject, including a bibliography and several charts and appendices covering such topics as the diseases and other conditions for which tobacco was used therapeutically and sample formulas of tobacco preparations from the materia medica literature.

521. Temkin, Owsei. "Historical Aspects of Drug Therapy." In *Drugs in Our Society*. ed. Paul Talalay, pp. 3-16. Baltimore: Johns Hopkins Press, 1964. 311 pp., index.

   Although very brief, this article is of interest because it expressed the views of one of the world's most distinguished medical historians. The author discusses general trends in the development of drug therapy from antiquity to the end of the nineteenth century.

522. Turner, Carlton E., Beverly S. Urbanek, G. Michael Wall, and Coy W. Walker. *Cocaine: An Annotated Bibliography*. 2 vols. Jackson: University Press of Mississippi, 1988.

   Contains over 5,000 citations, divided into pre-1950 and 1950-1986 sections, with author and subject indexes.

523. Valverde, José Luis, and José A. Pérez Romero. *Drogas Americanas en fuentes de escritores Franciscanos y Dominicos*. Estudios de la Cátedra de Historia de la Farmacia y Legislación Farmacéutica de la Universidad de Granada, España, no. 8.

Granada: Catedra de Historia de la Farmacia y Legislación Farmacéutica de la Universidad de Granada, 1988.

Largely a catalog of the indigenous materia medica of Latin America mentioned in the writings of 24 Franciscan and Dominican missionaries. Based on extensive research in primary documents in Spanish libraries and archives.

524. Van Tassel, R. "Bezoars." *Janus* 60 (1973): 241-59.

Reports on the chemical analysis of more than 200 bezoars from 20 museum collections. Discusses the different kinds of bezoars and the size of the stones. Includes a bibliography.

525. Vohora, S. B., and S. Y. Khan. *Animal Origin Drugs Used in Unani Medicine*. New Delhi: Vikas Publishing House, 1979. iv + 137 pp., illus., bibl.

Basically a therapeutic index of animal drugs used in Unani medicine, including the Unani and English names of the animal, the parts used, and the mode of administration. There is not much discussion of the history of the drugs. Includes a short bibliography.

526. Watson, Gilbert. *Theriac and Mithridatium: A Study in Therapeutics*. London: Wellcome Historical Medical Library, 1966. x + 165 pp., illus.

A thorough but dry history of the famous remedies from antiquity through the eighteenth century.

Pre-1600

527. Brunner, Theodore F. "Marijuana in Ancient Greece and Rome? The Literary Evidence." *Bulletin of the History of Medicine* 47 (1973): 344-55.

Based upon an examination of the Graeco-Roman literary evidence, Brunner concludes that certain properties of cannabis were known and used for medicinal purposes, but that there is no evidence that the plant was used as an intoxicant in ancient Greece and Rome.

528. Cooper, William C., and Nathan Sivin. "Man as Medicine: Pharmacological and Ritual Aspects of Traditional Therapy Using Drugs Derived from the Human Body." In *Chinese Science: Explorations of Ancient Tradition.* ed. Shigeru Nakayama, and Nathan Sivin, pp. 203-272. M. I. T. East Asian Science Series, 2. Cambridge: MIT Press, 1973.

This study uses drugs of human origin to examine the factors—pharmacological, theoretical, magical—that determined the incorporation and retention of drugs in the traditional Chinese pharmacopeia.

529. Cruz, Martin de la. *The Badianus Manuscript (Codex Barberini, Latin 241), Vatican Library: An Aztec Herbal of 1552. Introduction, Translation and Annotations by Emily Walcott Emmart.* . Baltimore: Johns Hopkins Press, 1940. xxiv + 341 pp., illus.

A reproduction of a 1552 illustrated manuscript of an Aztec herbal in Latin, with an English translation, introduction, and annotations by Emmart. A major source of information on Aztec materia medica. Includes a bibliography and several useful indexes.

530. Curtis, Robert I. *Garum and Salsamenta: Production and Commerce in Materia Medica.* Studies in Ancient Medicine, vol. 3. Leiden: E. J. Brill, 1991. xv + 226 pp., illus., bibl., index.

A detailed study of the production and commerce as well as the medicinal use of fermented fish products in the ancient world.

531. Debus, Allen G. "The Chemical Philosophers: Chemical Medicine from Paracelsus to Van Helmont." *History of Science* 12 (1974): 235-59.

Brief survey of chemical medicine in this period, identifying the major players and the basis for their doctrines. Shows the links between chemical medicine and physics.

532. Estes, J. Worth. *The Medical Skills of Ancient Egypt.* Canton, MA: Science History Publications, 1989. xii + 196 pp., illus.

A large part of the book is dedicated to the Egyptian materia medica, including an eighteen-page glossary of drug substances. Documented and indexed.

533. Florkin, Marcel, ed. *Materia Medica in the XVIIth Century. Proceedings of a Symposium of the International Academy of the History of Medicine Held at the University of Basel, 7th September 1964.* Analecta Medico-Historica, I. Oxford: Pergamon Press, 1966. v + 80 pp., illus.

Six papers of varying length and quality, three in French and three in English, on various aspects of materia medica in the sixteenth century. The topics range from the influence of Dioscorides to Indian and Chinese materia medica in the period.

534. Goltz, Dietlinde. *Studien zur altorientalischen und griechischen Heilkunde: Therapie, Arzneibereitung, Rezeptstruktur.* Sudhoffs Archiv, Supplement Number 16. Wiesbaden: Franz Steiner, 1974. xiv + 352 pp., bibl.

An extensive study of the drug therapy, pharmaceutical literature, and dosage forms of the ancient world. Includes a bibliography.

535. Hamarneh, Sami. "Development of Arabic Medical Therapy in the Tenth Century." *Journal of the History of Medicine and Allied Sciences* 27 (1972): 65-79.

Discusses the writings on therapeutics of such noted authors of tenth-century Islam as Rhazes, Haly Abbas, and Albucasis.

536. Hamarneh, Sami. "Origins of Arabic Drug and Diet Therapy." *Physis* 11 (1969): 267-86.

Examines the Greek, Chinese, Indian, Persian, Egyptian, and other roots of medieval Arabic drug therapy.

537. Hameed, Hakeem Abdul, ed. *Avicenna's Tract on Cardiac Drugs and Essays on Arab Cardiotherapy*. Karachi: Hamdard Foundation Press, 1983. 216 pp., illus., bibl.

This volume consists of an English translation of a treatise by Avicenna on cardiac drugs as well as twelve essays by various authors on the knowledge and treatment of heart diseases.

538. Harper, Donald J. "The *Wu Shih Erh Ping Fang*: Translation and Prolegomena." (Ph.D. dissertation, University of California, Berkeley,1982.)

This important dissertation deals with the silk manuscript buried in a Han tomb since 168 B.C. It was among several manuscripts excavated in 1973 near Ma-wang-tui. It contains fifty methods of treatment, including materia medica, external surgical techniques, and incantations.

539. Harrison, R. K. "Healing Herbs of the Bible." *Janus* 50 (1961): 9-54.

A useful and substantive discussion of the medicinal plants of the Bible, although based on translations and secondary sources.

540. Karnick, C. R. "Notes on Some Ancient Indian Medicinal Drug Plants with Special Reference to 'Soma'—The Rejuvenator and Promoter of Longevity." *Clio Medica* 5 (1970): 261-68.

A brief discussion of some of the plant drugs mentioned in such classic works of Indian literature as *Rig-Veda*.

541. Kuznicka, Barbara. "The Earliest Printed Herbals and Evolution of Pharmacy." *Organon* 16/17 (1980/81): 255-61.

    Discusses the role of herbals as well as describing specific Polish and other herbals.

542. Leake, Chauncey D. *The Old Egyptian Medical Papyri*. Logan Clendening Lectures on the History and Philosophy of Medicine, Second Series. Lawrence, KS: University of Kansas Press, 1952. 108 pp., appendix, bibl., index.

    This small book on the Egyptian medical papyri places significant emphasis on materia medica and therapeutics. Particular attention is given to the Hearst Papyrus, and an appendix lists the formulas in this document.

543. Levey, Martin. *The Medical Formulary or Aqrabadhin of Al-Kindi*. Madison, WI: University of Wisconsin Press, 1966. xiii + 410 pp., illus., bibl., index.

    A reproduction and translation of an important medieval Arabic manuscript, with an extensive introduction and discussion of the materia medica of the formulary by Martin Levey.

544. Levey, Martin. *Substitute Drugs in Early Arabic Medicine with Special Reference to the Texts of Masarjawaih, Al-Razi, and Pythagoras*. Veröffentlichungen der Internationalen Gesellschaft für Geschichte der Pharmazie e. V., Bd. 37. Stuttgart: Wissenschaftliche Verlagsgesellschaft, 1971. 102 pp.

    Contains the translation of three of the oldest extant treatises on drug substitution in Arabic, with notes and commentary by Levey.

545. Levey, Martin. "Some Facets of Medieaval Arabic Pharmacology." *Transactions and Studies of the College of Physicians of Philadelphia* Ser. 4. 30 (1962-63): 157-62.

   General summary of the assessment of the originality of form and content of Arabic pharmacology.

546. Manniche, Lise. *An Ancient Egyptian Herbal*. London: British Museum Publications, 1989. 176 pp., illus.

   A well-researched study of botanical drugs of ancient Egypt, including a bibliography and a list of Egyptian plant names quoted by Dioscorides.

547. McVaugh, Michael. "An Early Discussion of Medicinal Degrees at Montpellier by Henry of Winchester." *Bulletin of the History of Medicine* 49 (1975): 57-71.

   A study of a twelfth-century manuscript of Henry of Winchester, in which Henry discusses his concept of medicinal degrees (the degrees of intensity of properties of medicines, such as moistness).

548. McVaugh, Michael. "Quantified Medical Theory and Practice at Fourteenth-Century Montpellier." *Bulletin of the History of Medicine* 43 (1969): 397-413.

   About 1300, Arnald of Villanova developed a system attempting to apply definite mathematical relationships to the practice of compounding medicines from individual simples or herbs. This paper discusses the efforts of several fourteenth-century Montpellier physicians to incorporate Arnald's system into existing medical doctrine.

549. McVaugh, Michael. "Theriac at Montpellier 1285-1325." *Sudhoffs Archiv* 56 (1972): 113-44.

   Examines a tradition of academic discussion of theriac, moving towards a philosophical basis for academic medicine. Considers

Arnald of Villanova and contains text of "Questiones de tyriaca" of William of Brescia.

550. McVaugh, Michael. "Theriac at Montpellier 1285-1325 (with an Edition of the 'Questiones de Tyriaca' of William of Brescia)." *Sudhoffs Archiv* 56 (1972): 113-44.

An examination of the medico-philosophical discussion of theriac at Montpellier, initiated by Arnald of Villanova. The Latin text of a treatise on theriac by William of Brescia is included as an appendix.

551. Merlin, Mark David. *On the Trail of the Ancient Opium Poppy*. Rutherford, NJ: Associated University Presses, Inc., 1984. 324 pp., illus.

A detailed analysis of the origins and early history of the use of opium. The author surveys over 500 articles and books (which are compiled into a bibliography) from a variety of disciplines.

552. Meyerhof, M. "The Background and Origins of Arabian Pharmacology." *Ciba Symposia* 6, no. 5-6 (1944): 1847-67.

Describes the paths by which earlier medical and drug knowledge was transmitted to the Arabs at Alexandria.

553. Multhauf, Robert. "The Significance of Distillation in Renaissance Medical Chemistry." *Bulletin of the History of Medicine* 30 (1956): 329-46.

Discusses the important role of distillation in the preparation of chemical remedies in the sixteenth century.

554. Multhauf, Robert P. "John of Rupescissa and the Origin of Medical Chemistry." *Isis* 45 (1954): 359-67.

Discusses the alchemical origins of the adaptation of chemical processes to the preparation of medicines, particularly in thirteenth- and fourteenth-century texts attributed to John of Rupescissa.

555. Riddle, John M. *Dioscorides on Pharmacy and Medicine. History of Science Series*, no. 3. Austin: University of Texas Press, 1985. xxviii + 298 pp., illus., bibl.

   The definitive study of the materia medica of Dioscorides, shedding important new light on our understanding of the organizational principles behind Dioscorides' *De materia medica*. Includes an extensive bibliography. A second volume, dealing with the influence of Dioscorides on later generations, is planned.

556. Riddle, John M. *Quid pro quo: Studies in the History of Drugs*. Variorum Collected Studies Series, CS367. Brookfield, VT: Ashgate Publishing Co., 1992. 330 pp., index.

   A reprint collection of 15 papers by John Riddle, including a typescript of one previously unpublished essay, with an index to all.

557. Riddle, John M. "Amber in Ancient Pharmacy: The Transmission of Information About a Single Drug, a Case Study." *Pharmacy in History* 15 (1973): 3-17.

   A study of the description of the medicinal uses of amber in the writings of Dioscorides, Galen, Pliny, and other ancient authors, with emphasis on the linguistic problems involved.

558. Riddle, John M. "The Introduction and Use of Eastern Drugs in the Early Middle Ages." *Sudhoffs Archiv* 49 (1965): 185-98.

   Looks at medieval recipe literature, with an eye to the introduction of Eastern drugs. Also looks at the relation between pharmacy and trade.

559. Riddle, John M. "Lithotherapy in the Middle Ages." *Pharmacy in History* 12 (1970): 39-50.

   Based on a study of 616 lapidary manuscripts, Riddle characterizes this body of literature in terms of its uses, background, and relation to other medical literature.

560. Riddle, John M. "Pomum Ambrae: Amber and Ambergris in Plague Remedies." *Sudhoffs Archiv* 48 (1964): 111-22.

   Discussion of the medical use of amber and ambergris (which were frequently confused) in medieval times, especially in an effort to rid the air of plague infestation.

561. Sadek, M. M. *The Arabic Materia Medica of Dioscorides*. Quebec: Les Éditions du Sphinx, 1983. x + 229 pp., illus., bibl.

   A study of the Arabic translations of Dioscorides, with particular emphasis on the Leiden manuscript, which Sadek believes to be the earliest and most complete of all extant Arabic versions of Dioscorides.

562. Scarborough, John, ed. *Symposium on Byzantine Medicine*. Dumbarton Oaks Papers Number 38. Washington, DC: Dumbarton Oaks Research Library and Collection, 1985. xvi + 282 pp., illus.

   A collection of twenty-one papers, three of which focus specifically on the materia medica: John Riddle, "Byzantine commentaries on Dioscorides"; Jerry Stannard, "Aspects of Byzantine materia medica"; and John Scarborough, "Early Byzantine pharmacology."

563. Scarborough, John. "The Drug Lore of Asclepiades of Bithynia." *Pharmacy in History* 17 (1975): 43-57.

   A discussion of what is known of the drug theory and use of Asclepiades, who practiced medicine in Rome in the first century B. C. Surviving records provide much more information about

Asclepiades' external remedies than about those intended for internal use.

564. Scarborough, John. "Theophrastus on Herbals and Herbal Remedies." *Journal of the History of Biology* 11 (1978): 353-85.

An examination of the plant drug lore in the work of Theophrastus in fourth-century Greece.

565. Scarborough, John. "Theoretical Assumptions in Hippocratic Pharmacology." In *Formes de Pensée dans la Collection Hippocratique*. ed. François Lasserre, and Philippe Mudry, pp. 307-325. Université de Lausanne Publications de la Faculté des Lettres, Number 26. Geneva: Libraire Droz, 1983.

A study of the pharmaceutical theory of Hippocratic medicine within the context of Greek philosophy, examining the application of certain precepts of philosophical thinking to the understanding of the action of drugs.

566. Sivin, Nathan. *Chinese Alchemy: Preliminary Studies*. Cambridge: Harvard University Press, 1968. xxiv + 339 pp., illus.

A critical edition and English translation of the text of *Tan ching yao chueh*, attributed to Sun Ssu-mo (seventh century AD), a work belonging to the Chinese alchemical tradition concerned with the search for elixirs of immortality. Includes an extensive commentary by Sivin, a bibliography, and several appendices relevant to the pharmaceutical and medical aspects of the text.

567. Smith, Emilie Savage. "Drug Therapy in Trachoma and Its Sequelae as Presented by Ibn al-Nafis." *Pharmacy in History* 14 (1972): 95-110.

A detailed account of the drug therapy for trachoma described in the ophthalmological treatise of the thirteenth-century Islamic physician Ibn al-Nafis, including a translation of 19 recipes into English.

568. Stannard, Jerry. "Greco-Roman Materia Medica in Medieval Germany." *Bulletin of the History of Medicine* 46 (1972): 455-68.

An examination of the merger of the classical Graeco-Roman and native Germanic traditions of materia medica in medieval Germany.

569. Stannard, Jerry. "Hippocratic Pharmacology." *Bulletin of the History of Medicine* 35 (1961): 497-518.

A concise, useful overview of the drug lore of the Hippocratic Corpus, divided into sections on pharmacognosy, pharmacodynamics, and pharmacotherapy. Provides abundant examples of the vegetable, animal, and mineral materia medica of the Hippocratics.

570. Stannard, Jerry. "Marcellus of Bordeaux and the Beginnings of Medieval Materia Medica." *Pharmacy in History* 15 (1973): 47-53.

Uses the *Liber de medicamentis* (written sometime between AD 395 and 410) of Marcellus of Bordeaux to examine the transition from ancient to medieval materia medica. Some aspects go back to earlier Graeco-Roman texts, and some point ahead to future doctrines.

571. Stannard, Jerry. "Materia Medica and Philosophic Theory in Aretaeus." *Sudhoffs Archiv* 48 (1964): 27-53.

Examines the materia medica of this significant medical writer and places pharmacologic practice within the context of the pneumatic theories of this school of philosophy.

572. Stannard, Jerry. "Medicinal Plants and Folk Remedies in Pliny, *Historia Naturalis.*" *History and Philosophy of the Life Sciences* 4 (1982): 3-23.

The aim of this study is to examine some of the nonscientific grounds for the belief in an use of plants for therapeutic purposes, using the *Historia naturalis* of Pliny the Elder (AD 23-79) as a case study.

573. Stannard, Jerry. "Squill in Ancient and Medieval Materia Medica, With Special Reference to Its Employment for Dropsy." *Bulletin of the New York Academy of Medicine* 50 (1974): 684-713.

Discusses the early history of the medicinal use of squill, with extensive references to the primary literature.

574. Stannard, Jerry. "The Theoretical Basis of Medieval Herbalism." *Medical Heritage* 1, no. 3 (1985): 186-98.

Outlines theories such as the four humors, sympathy and magic, and astrology that provide a base for herbalism.

575. Stuart, G. A. *Chinese Materia Medica. Vegetable Kingdom.* Shanghai: American Presbyterian Mission Press, 1911; repr. NY: Gordon Press, 1977. 558+ pp.

Still available in many reprint versions, this work was often cited for identification of Chinese drugs. This is largely replaced by the work of Shiu-ying Hu (1980) (citation #500).

576. Teigen, Philip M. "Taste and Quality in 15th- and 16th-Century Galenic Pharmacology." *Pharmacy in History* 29 (1987): 60-68.

Teigen analyzes eight herbals of the fifteenth and sixteenth centuries and provides a frequency distribution of the drugs in terms of their Galenic qualities. He also examines the use of taste in assigning qualities to drugs (e.g., bitter taste is correlated with a hot quality).

577. Teigen, Philip M. "This Sea of Simples—The Materia Medica in Three Early English Receipt Books." *Pharmacy in History* 22 (1980): 104-108.

Teigen analyzes three books of recipes from the fourteenth, fifteenth, and sixteenth centuries by indexing them, identifying the simples therein, and providing a numerical summary of the frequency with which specific simples are mentioned. He identifies the most frequently used simples and demonstrates the close connection between diet and pharmacy in this period.

578. Temkin, Owsei. "Fernel, Joubert, and Erastus on the Specificity of Cathartic Drugs." In *Science, Medicine, and Society in the Renaissance: Essays to Honor Walter Pagel*. ed. Allen G. Debus, pp. 61-68, vol. 1. 2 vols. New York: Neale Watson Academic Publications, 1972.

The theoretical basis for the mode of action of cathartics is discussed for these three scientists who diverged from traditional views without revolutionary upheaval.

579. Unschuld, Paul U. "Ma-wang-tui *Materia Medica*. A Comparative Analysis of Early Chinese Pharmaceutical Knowledge." *Zinbun: Memoirs of the Research Institute for Humanistic Studies. Kyoto University* 18 (1982): 11-63.

In this article Paul U. Unschuld attempts to identify the drugs listed in a medical manuscript placed in a Han tomb in 168 B.C. Excavated in 1973 near Ma-wang-tui the manuscripts have become known collectively as the 'Ma-wang-tui manuscripts'. In this article the drugs mentioned are compared to drugs listed in other known works of a later period. [not seen].

580. Unschuld, Ulrike. "Traditional Chinese Pharmacology: An Analysis of Its Development in the Thirteenth Century." *Isis* 68 (1977): 224-48.

A discussion of the efforts to unite theoretical and empirical knowledge of drugs during the Chin and Yüan dynasties, focusing on one particular work on materia medica compiled in the thirteenth century. The author provides useful insights into the principles of drug use in classical Chinese medicine.

581. Yoke, Ho Peng, Beda Lim, and Francis Morsingh. "Elixir Plants: The Ch'un-yang Lü Chen-jen yao shih chih (Pharmaceutical Manual of the Adept Lü Ch'un-yang)." In *Chinese Science: Explorations of an Ancient Tradition*. ed. Nakayama Shigeru, and Nathan Sivin, pp. 153-202. M. I. T. East Asian Science Series, 2. Cambridge: MIT Press, 1973.

A detailed study of the plants in a Chinese elixir text of the fourteenth or fifteenth century. Alchemical texts on elixir plants are relatively scarce compared to those on metals and minerals.

Post-1600

582. Adams, David P. "Wartime Bureaucracy and Penicillin Allocation: The Committee on Chemotherapeutic and Other Agents, 1942-44." *Journal of the History of Medicine and Allied Sciences* 44 (1989): 196-217.

An examination of the policies and procedures for allocating the scarce supply of penicillin for civilian use in the United States during the Second World War.

583. "Antibiotics Number." *Journal of the History of Medicine and Allied Sciences* 6 (1951): 279-405.

This special issue contains six papers on the history of antibiotics and an introduction by John Fulton. One of the papers, by George Urdang, specifically discusses "The Antibiotics and Pharmacy."

584. Ayd, Frank J., and Barry Blackwell, eds. *Discoveries in Biological Psychiatry*. Taylor Manor Hospital Scientific Symposium, 2nd. Philadelphia: J. B. Lippincott, 1970. 254 pp., illus.

A collection of 18 papers offering accounts of discoveries in psychopharmacology, in most cases written by the discoverers themselves.

585. Berman, Alex. "The Heroic Approach in Nineteenth-Century Therapeutics." *Bulletin of the American Society of Hospital Pharmacists* 11 (1954): 320-27.

    A concise, readable, and useful summary of heroic therapy in America.

586. Berman, Alex. "The Persistence of Theriac in France." *Pharmacy in History* 12 (1970): 5-12.

    Discusses the history of theriac in France and its retention in the official materia medica of that country into the nineteenth century.

587. Berman, Alex. "A Striving for Scientific Respectability: Some American Botanics and the Nineteenth-Century Plant Materia Medica." *Bulletin of the History of Medicine* 30 (1956): 7-31.

    Berman examines the work of nineteenth-century American botanic practitioners with scientific pretensions, with attention to their efforts to influence the growth of the plant materia medica and to subject their plant medicinals to scientific verification.

588. Berman, Alex. "The Thomsonian Movement and Its Relation to American Pharmacy and Medicine." *Bulletin of the History of Medicine* 25 (1951): 405-28, 519-38.

    Includes a discussion of the botanical drugs used by the Thomsonians and their manufacture, sale, and distribution. Also includes a bibliography.

589. Berridge, Virginia. "Opium over the Counter in Nineteenth-Century England." *Pharmacy in History* 20 (1978): 91-100.

A discussion of the unrestricted sale of opiates in pharmacies, grocery stores, or other establishments in Victorian England.

590. Berridge, Virginia, and Griffith Edwards. *Opium and the People: Opiate Use in Nineteenth-Century England*. London: Allen Lane, 1981. xxx + 370 pp., bibl., index, illus.

    A comprehensive study of the medicinal use and abuse of opiates in nineteenth-century England.

591. Bickel, Marcel H. "The Development of Sulfonamides (1932-1938) as a Focal Point in the History of Chemotherapy." *Gesnerus* 45 (1988): 67-86.

    Provides a relatively brief overview of the introduction of the sulfonamides and the impact of their discovery on chemotherapy and drug regulation.

592. Bindra, Jasjit S., and Daniel Lednicer (eds.). *Chronicles of Drug Discovery*. New York: John Wiley and Sons, 1982-1983. 2 vols., illus.

    A series of essays on the development of modern drugs by the individuals most closely connected with their initial discovery. The essays tend to be very technical and to read like scientific review articles. The editors envision the possibility of future volumes in the series.

593. Blais, Gerard D., Jr., and George E. Osborne. "Drug Therapy at the Massachusetts Leper Colony 1905-1921." *Pharmacy in History* 18 (1976): 51-61.

    A look at an interesting leprosarium established by the state of Massachusetts at the beginning of the twentieth century, with particular emphasis on the drug therapy utilized there.

594. Bliss, Michael. *The Discovery of Insulin*. Chicago: University of Chicago Press, 1982. 304 pp., illus., bibl., index.

   A definitive account of the discovery of insulin, meticulously researched and eminently readable.

595. Borell, Merriley. "Brown-Séquard's Organotherapy and Its Appearance in America at the End of the Nineteenth Century." *Bulletin of the History of Medicine* 50 (1976): 309-20.

   A discussion of the role of Brown-Séquard's work on testicular extract in stimulating widespread interest in the therapeutic potential of "internal secretions" of animal organs.

596. Borell, Merriley. "Organotherapy, British Physiology and Discovery of the Internal Secretions." *Journal of the History of Biology* 9 (1976): 235-68.

   A discussion of the importance of the work of British physiologists on thyroid and adrenal extracts in advancing Brown-Séquard's organotherapy.

597. Bové, Frank J. *The Story of Ergot*. Basel: S. Karger, 1970. xiii + 297 pp., illus., bibl.

   Although only one chapter of this detailed study of ergot deals specifically with the history of the drug, the other chapters on the chemistry, pharmacology, etc., of ergot also contain significant historical information and many useful references. This book is fairly comprehensive, but lacks footnotes, even if it does have a large bibliography.

598. Bovet, Daniel. *Une chimie qui guérit: Histoire de la découverte des sulfamides*. Paris: Payot, 1988. 322 pp., illus.

   The most useful overview to date of the history of the sulfa drugs, by one of the participants in the story. Contains a historical chart of sulfa drug structures.

599. Brown, P. S. "Female Pills and the Reputation of Iron as an Abortifacient." *Medical History* 21 (1977): 291-304.

   A study of the "female pills" of the eighteenth and nineteenth centuries. Attention is given to the possible use of such preparations, which frequently contained iron (a presumed abortifacient), in an effort to induce abortion.

600. Burlingham, Robert. *The Odyssey of Modern Drug Research*. Kalamazoo, Michigan: Upjohn, 1951. 124 pp., illus.

   An introductory, popular text on drug discovery, with illustrations of medicine production. Although a public relations book for Upjohn, it includes a surprising number of references to the discoveries and developments of other companies.

601. Caldwell, Anne E. *Origins of Psychopharmacology from CPZ to LSD*. Springfield, IL: Charles C. Thomas, 1970. xiv + 225 pp., bibl., index.

   Largely tells the story of the introduction of chlorpromazine (not as well as Swazey's book [citation #676] on the subject, but the two works are complementary).

602. Carpenter, Kenneth J. *The History of Scurvy and Vitamin C*. Cambridge: Cambridge University Press, 1986. viii + 288 pp., illus., bibl.

   Contains two chapters on the discovery and uses of vitamin C, including a bibliography. A comprehensive and thoroughly referenced study of its subject.

603. Coley, Noel G. "The Preparation and Uses of Artificial Mineral Waters (ca. 1680-1825)." *Ambix* 31 (1984): 32-48.

A review of the manufacture and therapeutic uses of artificially produced mineral waters in Europe from the seventeenth through the nineteenth centuries.

604. Coulter, Harris L. *Homeopathic Influences in Nineteenth-Century Allopathic Therapeutics: A Historical and Philosophical Study.* Washington, DC: American Institute of Homeopathy, 1973. iii + 83 pp.

A supporter of homeopathy argues the case for homeopathic influence on the materia medica and therapeutic practices of nineteenth-century allopathic physicians.

605. Cowen, David L. "The British North American Colonies as a Source of Drugs." In *Die Vorträge der Hauptversammlung der Internationalen Gesellschaft für Geschichte der Pharmazie e. V. während des Internationalen Pharmaziegeschichtlichen Kongresses in London vom 1.-8. September 1965.* ed. Georg Edmund Dann, pp. 47-59. Veröffentlichungen der Internationalen Gesellschaft für Geschichte der Pharmazie e. V., 28. Stuttgart: Wissenschaftliche Verlagsgesellschaft, 1966.

A brief overview of the early drug trade, including the collection and cultivation of drugs, in the British North American colonies. Such botanicals as sassafras and ginseng were exported from the colonies to Britain.

606. Cowen, David L. "Squill in the 17th and 18th Centuries." *Bulletin of the New York Academy of Medicine* 50, no. Ser. 2 (1974): 714-22.

The many forms of squill used during this period and the various discussions of squill in the pharmaceutical literature are discussed. This is part of a "Symposium on Squill," (pp. 682-750) that includes: "Squill in the ancient and medieval materia medica, with special reference to its employment for dropsy," by Jerry Stannard, "A treatise on squill (Gottwald Schuster, 1757)," by Saul Jarcho, and "The pharmacology of squill," by Chalmers L. Gemmill, as well as the article by Cowen.

607. Cowen, David L. "A Store Mixt, Various, Universal." *Journal of the Rutgers University Library* 25 (1961): 1-9.

   Also reprinted in *Pharmacy in History* 29(1987):669-74. A broadside advertising products from Smith, Moore, & Co. (1784) reveals much about the drug trade in this period, as well as the relationship between the materia medica in American and Europe.

608. Crellin, John K. "Internal Antisepsis or the Dawn of Chemotherapy?" *Journal of the History of Medicine and Allied Sciences* 36 (1981): 9-18.

   A brief account of the effort to develop "internal antiseptics" in the late nineteenth century, forming part of the background to the development of modern chemotherapy by Paul Ehrlich at the beginning of the twentieth century.

609. Crellin, John K., and Jane Philpott. *Herbal Medicine Past and Present*. 2 vols. Durham, NC: Duke University Press, 1990. illus.

   The first volume of this set is a study of the beliefs and practices of Alabama herbalist Tommy Bass. The second volume, entitled *A Reference Guide to Medicinal Plants*, includes Bass's comments on a wide variety of herbs, and, more importantly for the historian, a useful historical commentary on each herb by the authors. Each volume contains an extensive annotated bibliography.

610. Davis, Audrey B. "The Role of the Vitamin-Medicinal as Illustrated by Vitamin D." *Pharmacy in History* 24 (1982): 59-72.

   Focuses on some of the issues involved in establishing the daily requirements and proper therapeutic doses of vitamins, using vitamins A and D as examples.

611. Dowling, Harry F. *Fighting Infection: Conquests of the Twentieth Century*. Cambridge: Harvard University Press, 1977. vii + 339 pp., illus.

A well-researched, highly readable account of the development of drugs and vaccines against infectious disease in the late nineteenth and twentieth centuries. The 74 pages of notes are a valuable guide to the primary literature.

612. Erichsen-Brown, Charlotte. *Use of Plants for the Past 500 Years*. Aurora, Ontario: Breezy Creeks Press, 1979. xxii + 510 pp., illus., bibl., index.

Basically a collection of quotations on selected North American plants from the works of various writers spanning several centuries (largely post-1600). The main value of the book is in alerting the reader as to what a particular writer on botanicals had to say about a plant and in the bibliography.

613. Estes, J. Worth. *Hall Jackson and the Purple Foxglove: Medical Practice and Research in Revolutionary America 1760-1820*. Hanover, N.H.: University Press of New England, 1979. xvi + 291 pp., illus., index.

Uses the introduction of foxglove into therapeutics as a case study of medical practice in the eighteenth century. Interweaves the story of Jackson's medical practice in eighteenth-century America with that of the introduction of foxglove into medicine in England and the United States.

614. Estes, J. Worth. "Drug Use at the Infirmary: The Example of Dr. Andrew Duncan, Sr." In *Hospital Life in Enlightenment Scotland: Care and Teaching at the Royal Infirmary of Edinburgh*. Guenter B. Risse, pp. 351-84. Cambridge: Cambridge University Press, 1986.

An analysis of the drugs used by one physician in an eighteenth-century hospital. Includes a glossary of the treatments prescribed and charts and tables providing quantitative information about treatment.

615. Estes, J. Worth. "John Jones's Mysteries of Opium Reveal'd (1701): Key to Historical Opiates." *Journal of the History of Medicine and Allied Sciences* 34 (1979): 200-209.

   Estes uses the 1701 work of Jones to evaluate the various strengths of opium preparations. An excellent example of a different approach to the history of therapeutics.

616. Florey, H. W., et al. *Antibiotics: A Survey of Penicillin, Streptomycin, and Other Antimicrobial Substances from Fungi, Actinomycetes, Bacteria, and Plants.* London: Oxford University Press, 1949. 2 vols., illus.

   Although dated, the historical chapters (one on penicillin and one on antibiotics in general) in these volumes are still extremely useful. The volumes are in themselves primary source documents as well.

617. Flückiger, Friedrich A., and Daniel Hanbury. *Pharmacographia: A History of the Principal Drugs of Vegetable Origin.* London: Macmillan & Co., 1874. xv + 704 pp.; 2nd ed., London: Macmillan, 1879. xx + 803 pp., index.

   This work is a compendium, following a systematic botanical organization, listing sources, history, methods of preparation, and clinical indications for each entry. Bibliographic references are minimalist. This classic book is still a valuable reference work on the history of the plant drugs of Britain and India.

618. Fye, W. Bruce. "Vasodilator Therapy for Angina Pectoris: The Intersection of Homeopathy and Scientific Medicine." *Journal of the History of Medicine and Allied Sciences* 45 (1990): 317-40.

   Discusses the introduction of nitroglycerin and amyl nitrite for the treatment of angina pectoris in the nineteenth century. Fye points out that while the homeopaths were responsible for introducing nitroglycerin as a remedy, it was an allopathic physician who first suggested its use for the treatment of angina.

619. Gifford, George E., Jr. "Botanic Remedies in Colonial Massachusetts, 1620-1820." In *Medicine in Colonial Massachusetts, 1620-1820*. ed. Philip Cash, Eric H. Christianson, and J. Worth Estes, pp. 263-88. Boston: Colonial Society of Massachusetts, 1980.

This paper provides a good overview of many rationales for drug usage in the seventeenth and eighteenth centuries. Discusses the use of plant drugs, derived from both British and American Indian traditions, in colonial Massachusetts.

620. Goldwater, Leonard J. *Mercury: A History of Quicksilver*. Baltimore: York Press, 1972. xi + 318 pp., illus.

A potpourri of miscellaneous information on the many facets of mercury's history, including its use in therapy.

621. Griffenhagen, George. "Medicines in the American Revolution." In *American Pharmacy in the Colonial and Revolutionary Periods: A Bicentennial Symposium*. ed. George A. Bender, and John Parascandola, pp. 27-36. Madison, WI: American Institute of the History of Pharmacy, 1977.

A brief review of the most important items in the drug armamentarium of the American Revolutionary forces.

622. Haggis, A. W. "Fundamental Errors in the Early History of Cinchona." *Bulletin of the History of Medicine* 10 (1941): 417-59, 568-92.

A lengthy discussion of the early history of cinchona, correcting some of the erroneous beliefs concerning the origin of the word "quina" (from which quinine derives) and the introduction of cinchona into Europe.

623. Haller, John S., Jr. "The History of Strychnine in the Nineteenth-Century Material Medica." *Transactions and Studies of the College of Physicians of Philadelphia* 40 (1973): 226-38.

   An overview of the therapeutic use of strychnine in the nineteenth century, with particular emphasis on the role that it played in the "dosimetric" therapeutics introduced by the Belgian physician Adolphe Burggraeve.

624. Haller, John S., Jr. "Opium Usage in Nineteenth-Century Therapeutics." *Bulletin of the New York Academy of Medicine* 65 (1989): 591-607.

   An overview of the therapeutic use of opium and of opium addiction in the nineteenth century, focusing on the United States.

625. Haller, John S., Jr. "Samson of the Materia Medica: Medical Theory and the Use and Abuse of Calomel in Nineteenth-Century America." *Pharmacy in History* 13 (1971): 27-34, 67-76.

   A discussion of the rise and fall of calomel in American therapeutics.

626. Haller, John S., Jr. "Smut's Dark Poison: Ergot in History and Medicine." *Transactions and Studies of the College of Physicians of Philadelphia* series V, 3 (1981): 62-79.

   A discussion of the use of ergot in medicine, with emphasis on John Stearns and the American use of ergot in the nineteenth century.

627. Haller, John S., Jr. "Therapeutic Mule: The Use of Arsenic in the Nineteenth-Century Materia Medica." *Pharmacy in History* 17 (1975): 87-100.

   Discusses the extensive use of arsenic (e.g., in the form of Fowler's Solution) in nineteenth-century therapeutics.

628. Haller, John S., Jr. "The Use and Abuse of Tartar Emetic in the 19th-Century Materia Medica." *Bulletin of the History of Medicine* 49 (1975): 235-57.

A detailed look at the therapeutic uses of tartar emetic in the nineteenth century, with some attention to its use as a poison for criminal purposes.

629. Hare, Ronald. *The Birth of Penicillin and the Disarming of Microbes*. London: George Allen and Unwin, 1970. 236 pp., illus., bibl., index.

A readable and useful general account of the story of penicillin written by a colleague of Alexander Fleming. Includes a description of Hare's experiments attempting to recreate Fleming's discovery to better understand how it came about.

630. Hare, Ronald. "New Light on the History of Penicillin." *Medical History* 26 (1982): 1-24.

Drawing upon information that had become available in the previous decade, Hare offers his view of the probable reasons for Fleming's failure to prove the therapeutic value of penicillin.

631. Harris, Michael R. "Iron Therapy and Tonics." In *Fitness in American Culture: Images of Health, Sport, and the Body, 1830-1940*. ed. Kathryn Grover, pp. 67-85. Amherst, MA: University of Massachusetts Press, 1989.

An examination of the use of iron in therapy, especially in tonics, focusing largely on the eighteenth through the twentieth centuries. Consideration is given to iron's place in mass culture as a symbol of health and vitality.

632. Hershenson, Benjamin R. "A Botanical Comparison of the United States Pharmacopoeias of 1820 and 1960." *Economic Botany* 18 (1964): 342-56.

Records the results (largely in tabular form) of a botanical comparison of the U. S. P. of 1820 with that of 1960. Brief historical statements are provided for some twenty selected drugs.

633. Hobby, Gladys L. *Penicillin: Meeting the Challenge.* New Haven, CT: Yale University Press, 1985. xxii + 319 pp., illus., bibl., index.

The penicillin saga as told by a participant in the process. Parts 2 and 3, dealing with the mass production and later history of penicillin, are the most valuable portions of the book as they cover ground that has been less well tread by historians.

634. Ihde, Aaron J. "Studies on the History of Rickets. II. The Roles of Cod Liver Oil and Light." *Pharmacy in History* 17 (1975): 13-20.

Discusses the history of the use of cod liver oil and of sunlight in the treatment of rickets and the relationship of these therapeutic measures to the understanding of the vitamin concept in the early twentieth century.

635. Issekutz, Béla. *Geschichte der Arzneimittelforschung.* trans. Adám Faragó. Budapest: Akadémiae Kiadó, 1971. 651 pp., illus.

An encyclopedic, technical reference work on the history of drug research (largely nineteenth and twentieth centuries), organized by classes of drugs. It includes a chronology of drug research and thousands of references to the primary literature.

636. Jarcho, Saul. "Drugs Used at Hudson Bay in 1730." *Bulletin of the New York Academy of Medicine* 47 (1971): 838-42.

Publication of and brief commentary on a list of drugs from the Hudson's Bay Company post at Fort Albany, compiled by one of the company's surgeons in 1730.

637. Johnson, F. Neil. *The History of Lithium Therapy*. London: Macmillan, 1984. xvii + 198 pp., illus.

   An "insider's" account of the development of lithium therapy, based on significant research in the primary literature. The extensive references provide a useful bibliography on the subject.

638. Keating, Peter. "Vaccine Therapy and the Problem of Opsonins." *Journal of the History of Medicine and Allied Sciences* 43 (1988): 275-96.

   A study of the rise and fall of Almroth Wright's vaccine therapy in the first quarter of the twentieth century.

639. Kendall, Edward C. *Cortisone*. New York: Charles Scribner's Sons, 1971. 175 pp., illus.

   A personal narrative by Nobel Laureate Kendall focusing on his research on cortisone and other cortical hormones.

640. Klinkenberg, Norbert. *Cortison: Die Geschichte des Cortisons und der Kortikosteriodtherapie—Ein Beitrag zur Forschungs- und Therapiegeschichte heutiger Medizin*. Pahl-Rugenstein Hochschulschriften Gesellschafts- und Naturwissenschaften, no. 238. Cologne: Pahl-Rugenstein, 1987. 187 pp., illus.

   An account of the discovery of cortisone and its introduction into therapeutics. Includes a bibliography.

641. Knightley, Phillip, et al. *Suffer the Children: The Story of Thalidomide*. New York: Viking Press, 1979. vi + 309 pp., illus.

   A journalistic but thorough account of the discovery, use, and tragedy of thalidomide by the Insight team of the *Sunday Times of London*.

642. Liebenau, Jonathan. "The British Success with Penicillin." *Social Studies of Science* 17 (1987): 69-86.

   A discussion of the large-scale production of penicillin in Britain during World War II, contrasting the British and American approaches and results.

643. Liebenau, Jonathan. "Public Health and the Production and Use of Diphtheria Antitoxin in Philadelphia." *Bulletin of the History of Medicine* 61 (1987): 216-36.

   An examination of the early production and use of diphtheria antitoxin in the United States, with special emphasis on Philadelphia. Discusses the transfer of production from public to commercial laboratories.

644. Mann, Ronald D. *Modern Drug Use: An Enquiry on Historical Principles*. Lancaster: MTP Press Limited, 1984. xxii + 769 pp., illus., index.

   The word "modern" in the title of this work is misleading, as the book covers the subject from antiquity to the present. Its encyclopedic scope and 2,550 footnotes give it significant value as a reference work. Unfortunately, the book tries to cover too much of medical history in general and consequently fails to provide a focused, balanced account of the history of drug use. The work includes an appendix listing the materia medica of the 1789 London Pharmacopeia.

645. Marcum, James A. "William Henry Howell and Jay McLean: The Experimental Context for the Discovery of Heparin." *Perspectives in Biology and Medicine* 33 (1990): 214-30.

   Situates the discovery of the anticoagulant heparin in 1916 by McLean in the milieu of experimental research conducted in the laboratory of his mentor Howell and evaluates the contributions of both men to the discovery.

646. Maxwell, Robert A., and Shohreh B. Eckhardt. *Drug Discovery: A Casebook and Analysis*. Clifton, NJ: Humana Press, 1990. xxv + 438 pp., illus.

The authors provide brief case studies of some 28 drug discoveries of the post-World War II era, and then attempt a quantitative analysis of various factors involved in the discovery (e.g., type of research institution, country of origin, whether the discovery was "orderly" or "serendipitous," etc.). An interesting and significant effort in spite of the difficulties of classifying complex discoveries into neat categories.

647. McFadyen, Richard E. "Thalidomide in America: A Brush with Tragedy." *Clio Medica* 11 (1976): 79-93.

Examines the effort to get thalidomide approved for use in the United States, with emphasis on the key role played by Dr. Frances Kelsey of the Food and Drug Administration in preventing the drug from reaching the American market.

648. McIntyre, A. R. *Curare: Its History, Nature, and Clinical Use*. Chicago: University of Chicago Press, 1947. vii + 240 pp., illus., index.

A significant proportion of this book is devoted to the history of curare, including its use in medicine. Contains numerous references to the primary literature.

649. McTavish, Jan R. "Aspirin in Germany: The Pharmaceutical Industry and the Pharmaceutical Profession." *Pharmacy in History* 29 (1987): 103-15.

An excellent analysis of an early example of the brand name versus generic drug and the drug substitution controversies.

650. McTavish, Jan R. "What's in a Name? Aspirin and the American Medical Association." *Bulletin of the History of Medicine* 61 (1987): 343-66.

An excellent case study of the marketing of aspirin in the United States in the early twentieth century. Sets the story within the context of the contemporary dominance of the synthetic pharmaceuticals industry by German dye and drug firms and the concern within the American medical profession over patenting and trademarking drugs.

651. Morton, Julia F. *Major Medicinal Plants: Botany, Culture and Uses*. Springfield, IL: Charles C. Thomas, 1977. xix + 431 pp., illus.

Brief descriptions, including some historical information (mostly post-1600), of 92 major medicinal plants. Includes a useful bibliography of over 600 references and a table of medicinal plants that are no longer "official" in the United States but do still find some use in medicine.

652. Needham, Joseph, and Lu Gwei-Djen. "Chinese Medicine." In *Medicine and Culture*. ed. F. N. L. Poynter, pp. 255-314. London: Wellcome Institute of the History of Medicine, 1969.

Because Chinese medicine is so closely linked to culture, the authors describe the general position of medicine in Chinese society, the influence of philosophical and religious doctrines on the medicine, and the effects of the transition from a traditional society to Marxist Socialism. With discussion following.

653. Neill, John R. "'More than Medical Significance': LSD and American Psychiatry 1953 to 1966." *Journal of Psychoactive Drugs* 19 (1987): 39-45.

A brief discussion of the history of LSD in American psychiatry and the problems that the drug posed for the psychiatric profession.

654. Palliser, Susan M. *The Use of Plants in English Folk Medicine: 1600 to 1800*. Monographs in Folk Life Studies, no. 1. Leeds: Leeds Folklore Group, 1984. 122 pp.

A cheaply printed but useful discussion of English botanical folk remedies used to treat various conditions.

655. Palmieri, Anthony III, and Daniel J. Hammond. "Drug Therapy at a Frontier Fort Hospital: Fort Laramie, Wyoming Territory, 1870-1889." *Pharmacy in History* 21 (1979): 35-44.

Based on surviving records from Fort Laramie, the authors analyze the drug therapy used to treat illnesses there in the nineteenth century. Includes a standard list of medical supplies for a military post of Fort Laramie's size.

656. Panem, Sandra. *The Interferon Crusade*. Washington, DC: Brookings Institution, 1984. x + 109 pp., illus., index.

This brief book uses the history of interferon as a case study to examine policy issues raised by the biotechnology revolution.

657. Parascandola, John, ed. *The History of Antibiotics: A Symposium*. Madison, WI: American Institute of the History of Pharmacy, 1980. vi + 137 pp., illus.

A collection of ten papers ranging in scope from antibiosis in the nineteenth century to the development of concern over the misuse of antibiotics. Several of the papers are by historians and the rest are by scientists who were personally involved in the antibiotic history that they discuss.

658. Parascandola, John. "A Brief History of Drug Use." In *Perspectives on Medicines in Society*. edited by Albert I. Wertheimer, and Patricia J. Bush, pp. 3-35. Hamilton, IL: Drug Intelligence Publications, 1977.

A general but comprehensive overview of drug use from ancient to modern times. Provides historical context for other essays in this book.

659. Parascandola, John. "The Theoretical Basis of Paul Ehrlich's Chemotherapy." *Journal of the History of Medicine and Allied Sciences* 36 (1981): 19-43.

   A discussion of the theoretical principles behind Ehrlich's concept of chemotherapy, including an account of the development of Salvarsan.

660. Parish, H. J. *A History of Immunization*. Edinburgh: E. & S. Livingstone, 1965. vii + 356 pp., illus., index.

   A useful reference work for information on the development of immunological agents against various infectious diseases.

661. Porter, Roy, ed. *The Medical History of Waters and Spas. Medical History*, Supplement Number 10. London: Wellcome Institute for the History of Medicine, 1990. xii + 150 pp., illus., index.

   Although the ten papers in this volume focus more on the bathing aspects of spas than on the consumption of spa waters, some attention is given to the latter subject. Of particular interest to historians of pharmacy is Noel Coley's paper on the chemical analysis of mineral waters.

662. Risse, Guenter B. "Calomel and the American Medical Sects During the Nineteenth Century." *Mayo Clinic Proceedings* 48 (1973): 57-64.

   A brief but clear and informative discussion of the use of calomel in nineteenth-century therapeutics and its relationship to the rise of medical sects in the United States.

663. Rosenberg, Charles E. "The Therapeutic Revolution: Medicine, Meaning, and Social Change in Nineteenth-Century America." In *The Therapeutic Revolution: Essays in the Social History of Medicine*. ed. Morris J. Vogel, and Charles E. Rosenberg, pp. 3-25. Philadelphia: University of Pennsylvania Press, 1979.

A relatively brief but perceptive essay by a distinguished medical historian on the fundamental changes in traditional therapeutics that occurred over the course of the nineteenth century.

664. Sakula, Alex. "Doctor Nehemiah Grew (1641-1712) and the Epsom Salts." *Clio Medica* 19 (1984): 1-21.

Discusses the extraction of Epsom Salts from the spa waters and their chemical analysis by Grew, who became involved in a controversy over his attempt to patent the production and sale of Epsom Salts.

665. Schmitz, Rudolf. "Friedrich Wilhelm Sertürner and the Discovery of Morphine." *Pharmacy in History* 27 (1985): 61-74.

Provides biographical information on Sertürner and a brief discussion of the isolation of morphine and its consequences. Includes a substantial bibliography in addition to the footnotes.

666. Simon, William J. "A Luso-African Formulary of the Late Eighteenth Century: Some Notes on Angolan Contributions to European Knowledge of Materia Medica." *Pharmacy in History* 18 (1976): 103-14.

A study of a late-eighteenth-century inventory of a shipment of Angolan materia medica prepared by a Portuguese naturalist. Simon provides an English translation of the inventory (which describes the medicinal virtues of the drugs) and discusses and attempts to identify the drugs.

667. Smith, Dale C. "Quinine and Fever: The Development of the Effective Dosage." *Journal of the History of Medicine and Allied Sciences* 31 (1976): 343-67.

Discusses the use of quinine in the treatment of fevers, with emphasis on the development of large-dose therapy for the effective treatment of malarial fevers in the United States in the nineteenth century.

668. Smith, Emilie Savage. "Drug Therapy of Eye Disease in Seventeenth-Century Islamic Medicine: The Influence of the 'New Chemistry' of the Paracelsians." *Pharmacy in History* 29 (1987): 3-28.

Although the focus of this informative article is the pharmacological treatment of eye diseases, the subject is set within the broader context of the influence of Paracelsian chemical remedies on seventeenth-century Islamic therapeutics.

669. Smith, Mickey C. *Small Comfort: A Social History of the Minor Tranquilizers.* New York: Praeger, 1985. viii + 265 pp., illus., bibl.

This book is as much a social analysis as a history of the minor tranquilizers. It provides a useful entry into the subject and includes a 25-page bibliography.

670. Sneader, Walter. *Drug Discovery: The Evolution of Modern Medicines.* Chichester: John Wiley and Sons, 1985. x + 435 pp., illus., bibl.

An overview of the development of modern medicines, largely focused on the nineteenth and twentieth centuries, which includes a substantial bibliography. Sneader writes clearly and succinctly, but the extensive use of technical terminology and structural formulas may make the book difficult going for the chemically uninitiated.

671. Spink, Wesley W. *Infectious Diseases: Prevention and Treatment in the Nineteenth and Twentieth Centuries.* Minneapolis: University of Minnesota Press, 1978. xx + 577 pp., illus., bibl., index.

Useful mainly as a reference work on the prevention and treatment of infectious diseases in modern times. Dowling's *Fighting Infection* covers largely the same ground in a more readable and synthetic fashion. Spink's 60-page bibliography adds considerably to the value of this book.

672. Swain, Tony, ed. *Plants in the Development of Modern Medicine*. Cambridge: Harvard University Press, 1972. xii + 367 pp., illus.

   This volume, which developed out of a 1968 symposium, contains 11 papers on a variety of themes. Several of the papers are specifically historical in content, but almost all contain some historical information.

673. Swann, John P. "Arthur Tatum, Parke-Davis and the Discovery of Mapharsen as an Antisyphilitic Agent." *Journal of the History of Medicine and Allied Sciences* 40 (1985): 167-87.

   Examines the discovery of the antisyphilitic therapeutic value of the organic arsenical drug Mapharsen and places it within the context of collaborative research between university scientists and the pharmaceutical industry.

674. Swann, John P. "Insulin: A Case Study in the Emergence of Collaborative Pharmacomedical Research." *Pharmacy in History* 28 (1986): 3-13, 65-74.

   Examines the collaborative arrangement of the University of Toronto and Eli Lilly and Company in the development and production of insulin after its initial discovery.

675. Swann, John P. "The Search for Synthetic Penicillin During World War II." *British Journal for the History of Science* 16 (1983): 154-90.

   A discussion of the efforts to synthesize penicillin in Britain and the United States during World War II. The paper also provides useful information on the wartime organization of research on penicillin and on the history of the understanding of the chemistry of penicillin.

676. Swazey, Judith P. *Chlorpromazine in Psychiatry: A Study of Therapeutic Innovation.* Cambridge: MIT Press, 1974. xvi + 340 pp., illus., bibl.

A detailed study of the discovery of chlorpromazine and its introduction into therapeutics.

677. Taberner, P. V. *Aphrodisiacs: The Science and the Myth.* Philadelphia: University of Pennsylvania Press, 1985. x + 276 pp., illus., bibl.

A useful and readable introduction to the subject. Includes a list of supposed aphrodisiacs and a bibliography.

678. Taylor, Norman. *Plant Drugs that Changed the World.* New York: Dodd, Mead and Company, 1965. viii + 275 pp., illus., bibl.

A popular and undocumented history (largely post-1600) that is more suited to the lay reader than to the historian. The bibliography of some 180 references, however, is of value even to the serious scholar.

679. Vogel, Virgil J. *American Indian Medicine.* Norman, OK: University of Oklahoma Press, 1970. xx + 583 pp., illus., bibl.

Vogel includes a substantial chapter on therapeutic practices. Perhaps the most useful parts of the book for the historian of materia medica are the bibliography and the lengthy appendix discussing some 170 American Indian drugs that were at one time or another included in the Pharmacopoeia of the *United States of America* or the *National Formulary.*

680. Vos, Rein. *Drugs Looking for Diseases: Innovative Drug Research and the Development of the Beta Blockers and the Calcium Antagonists.* Developments in Cardiovascular Medicine, volume 120. Dordrecht: Kluwer Academic Pubishers, 1991. xxix + 374 pp., illus., bibl.

The aims of this study are to develop a theory to describe the drug discovery process, to demonstrate the contributions of medical practice to that process, and to provide a history of the development of the beta blockers and calcium antagonists in the 1960s and 1970s. Includes an extensive bibliography.

681. Wainwright, Milton. "The History of the Therapeutic Use of Crude Penicillin." *Medical History* 31 (1987): 41-50.

    Discusses the development of the therapeutic use of crude penicillin from Fleming's discovery to its eventual demise when the partially purified product became more widely available in the early 1940s.

682. Wainwright, Milton. "Streptomycin: Discovery and Resultant Controversy." *History and Philosophy of the Life Sciences* 13 (1991): 97-124.

    An examination of the discovery of streptomycin in the laboratory of Selman Waksman, with particular emphasis on the role played by his graduate student, Albert Schatz.

683. Wainwright, Milton, and Harold T. Swan. "C. G. Paine and the Earliest Surviving Clinical Records of Penicillin Therapy." *Medical History* 30 (1986): 42-56.

    Based on surviving case records of the Royal Infirmary in Sheffield, England, the authors document the clinical use of crude penicillin in the external treatment of eye disorders as early as 1930 by C. G. Paine and A. B. Nutt.

684. Ward, Patricia Spain. "The American Reception of Salvarsan." *Journal of the History of Medicine and Allied Sciences* 36 (1981): 44-62.

    An excellent study of the introduction of Salvarsan into American medical practice, examining use of an reaction to the drug by physicians. Problems encountered in administering the drug are also considered.

685. Warner, John Harley. *The Therapeutic Perspective: Medical Practice, Knowledge, and Identity in America, 1820-1885.* Cambridge: Harvard University Press, 1986. x + 367 pp., illus.

Drawing upon hospital records and other manuscript materials as well as the published literatuare, Warner provides an excellent analysis of therapeutic practice and its relationship to medical theory in nineteenth-century America. Emphasis is placed on the cities of Boston, Cincinnati, and New Orleans as case studies.

686. Warner, John Harley. "Physiological Theory and Therapeutic Explanation in the 1860s: The British Debate on the Medical Use of Alcohol." *Bulletin of the History of Medicine* 54 (1980): 235-57.

Using the medicinal use of alcohol in Britain as a case study, Warner examines the relationship between theory and practice in therapeutics.

687. Weatherall, M. *In Search of a Cure: A History of Pharmaceutical Discovery.* Oxford: Oxford University Press, 1990.

A very readable account of the development of drugs, largely from about 1800 up to recent times. The notes provide some access to the primary and secondary literature.

688. Wray, Susan, D. A. Eisner, and D. G. Allen. "Two Hundred Years of the Foxglove." In *The Emergence of Modern Cardiology.* ed. William F. Bynum, C. Lawrence, and V. Nutton, pp. 132-50. *Medical History*, Supplement Number 5. London: Wellcome Institute for the History of Medicine, 1985.

A review of the therapeutic use of digitalis from before Withering to the present, with emphasis on the nineteenth and twentieth centuries.

689. Young, James Harvey. *The Medical Messiahs: A Social History of Health Quackery in Twentieth-Century America.* Princeton, NJ: Princeton University Press, 1967. xx + 460 pp., illus.

The sequel to *The Toadstool Millionaires*, and an equally valuable study. Although the work examines health quackery broadly, patent medicines receive the major attention.

690. Young, James Harvey. *American Self-Dosage Medicines: An Historical Perspective.* Logan Clendening Lectures on the History and Philosophy of Medicine, New Series, Number 1. Lawrence, KS: Coronado Press, 1974. xiv + 75 pp.

Although Young covered the subject in more detail in his two earlier books, there is some new material in this work, most notably the author's appraisal of the proprietary medicine situation in the 1970s.

2d—Laws and Regulations

691. Anderson, Jr., Oscar Edward. *The Health of a Nation: Harvey W. Wiley and the Fight for Pure Food.* Chicago: University of Chicago Press, 1958. 332 pp., notes, index, illus.

A well-documented account of Wiley's life and work on behalf of pure food, and to a much lesser extent, pure drugs.

692. Anderson, Jr., Oscar E. "Pioneer Statute: The Pure Food and Drugs Act of 1906." *Journal of Public Law* 13 (1964):189-96.

A short, undocumented introduction to the complex factors that went into the creation of the act.

693. Bailey, Thomas A. "Congressional Opposition to Pure Food Legislation, 1879-1906." *American Journal of Sociology* 36 (1930): 52-64.

This short article is well documented to contemporary literature.

694. Barkan, Ilyse D. "Industry Invites Regulation: The Passage of the Pure Food and Drugs Act of 1906." *American Journal of Public Health* 75 (1985): 18-26.

   A provocative, if flawed, look at the 1906 Act. The author argues that market conditions forced manufacturers to support passage of the landmark act. The author's knowledge of pharmacy issues is slight.

695. Bartels, Karl H. *Drogenhandel und apothekenrechliche Beziehungen zwischen Venedig und Nürnberg; das Eindringen italienische Elemente in die deutsche Apothekengesetzgebung als Folge des Drogenhandels* . . . Frankfurt am Main: Govi, 1966. 226 pp., index.

   Part III includes a study of municipal ordinances pertaining to pharmacy in the late Middle Ages.

696. Beal, J. H. "The American Pharmaceutical Association as a Factor in American Food and Drug Regulation." *Journal of the American Pharmaceutical Association* 26 (1937): 747-51.

   In this undocumented piece, the author ties together the history of the pursuit of drug quality and that of the American Pharmaceutical Association. A good, quick summary.

697. Berman, Alex. "Drug Control in Nineteenth-Century France: Antecedents and Directions." In *Safeguarding the Public: Historical Aspects of Medicinal Drug Control.* ed. John B. Blake, pp. 3-14. Baltimore: Johns Hopkins Press, 1970.

   A history of legislation in France governing the quality of drugs from its eighteenth-century origins through a decree of 1926, with special reference to the role of the French Codex.

698. Bernsmann, W. "Die Entwicklung des Gesetzes über den Verkehr mit Arzneimitteln in der Bundesrepublik Deutschland:

Arzneispezialitäten-Registrierung." *Deutsche Apotheker-Zeitung* 111, no. No. 39 (1971): 1435-42.

A survey of the laws regulating manufactured, pre-packaged medicinals in the Federal Republic of Germany.

699. Cavers, David B. "The Evolution of the Contemporary System of Drug Regulation under the 1938 Act." In *Safeguarding the Public: Historical Aspects of Medicinal Drug Control*. ed. John B. Blake, pp. 158-70. Baltimore: Johns Hopkins Press, 1970.

The evolution of drug controls in the United States from the Food Drug and Cosmetic Act of 1938 through the Kefauver-Harris Amendments of 1962.

700. Colapinto, Leonardo, and Marcello Marchetti. "Note di legislazione negli ex stati Italiani." Extract from *Notiziario dei Farmacisti Ospedalieri Romani*, July, 1974.

Compilations of the portions pertaining to pharmacy of the 1865 law (the first health law passed in the then-new kingdom of Italy), and of the laws pertaining to pharmacy of various pre-unification Italian jurisdictions. [not seen].

701. Cook, Harold. "The Rose Case Reconsidered: Physicians, Apothecaries, and the Law in Augustan England." *Journal of the History of Medicine and Allied Sciences* 45 (1990): 527-55.

Rather than having secured the apothecaries' right to prescribe, the Rose Case of 1704 is credited with having confirmed the status quo: the apothecaries had long been prescribing. Moreover, the decision did not prevent the apothecaries from charging for medical advice: they had been doing so and continued to do so.

702. Cowen, David L. "America's First Pharmacy Laws." *Journal of the American Pharmaceutical Association, Practical Pharmacy Edition* 3 (1942): 162-69, 214-21.

The laws in the only four states to regulate pharmacy statewide before the Civil War—Louisiana, South Carolina, Georgia, and Alabama—are described.

703. Cowen, David L. "Colonial Laws Pertaining to Pharmacy." *Journal of the American Pharmaceutical Association* 23 (1934): 1236-42.

A Virginia statute of 1736 that regulated the apothecary as well as the physician; the slave laws of Virginia, South Carolina, and Georgia that prohibited the imparting of pharmaceutical knowledge or skills to or by non-whites; and the South Carolina statute of 1751 that prohibited the employment of non-whites by physicians, apothecaries, and druggists are described. The complete text of the Virginia 1736 statute and a partial text of the South Carolina 1751 statute are given.

704. Cowen, David L. "Liberty, Laissez-faire and Licensure in Nineteenth-Century Britain." *Bulletin of the History of Medicine* 43 (1969): 30-40.

The impact of liberal political and economic thought and outlook on the regulation of medicine and pharmacy is described.

705. Cowen, David L. "Louisiana, Pioneer in the Regulation of Pharmacy." *Louisiana Historical Quarterly* 26, no. 2 (1943): 330-40.

The history of pharmaceutical legislation in Louisiana from 1808 (when the first pharmacy law was passed in an American jurisdiction) until 1852, after which there was no enforcement until a modern law was enacted, is recounted.

706. Dillemann, Georges. "La remèdes secrets et la réglementation de la pharmacopée française." *Revue d'histoire de la pharmacie* 23, no. 228 (1976): 37-48.

Laws and Regulations 175

>The regulation of "secret remedies," i.e., those not in the *Codex* and whose formula had not been published, from the Ancien Regime until 1926, and their relation to the Pharmacopoeia.

707. Fischelis, Robert P. "A Study of State Pharmacy Laws with Reference to the Sale of Drugs and Medicines by General Merchants." *Journal of the American Pharmaceutical Association* 20 (1931): 1331-41.

>The laws governing the sale of drugs by general merchants are given state by state and are also presented in tabular fashion. There are also lists of patent and proprietary medicines named in the laws.

708. Grapes, Z. T., and T. R. Brown. "Drugs with Abuse Potential: A 70-year History of Increasing Government Control." *Hospital Formulary* 11 (1976): 608, 611-13.

>A survey of federal legislation from the Harrison Narcotic Act of 1914 through the Comprehensive Drug Abuse Prevention and Control Act of 1970.

709. Guislain, André. "Origine et évolution des premières réglimenatations en pharmaceutiques en Belgique." *La Revue de Médicine et de Pharmacie (Section de Pharmacie)* no. 4 (1962): 129-35.

>A historical review of the regulations affecting pharmacy in Belgium, including a tabular presentation of the regulations in various Belgian cities from 1229 to 1785. [not seen].

710. Harris, Richard. *The Real Voice*. New York: Macmillan, 1964. 245 pp.

>A sympathetic account of Senator Estes Kefauver's campaign to investigate the drug industry and secure the 1962 amendments to the 1938 Food, Drug, and Cosmetic Act.

711. Hein, Wolfgang-Hagen. "Einige Bemerkungen zu den frühen Apothekerstatuten im Königreich Sizilien und im Arelat." *Pharmazeutische Zeitung* 116 (1971): 1901-1905.

A survey of the ordinances relating to pharmacy in the late Middle Ages in the Kingdom of the Two Sicilies and in various municipalities in northern Italy and France and their interrelations.

712. Hein, Wolfgang-Hagen. "Über einige Arzneitaxen des späten Mittelalters." In *Die Vorträge der Hauptversammlung der Internationalen Gesellschaft für Geschichte der Pharmazie während des Internationalen Pharmaziegeschichtlichen Kongresses in Rom, vom 6.-10. September 1954.* pp. 99-110. Veröffentlichungen der Internationalen Gesellschaft für Geschichte der Pharmazie, NF Bd.8. Eutin: Internationale Gesellschaft für Geschichte der Pharmazie, 1956.

The study describes fifteen Arzneitaxen—official price lists—in ten German-speaking cities between 1350 and 1500.

713. Hein, Wolfgang-Hagen, and Kurt Sappert. *Die Medizinalordnung Friedrich II.* Veröffentlichungen der Internationalen Gesellschaft für Geschichte der Pharmazie, NF Bd.12. Eutin: Internationale Gesellschaft für Geschichte der Pharmazie, 1957. 112 pp. + 22 plates.

The Edicts promulgated by the Holy Roman Emperor Friedrich II between 1231 and 1240 regulating medicine included the first legal separation of pharmacy from medicine and established features in the regulation of pharmacy found on the continent. This detailed historical study is followed by transcripts of the original Latin and translations into German and facsimiles of pertinent documents.

714. Holloway, S. W. F. *Royal Pharmaceutical Society of Great Britain 1841-1991: A Political and Social History.* London: The Pharmaceutical Press, 1991. xvii + 440 pp., illus. index.

Laws and Regulations 177

> Largely a very detailed history of the background of each of the major pharmaceutical statutes in Great Britain from 1852 on.

715. Jackson, Charles O. *Food and Drug Legislation in the New Deal.* Princeton: Princeton University Press, 1970. xi + 249 pp., bibl, index.

> A study of the inadequacies of the 1906 law is followed by a detailed account of a five-year struggle that led to the passage of the Food and Cosmetic Act of 1938, with particular emphasis on the political and administrative complications that were involved.

716. Janssen, Wallace F. "The Story of the Laws Behind the Labels." *FDA Consumer* 15, no. 5 (1981): 32-45.

> A survey of early state pure food and drug laws and a history of the federal 1906 and 1938 Acts, the 1962 amendments, and subsequent developments, with many illustrations.

717. Kebler, Lyman F. "The Work of Three Pioneers in Initiating Food and Drug Legislation." *Journal of the American Pharmaceutical Association* 19 (1930): 59-96.

> Hendrick B. Wright, Richard Lee T. Beale, H. Casey Young and late-nineteenth-century pure food bills.

718. Kondratas, Ramunas A. "Biologics Control Act of 1902." In *The Early Years of the Federal Food and Drug Control.* ed. James Harvey Young, pp. 8-27. Madison, WI: American Institute of the History of Pharmacy, 1982.

> An account of the background of the Biologics Control Act of 1902 with special reference to the work of the federal Hygienic Laboratory. A copy of the Act is appended.

719. Lamb, Ruth deForest. *American Chamber of Horrors: The Truth about Food and Drugs.* New York: Farrar & Rinehart, 1936. 418 pp., illus., bibl.

   Examines questions of regulation and quality of food and drugs during early quest for regulation. Includes numerous descriptions of poorly regulated products.

720. Muñoz Calvo, Sagrario. "Ordenación farmacéutica en España." *Boletin de la Sociedad Espanola de Historia de la Farmacia* 30, no. 120 (1979): 305-17.

   A survey of the historical writing on pharmaceutical legislation in Spain.

721. Muñoz Calvo, Sagrario. "Ordenación legislative de la farmacia en España durante la primera mitad del siglo XIX." *Boletin de la Sociedad Espanola de Historia de la Farmacia* 36, no. 141-42 (1985): 109-29.

   A chronological listing and description of the various regulations pertaining to pharmacy in Spain in the first half of the nineteenth century.

722. Musto, David F. *The American Disease: Origins of Narcotic Control.* Expanded edition. New York: Oxford University Press, 1987. xvi + 384 pp., index.

   Includes histories of the Harrison Narcotic Act, of state and local legislation for the control of narcotics, and of federal enforcement of the Harrison Act.

723. Paterson, G. R. "Canadian Pharmacy in Preconfederation Medical Legislation." *Journal of the American Medical Association* 200 (1967): 849-52.

   The history of the medical legislation in Canada that sought to control pharmacy and pharmacists from 1750 until pharmacy laws were passed in Quebec in 1870 and Ontario in 1871 is presented.

724. Penn, R. G. "The State Control of Medicines: The First 3000 years." *British Journal of Clinical Pharmacology* 8 (1979): 293-305.

A rapid survey of the control of medicines from ancient times on is followed by a history of the control of medicine in Great Britain with special attention to the British Pharmacopoeia, the Therapeutic Substances Act of 1925, the impact of the thalidomide episode, and the Medicines Act of 1968.

725. Pugsley, L. I. "The Administration and Development of Federal Statutes on Food and Drugs in Canada." *Medical Services Journal Canada* 23 (1967): 387-449.

A survey of Canadian legislation from 1874 on. [not seen]

726. Sappert, Kurt. "Vergleich des Niederlassungsrechtes der Apotheker in 56 Staaten der Erde." *Pharmazeutische Zeitung* 90 (1954): 923-28.

A discussion and presentation in tabular form of the ownership arrangements, educational requirements, registration and licensing requirements, restrictions or lack of restrictions on the number of pharmacies and their location, and who may open a pharmacy, in 56 countries.

727. Sciortino, T. *Evoluzione storica della legislazione farmaceutica in Italia*. Trieste: LINT, 1969. 174 pp.

A brief historical sketch is followed by portions of selected documents from 1249 to 1945.

728. Soldi, A. *Origini ed evoluzione della legislazione farmaceutica in Italia*. Milan: Guadagni, 1976. xv + 371 pp.

The legislative history of the various pre-unification states is followed by an account of the national laws governing pharmacy. [not seen].

729. Sonnedecker, Glenn. "Drug Standards Become Official." In *The Early Years of the Federal Food and Drug Control.* ed. James Harvey Young, pp. 28-39. Madison, WI: American Institute of the History of Pharmacy, 1982.

A study and evaluation of the impact of the official status given to the USP and NF under the 1906 Pure Food and Drugs Act.

730. Stevenson, Lloyd G. "Official Control of the Administration of Drugs: Historical Notes on Early Attempts at Regulation." *Experimental Medicine and Surgery* 22 (1964): 147-54.

A kaleidoscopic overview of attempts to control the administration of drugs from classical, Arabic, and early modern times. [not seen].

731. Stieb, Ernst W. "Drug Adulteration and Control in Canada. II. A Step Forward: The Adulteration Act of 1884." *Pharmacy in History* 18 (1976): 17-24.

The inadequacies of the 1875 Act and the provision of the 1884 Act are described and the latter's similarities to and differences from the British and New York State legislation are pointed out.

732. Stieb, Ernst W. "Drug Control in Britain, 1850-1914." In *Safeguarding the Public: Historical Aspects of Medicinal Drug Control.* ed. John B. Blake, pp. 15-26. Baltimore: Johns Hopkins Press, 1970.

The history of the Adulteration Acts in Britain and the impact of the *British Pharmacopoeia* in establishing drug standards.

733. Stieb, Ernst W., with the collaboration of Glenn Sonnedecker. *Drug Adulteration: Detection and Control in Nineteenth-Century*

Britain. Madison: University of Wisconsin Press, 1966. 335 pp., illus., index.

A comprehensive study of the economic, political, and social aspects of the adulteration of drugs is followed by an account of the legislation that sought to control the problem.

734. Stieb, Ernst W., and Elizabeth J. Quance. "Drug Adulteration: Detection and Control in Canada. I. Beginnings: The Inland Revenue Act of 1875." *Pharmacy in History* 14 (1972): 18-24.

The background of the "first food and drug legislation" in Canada is described and its similarity to British rather than United States precedents is pointed out.

735. Stürzbecher, Manfred. "Einige Bemerkungen zur Geschichte der Medizinalgesetzgebung im deutschen Sprachgebiet." *Veröffentlichungen der Internationalen Gesellschaft für Geschichte der Pharmazie e.V.* 24 (1964): 123-32.

A discussion of the relationship of the Edicts of Friedrich II to the medical (and pharmaceutical) ordinances of the German cities in the later Middle Ages and Renaissance that contends that the ordinances derived from the practical social requirements of the cities and not from the Edicts.

736. Suñé Arbussa, José María, and José Luis Valverde. "Del remedio secreto a la especialidad farmacéutica: Evolución legal en España." In *Farmacia e Industrializacion: Libro homenaje al Doctor Guillermo Folch Jou*. ed. F. Javier Puerto Sarmiento, pp. 83-93. Madrid: Sociedad Española de Historia de la Farmacia, 1985.

A chronological presentation and description of each regulation in Spain pertaining to industrially produced and proprietary medicines from 1788 to the 1940s.

737. Temin, Peter. *Taking Your Medicine: Drug Regulation in the United States*. Cambridge: Harvard University Press, 1980. xi + 274 pp., bibl., index.

A distinguished economic historian views the history of drug regulation in the United States within the context of the growth and development of the pharmaceutical manufacturing industry. Both the historical work and the economic analysis are impressive.

738. Valverde, José Luis. "Regulaciones de farmacia contenidas en las Ordinanzas Municipales de las Ciudades españolas." *Veröffentlichungen der Internationalen Gesellschaft für Geschichte der Pharmazie e.V.* NF 36 (1970): 135-58.

A detailed study of the municipal ordinances pertaining to pharmacy in the cities of medieval and Renaissance Spain.

739. Wardell, William M., and Louis Lasagna. *Regulation and Drug Development*. Washington: American Enterprise Institute for Public Policy Research, 1975. 181 pp., refs.

Includes a chapter on pre-1962 regulations, and examines the changing mechanisms of regulation.

740. Welch, Henry, and Felix Marti-Ibañez, eds. *The Impact of the Food and Drug Administration on Our Society: A Fiftieth Anniversary Panorama*. New York: MD Publications, 1956. 144 pp., index.

A symposium with a section on the FDA and drugs.

741. Whittet, T. Douglas. "Drug Control in Britain: From World War I to the Medicines Bill of 1968." In *Safeguarding the Public: Historical Aspects of Medicinal Drug Control*. ed. John B. Blake, pp. 27-37. Baltimore: Johns Hopkins Press, 1970.

The effect of the *British Pharmacopoeia* and of the *British Pharmaceutical Codex* on drug quality, on the report of the

Ministry of Health Committee on Control of Certain Therapeutic Substances and the Therapeutic Substances Act of 1925 that resulted from the report, and on the Medicines Bill of 1968 under consideration at the time.

742. Wolfe, Margaret Ripley. *Lucius Polk Brown and Progressive Food and Drug Control: Tennessee and New York City, 1908-1920.* Lawrence, KS: Regents Press of Kansas, 1978. 194 pp., index.

A study of food and drug regulation on state and urban levels.

743. Young, James Harvey, ed. "The American Drug Scene." *Emory University Quarterly* 21 (1965): 71-141.

Papers presented at a symposium: drug manufacturing in America, appraising drug safety and efficacy, doctors and drugs, proper limits of self-medication, pharmacists and public health, and what new medicines we may expect.

744. Young, James Harvey. *Pure Food: Securing the Federal Food and Drugs Act of 1906.* Princeton: Princeton University Press, 1989. xiii + 312 pp., illus., index, bibliographic essay.

A detailed account of the conditions that led to the passage of the Food and Drugs Act of 1906 and that includes the struggles of the various consumer groups and special interest groups, the roles of the leadership, the political problems involved. A historiographical survey of the literature and on the Act makes up a final chapter.

745. Young, James Harvey. "Drugs and the 1906 Law." In *Safeguarding the Public: Historical Aspects of Medicinal Drug Control.* ed. John B. Blake, pp. 147-57. Baltimore: Johns Hopkins Press, 1970.

An account of the problems involved in the enforcement of the 1906 law up to the passage of the 1938 law.

746. Young, James Harvey. "The Government and the Consumer: Evolution of Food and Drugs Laws. The 1938 Food, Drug, and Cosmetic Act." *Journal of Public Law* 13 (1964): 197-204.

An entertaining look at the 1938 Act, comparing aspects of its passage to those of the 1906 Act. Fully documented.

747. Young, James Harvey. "Public Policy and Drug Innovation." *Pharmacy in History* 24 (1982): 3-31.

A history of government as guarantor, guardian, and generator of food and drug supplies. Emphasis is on American examples.

748. Young, James Harvey. "Social History of American Drug Regulation." In *Drugs in Our Society*. ed. Paul Talalay, pp. 217-19. Baltimore: Johns Hopkins Press, 1964.

Examines the social history of drug regulation in America in terms of "change, complexity, competition, crusading, compromise, catastrophe," with documentation.

2e—Professional Pharmaceutical Literature

Classics

749. Avicenna (Ibn Sina). *Zusammengesetzte Heilmittel der Araber. Nach dem fünften Buch des Canons von Ibn Sina aus dem Arabischen übersezt*. ed. Sontheimer. Freiburg im Breisgau: 1845. 289 pp., index.

The book of the Canon on the materia medica.

750. Baumé, Antoine. *Elémens de pharmacie théoretique et pratique*. Paris: Damonneville & Musier, 1762. xvi + 853 pp.

A very popular review of the entire field of pharmaceutical chemistry, it also describes pharmaceutical apparatus and procedures.

751. Beguin, Jean. *Tyrocinium chymicum*. Paris: 1608. [Modern printing of an English version with a preface by Hans W. Nintzel. Gillette, NJ: Heptangle Books, 1983. xv + 145 pp., index.].

   A very popular work that illustrates the growing rapport between chemistry and pharmacy.

752. Cordus, Valerius. *Dispensatorium pharmacopolarium*. Facsimile: *Das Dispensatorim des Valerius Cordus; Faksimile des im Jahre 1546 erschienenen ersten Druckes durch Joh. Petreium in Nürnberg. Hersg. von der Gesellschaft für Geschichte der Pharmazie*. Mittenwald: Neymayer, 1934. 20 pp., 273 cols., illus.

   This dispensatory became the first to be recognized as an official pharmacopoeia when the city of Nuremberg gave it such recognition in 1546.

753. Croll, Oswald. *Basilica chymica* . . . Francoforti: Claud. Marnium & herendes Joannis Aubrii, 1609. illus.

   A very popular work that strongly defended Paracelsus; included an essay on the doctrine of signatures and a list of drugs and the methods for preparing them.

754. Cruz, Martin de la. *The Badianus Manuscript (Codex Barberini, Latin 241), Vatican Library: An Aztec Herbal of 1552. Introduction, Translation and Annotations by Emily Walcott Emmart*. Baltimore: 1940. xxiv + 341 pp., illus.

   A facsimile reproduction and an English translation from the Latin translation by Badianus of a manuscript on American materia media by an Aztec.

755. Dioscorides. *De materia medica*. Translated by Pietro Andrea Mattioli. Venice: Bascarini, 1544. 443 pp.

The first of the many editions of Dioscorides put out by Mattioli. It offered marginal annotations, and synonyms in Greek, Arabic, German, and French.

756. Dioscorides. *De materia medica*.

Two modern language renditions have appeared, each with limitations: Berendes, J. *Des Pedanios Dioskurides aus Anazarbos Arzneimittellehre in fünf Büchern*. Stuttgart: 1902; and Gunther, Robert T. *The Greek Herbal of Dioscorides. Illustrated by a Byzantine A. D. 512. Englished by John Goodyer A. D. 1655. Edited and First Printed A. D. 1933.* New York: Hafner Publishing Co., 1968 (ix + 701 pp., index, supplemental index, illus.).

757. Dioscorides. *De medicinali materia libri quinque.* translated by Jean Ruel. [Paris]: Stephani, [1516]. 159 ff.

Many editions and translations of Dioscorides were issued in the Renaissance; this was the first of Ruel's influential translations into Latin. [not seen]

758. Frampton, John. *Joyfull Newes out of the Newe Founde Worlde wherein is Described the Rare and Singular Vertues of Diverse and Sundrie Hearbes, Trees, Oyles, Plantes, and Stones . . . Englished by J. Frampton*. London: William Norton, 1577. 109 ff.; Facsimile, Amsterdam: Theatrum Orbis Terarum; New York, De Capo, 1970.

An English version of the first treatise on American drugs, from the Seville, 1574 edition of Nicholas Monardes, *Primera y Segunda y Tercera Partes de la Historia Medicinal de las Cosas que se Traen de Nuestras Indias Occidentales . . .* [not seen].

Dioscorides and Theophrastus were major contributors to knowledge about plants and their uses, as indicated by their important positions on the title page for The Herball or General History of Plants *(London, 1636).*

759. Galen. *Claudii Galeni Opera Omni.* Edited by C. G. Kühn. 20 vols. in 22. Leipzig: 1821-33; Reprint, Hildesheim: Olms, 1964-65.

The pharmaceutical texts are: *De antidotis*, vol. 15, 1-209 *Die glauconem de medendi methodo*, vol. 11, 1-146; *De compositione medicamentorum secundum locos libri X*, vol. 12, 378-1007, vol. 13, 1-361; *De compositione medicamentorum per genera libri VII*, vol. 13, 362-1058; and *De simplicium medicamentorum facultate libri XI*, vol. 11, 379-892. These have not been translated into a modern language.

760. Geoffroy, Etienne-François. *Tractatus de materia medica.* 3 vols. Paris: Sumptibus & Empensis Joannes Desaint & Caroli Saillant, 1741.

Considered to be the first book to present pharmacognosy—the identification and description of crude drugs—in a systematic way.

761. Hagen, Karl G. *Lehrbuch der Apothekerkunst.* 2nd ed. Königsberg: Hartung, 1781. 9 lvs., 832 pp., 30 lvs.

The first edition appeared in 1778 and was a most popular textbook in pharmacy in Germany for seventy-five years. [not seen].

762. LeFebvre, Nicaise. *Traicté de Chymie.* 2 vols. Paris: Jolly, 1660. 1092 pp., illus.

The best chemistry textbook of the period. Written by a pharmacist, it was essentially a work in pharmaceutical chemistry. [not seen].

763. Lémery, Nicolas. *Cours de chymie.* Paris: By the author, 1675. 534 pp.

Perhaps the most widely used textbook for a century, the bulk of the treatise concerned the preparation of chemical remedies, although an interest in pure chemistry is pronounced.

764. Lémery, Nicolas. *Pharmacopée universelle*. Paris: Laurent D'Houry, 1697. xvi + 1050 pp., tables.

   A widely translated and published general treatise on drugs and medicines.[not seen].

765. Lémery, Nicolas. *Traité universel des drogues simples*. Paris: Laurent d'Houry, 1698. [14] + 838 pp. + [4] + [51 pp.].

   A widely translated and published list, with synonyms, descriptions, locations, literary references, virtues, etymology, and so forth. There is a list of seeds "recently brought over from the American islands." [not seen].

766. Manliis, Joannes Jacobus de. *Luminare maius*. Venice: Impressum per Albertinum Vercellensem, 1504 (or later). [1] + 94 + [4] pp.

   A pharmaceutical handbook by a pharmacist; the "Greater Luminary" was recognized as authoritative in several European cities. [not seen].

767. Monardes.

   See Frampton (citation #758).

768. Orta, Garcia da. *Coloquios dos simples, e drogas he cousas medicinais da India*. Goa: J. de endem, 1563. 159 ff.

   The first published work on the materia medica of the East Indies. [not seen].

Historical Studies

769. Anderson, Frank J. *An Illustrated History of the Herbals.* New York: Columbia University Press, 1977. xiv + 270 pp., illus., bibl., index.

    Analyses of 32 important first- to sixteenth-century herbals in the Library of the New York Botanical Garden. Bibliographic notes are particularly significant.

770. Arber, Agnes R. *Herbals: Their Origin and Evolution: A Chapter in the History of Botany 1470-1670.* 3rd ed. with an introduction and annotations by William T. Stearn. Cambridge: Cambridge University Press, 1986. xxxii + 358 pp., illus., index.

    This edition of Arber's germinal study of herbals is followed by important appendices: (1) a chronological list of herbals with brief bibliographic information; (2) an extensive bibliography and (3) an index to it; (4) annotations by W. T. Stearn; (5) two essays by Arber, one on the coloring of sixteenth-century herbals (1940) and the other entitled "From Medieval Herbalism to the Birth of Modern Botany" (1944).

771. Blunt, Wilfred, and Sandra Raphael. *The Illustrated Herbal.* New York: Metropolitan Museum of Art, 1979. 187 pp. + index.

    With more than 150 illustrations, many in full color, this book conveys the artistry of the herbals. The illustrations are well documented and the book contains a short bibliography and index.

772. Cowen, David L. *America's Pre-Pharmacopoeial Literature.* Madison: American Institute of the History of Pharmacy, 1961. 40 pp.

    A description of the European dispensatory and pharmacopoeial literature used in North American and of the veterinary, popular, and professional works of this genre published in North America between 1720 and 1820.

773. Cowen, David L. *The Spread and Influence of British Pharmacopoeial and Related Literature: An Historical and Bibliographic Study. Mit einer Einführung von Erika Hickel.* Veröffentlichungen der Internationalen Gesellschaft für Geschichte der Pharmazie, NF Bd. 41. Stuttgart: Wissenschaftliche Verlagsgesellschaft MBH, 1974. xviii + 105 pp.

An account of British dispensatories and pharmacopoeias published outside of Great Britain (1677-1871), with a checklist and selected library holdings indicated. Maps, tables, and illustrations of selected title pages are appended.

774. Cowen, David L. "The Boston Editions of Nicholas Culpeper." *Journal of the History of Medicine and Allied Sciences* 11 (1956): 156-65.

A description of the two works attributed to Culpeper published in Boston: *The English Physician* (1708) and the *Pharmacopoeia Londinensis* (1720), the latter the first full-sized medical book published in North America.

775. Cowen, David L. "The Edinburgh Dispensatories." *Papers of the Bibliographic Society of America* 45 (1951): 85-96.

An historical account of the *New Dispensatory* and the *Edinburgh New Dispensatory* (1753-1847), with a check list.

776. Cowen, David L. "The Edinburgh Pharmacopoeia: I. Historical Development and Significance; II. Bibliography." *Medical History* 1 (1957): 123-39, 340-51.

A history of the Edinburgh Pharmacopoeia, 1699-1847, with a check list.

777. Feldmann, Edward G. "The NF-USP Merger: Controversies and Consequences." In *One Hundred Years of the National*

Formulary: A Symposium. ed. Gregory J. Higby, pp. 43-53. Madison: American Institute of the History of Pharmacy, 1989.

The controversies that arose and were resolved in the merger are discussed and a sanguine appraisal of the consequences presented.

778. Goltz, Dietlinde. "Zur Entwicklungsgeschichte der Arzneibücher—Form—Inhalt—Problematik." *Pharmazeutische Zeitung* 114 (1969): 1819-27, 2009-2014.

In the first part, an intensive survey of pharmaceutical literature of the Middle Ages and of the sixteenth century precedes a study of the contents and structure of the "official" pharmacopoeias, particularly the Florentine *Receptario* and the *Dispensatorium* of Valerius Cordus. Special attention is given to the handling of simples and composites, the methods of compounding, indications for use, and legal arrangements. The second part discusses the impact of the introduction of the binomial system of plant classification upon pharmacy and the meaning of the term "pharmacopoeia" historically.

779. Hamarneh, Sami. "The Climax of Medieval Arabic Professional Pharmacy." *Bulletin of the History of Medicine* 42 (1968): 450-61.

A discussion of Arabic pharmaceutical literature mainly concerned with Ibn al-Attar's *Minhâj al-Dukkân wa Dustûr al-'yân* (Handbook for the Apothecary Shop). Composed in 1259 or 1260, this popular handbook (printed as late as 1932) included recipes, weights, synonyms, the acquiring and storing of drugs, the examination and testing of drugs, and the duties, social responsibilities, moral conduct, and shop practices of the pharmacist.

780. Hamarneh, Sami, and Glenn Sonnedecker. *A Pharmaceutical View of Albucasis al-Zahrâwî in Moorish Spain. Janus,* suppl., vol. 5. Leiden: Brill, 1963. xii + 176 pp., index, illus.

A study of the various Albucasis manuscripts. Included is a reconstructed Arabic text of excerpts from the 25th treatise and an English translation of it.

781. Higby, Gregory J. "Publication of the National Formulary: A Turning Point for American Pharmacy." In *One Hundred Years of the National Formulary: A Symposium*. ed. Gregory J. Higby, pp. 3-19. Madison: American Institute of the History of Pharmacy, 1989.

A study of the background of the *National Formulary* (with special reference to the work of Charles Rice), the reasons for its coming into existence, and its significant impact on the practice of pharmacy.

782. Levey, Martin. "The Italian Pharmacopoeia and the Influence of Medieval Arabic Pharmacy." *Pharmacy in History* 12 (1970): 13-15.

Very brief introduction to the study of the Arabic influence on European medicine. With a translation of the preface of the *Nuovo Receptario* (Florence, 1498).

783. Lutz, Alfons. "Studien über pharmazeutische Inkunabel 'Nuovo Receptario' von Florenz." *Veröffentlichungen der Internationalen Gesellschaft für Geschichte der Pharmazie e.V.* NF 13 (1958): 113-28.

A comparison of the two incunabula editions, dated 10 January and 21 January 1498 (but actually 1499) of the Florentine *Nuova Receptario*.

784. Matthews, Leslie G. "Herbals and Formularies." In *The Evolution of Pharmacy in Britain*. ed. F. N. L. Poynter, pp. 187-213. London: Pitman, 1965.

A survey of herbals and formularies with special emphasis on those of Great Britain.

785. Scarborough, John. "Texts and Sources in Ancient Pharmacy." *Pharmacy in History* 29 (1987): 81-84, 133-39.

   An analytical, critical, and thorough bibliography of works, mainly in English and German, pertaining to ancient Near Eastern, Greek, and Hellenistic pharmacy.

786. Schmitz, Rudolf. "Formen pharmazeutischen Schrifttums." *Veröffentlichungen der Internationalen Gesellschaft für Geschichte der Pharmazie e.V.* NF 45 (1978): 97-113.

   An analytical historical survey of pharmaceutical literature arranged on the basis of forms, viz., corpus, canon, tractate, herbal, technical, domestic medicine, and such special forms as literature on substitutions and on inter- and intraprofessional relations.

787. Schneider, Wolfgang. *Mein Umgang mit Paracelsus and Paracelsisten: Beitrage zur Paracelsus-Forschung, besonders auf arzneimittelgeschichtlichem Gebiet*. Frankfurt/M: Govi, 1982. 199 pp.

   A collection of essays on Paracelsus with particular regard to the pharmaceutical aspects of Paracelsianism. [not seen].

788. Smola, Gertrud. *Alte Kräuterbucher Pflanzbild und Heilkunde: Bestände aus steirischen Bibliotheken und Sammlungen*. Graz: Landesmuseum Joanneum Abteiling für Kunstgewerbe, 1972. 47 pp., illus.

   Descriptions, bibliographic details, and annotations of 209 herbals, starting with the Dioscorides *Codex* and ending with an 1895 publication. [not seen].

789. Sonnedecker, Glenn. "The Changing Character of the National Formulary (1890-1970)." In *One Hundred Years of the National Formulary: A Symposium*. ed. Gregory J. Higby, pp. 21-42. Madison: American Institute of the History of Pharmacy, 1989.

A detailed study of the NF and the impact on it of the official status it received, of the progress of pharmaceutical science and technology, of the industrialization of drug making, and of the status of the USP.

790. Stannard, Jerry. "The Herbal as a Medical Document." *Bulletin of the History of Medicine* 43 (1969): 212-20.

   The text as well as the illustrations in herbals were meant to convey important medical information. The arrangement of plants within the herbals and their content is considered.

791. Urdang, George. *Pharmacopoeia Londinensis of 1618 Reproduced in Facsimile with a Historical Introduction*. Madison: State Historical Society of Wisconsin, 1944. vii + 299 pp.

   The introduction presents the background of the London Pharmacopoeia in detail and compares the two issues of the Pharmacopoeia. The first issue, of 7 May 1618, is presented in facsimile.

792. Urdang, George. "Pharmacopoeias as Witnesses of World History." *Journal of the History of Medicine and Allied Sciences* 1 (1946): 46-70.

   This seminal study covers European pharmacopoeial publications from the Florentine *Receptario* to modern times, pointing out the historical context in which they appeared.

793. Valverde, José Luis. "The Aztec Herbal of 1552: Martin de la Cruz' 'Libellus de Medicinalibus Indorum Herbis': Context of the Sources on Nahautl Materia Medica." *Veröffentlichungen der Internationalen Gesellschaft für Geschichte der Pharmazie e.V.* NF 53 (1984): 9-30.

   A critical historiographical study [in English] of an Aztec manuscript (known as the Badianus Manuscript) and its subsequent translations, commentaries, and printings, followed by a review of the pharmaceutical techniques and forms noted in the manuscript, and by an evaluation of the relation of this *Libellus* to other texts of Nahautl medicine.

794. Valverde, José Luis, and José A. Pérez Romero. *Drogas Americanas en fuentes de escritores Franciscanos y Dominicos*. Estudios de la Cátedra de Historia de la Farmacia y Legislación Farmacéutica de la Universidad de Granada, España, no. 8. Granada: Catedra de Historia de la Farmacia y Legislación Farmacéutica de la Universidad de Granada, 1988.

Bio-bibliographic accounts of 24 Franciscans and Dominicans (two of whom are from this century, the others from the sixteenth through the eighteenth centuries) whose writings are original sources of information on drugs encountered in the New World. These accounts are followed by a compilation and consolidation of the descriptions and comments on 441 Spanish-American drugs found in their writings. A cross-index and a list of synonyms (mainly of Indian names) are provided.

2f—Professional and Social Aspects

795. Anderson, Lee. *Iowa Pharmacy, 1880-1905, An Experiment in Professionalism*. Iowa City: University of Iowa Press, 1989. 178 pp., index.

A study of the formative years of pharmacy in Iowa, including discussion of legislation, organization, and education.

796. Ballard, Charles W. "Historical Background of the Founding of the APhA." *Journal of the American Pharmaceutical Association, Practical Pharmacy Edition* 12 (1951): 695-98.

A succinct review of the conditions and events leading to the founding of the American Pharmaceutical Association in 1851.

797. Bender, George A. *A History of Arizona Pharmacy*. Tucson: Arizona Pharmacy, 1985. 727 pp., illus., index.

Comprehensive account of the growth of pharmacy in Arizona, covering all aspects of professional development and including details of the program and business of each annual meeting of the Arizona Pharmaceutical Association.

798. Berman, Alex. "American Hospital Pharmacy: A Bicentennial Perspective." *American Journal of Hospital Pharmacy* 33 (1976): 129-33.

Review of the evolution of hospital pharmacy in the United States from its emergence at the turn of the twentieth century through its maturation in the 1930s and into the 1970s. Emphasis is placed on the importance of hospital pharmacy for the elevation of professional standards above commercialism.

799. Berman, Alex. "Conflict and Anomaly in the Scientific Orientation of French Pharmacy, 1800-1873." *Bulletin of the History of Medicine* 37 (1963): 1963.

This analysis of professional trends in nineteenth-century France examines the tensions between the scientific investigators at the head of the profession and the more mundane preoccupations of retail pharmacists, stressing the growing estrangement between the two. It also covers the impact of the Paris clinical school on French scientific pharmacy. Finally, the article discusses the debate over recognition of military pharmacy, which physicians opposed.

800. Berman, Alex. "Historical Currents in American Hospital Pharmacy." *Drug Intelligence and Clinical Pharmacy* 6 (1972): 441-47.

Survey of some of the major trends affecting the development of institutional pharmacy in America, including the hospital environment, the roles of the hospital, and the influence of the American Association of Hospital Pharmacists.

801. Berman, Alex, Gloria Niemeyer, and Donald E. Francke. "Ten Years of the American Society of Hospital Pharmacists." *Bulletin of the American Society of Hospital Pharmacists* 9 (1952): 277-421.

Thorough coverage of the first decade of the Society, divided into six sections: the formative period (the background of hospital pharmacy in the 1920s and 1930s); founding and growth; establishment of standards; the Society's *Bulletin*; education and training; and evaluation and interpretation. Appendices record the Society's officers, committees, programs, and constitution. Immediately preceding this work (pp. 249-75) are a number of short articles by various authors discussing the history of hospital pharmacy in distinct settings such as the Army, the Navy, and the Veterans Administration.

802. Bono, James, and Charles Schmitt. "An Unknown Letter of Jacques Daléchamps to Jean Fernel: Local Autonomy Versus Centralized Government." *Bulletin of the History of Medicine* 53 (1979):100-27.

A letter between two prominent medical practitioners is translated and analyzed for insight into physician-apothecary relations in sixteenth-century France. The letter portrays apothecaries as taking the practice of medicine into their own hands, dispensing inferior and corrupt remedies, and abusing physicians.

803. Burnby, Juanita G. L. *A Study of the English Apothecary from 1660 to 1760. Medical History*, Supplement No.3. London: Wellcome Institute for the History of Medicine, 1983. 128 pp., index.

A careful treatment of the professional life and social status of the apothecary in seventeenth- and eighteenth-century England, which integrates the pharmacist's work with that of other health professionals.

804. Bynum, William F. *An Early History of the British Pharmacological Society*. [London]: British Pharmacological Society, 1981. 59 pp., index.

Booklet outlining the activities of the Society since its founding in 1931; includes lists of members and officers.

805. Campbell, Leslie Caine. *Two Hundred Years of Pharmacy in Mississippi*. Jackson, MS: University Press of Mississippi, 1974. 192 pp. + index, bibliography.

A well-done state history with some specific information about practice and education.

806. Cook, Harold. "The Rose Case Reconsidered: Physicians, Apothecaries, and the Law in Augustan England." *Journal of the History of Medicine and Allied Sciences* 45 (1990): 527-55.

The reevaluation of the famous conflict between doctors and druggists in early eighteenth-century London argues the Rose case confirmed rather than altered the status quo with respect to apothecaries practicing physic and did not prevent apothecaries from charging for medical advice. In the process, a detailed account of the circumstances of the case is provided.

807. Copeman, W. S. C. *The Worshipful Society of Apothecaries of London. A History 1617-1967*. London: Pergamon Press, 1967. 94 pp., illus., append.

Short but substantive account of the first 350 years of the Worshipful Society, which also provides a good overview of the professional growth of English pharmacy generally during this period.

808. Cowen, David L. "The Foundations of Pharmacy in the United States." *Journal of the American Medical Association* 236 (1976): 83-87.

Concise survey of pharmacy in colonial America, concentrating on the overlap of drug dispensing among apothecaries, physicians, druggists, and merchants, and discussing the emergence of recognition of the necessity of an independent and specialized pharmaceutical profession.

809. Cowen, David L., and William H. Helfand. "The Progressive Movement and Its Impact on Pharmacy." *Pharmaceutica Acta Helvetiae* 54 (1979): 317-23.

Discussion of the influence of the 1906 Food and Drugs Act and the 1914 Harrison Narcotic Act on the professional status of pharmacy, emphasizing the importance of the new trust placed in the pharmacist for enforcement of the laws and protection of public health.

810. Crellin, John K. "Apothecaries, Dispensers, Students and Nineteenth-Century Pharmacy at St. George's Hospital, London." *Medical History* 6 (1962): 131-45.

This article discusses the pharmaceutical (and medical) duties of apothecaries working at a major London hospital, demonstrating the complexity, sometimes confusion, of British pharmacy in the mid-nineteenth century.

811. Crellin, John K. "Eighteenth-Century Pharmacy at St. George's Hospital, London." *Medical History* 5 (1961): 327-40.

Useful article for insight into the duties of early hospital pharmacists and their relations with physicians.

812. Crellin, John K. "Leicester and the Nineteenth-Century Provincial Pharmacy." *Pharmaceutical Journal* 195 (1965): 417-20.

Although restricted to a single English town, this article provides an informative perspective on the status and activities of pharmacists in the mid-1800s and the profession's concern to elevate standards of training and practice in a period when its best and brightest members were moving into general medical practice and abandoning drug compounding and dispensing.

813. Crellin, John K. "Pharmaceutical History and its Sources in the Wellcome Collections. The Growth of Professionalism in Nineteenth-Century British Pharmacy." *Medical History* 11 (1967): 215-27.

Condensed account of English pharmacy's professionalization, integrated with discussion of pamphlets, prints, artifacts, and other items illustrative of the professionalization process, maintained in the collections of the Wellcome Historical Medical Museum.

814. Crellin, John K., and William Helfand. "Picture Postcards—A Resource for the Social History of Pharmacy." *Pharmacy in History* 25 (1983): 116-30.

A thorough exploration of the depiction of pharmacies and pharmaceutical themes on postcards, and discussion of what the cards tell us about pharmacy in different periods, and how the profession and the public viewed each other.

815. Einbeck, Arthur. "Pharmacy in the Army and Navy." *Merck Report* 56 (January 1947): 22-26.

Discussion of pharmacy in the military in World War II and after, concentrating on the struggle to establish pharmacy practice on the same professional plane as in civilian life.

816. Ellis, Frank. "The Background of the London Dispensary." *Journal of the History of Medicine and Allied Sciences* 20 (1965): 197-212.

This treatment of the events leading to the opening of London's first free out-patient clinic includes discussion of apothecaries' encroachment on the privileges of physicians, the strained relations between the two sides, and the battle which resulted in the Dispensary.

817. Ferguson, Thomas. "Early History of Pharmacy and the Apothecary in Scotland." *Chemist and Druggist* 116 (1932): 695-702.

Outline of the growth of pharmaceutical activities in Scotland from the late Middle Ages into the nineteenth century. The article includes discussion of developments in training, literature, regulation, and relations with surgeons.

818. Forbes, Thomas. "Apprentices in Trouble: Some Problems in the Training of Surgeons and Apothecaries in Seventeenth-Century London." *Yale Journal of Biology and Medicine* 52 (1979): 227-37.

Interesting discussion of the conditions of apprenticeship, and the relations of master and apprentice, in the 1600s; based on court records of disputes between the two sides.

819. Griffenhagen, George. *The Story of California Pharmacy.* Madison, WI: American Institute of the History of Pharmacy, 1950. 58 pp., illus., append., index.

Compact survey of the development of the pharmaceutical profession in California, with particular attention to literature and organizations.

820. Griffenhagen, George. "125th APhA Anniversary... Predictions or Prologue." *Journal of the American Pharmaceutical Association* N.S. 17 (1977): 614-16.

Account of the 1852 founding of the American Pharmaceutical Association and the organizational evolution of the Association to the present.

821. Griffenhagen, George. "American Pharmacists in Political Life." *Journal of the American Pharmaceutical Association* N.S. 6 (1966): 376-82.

Review of the political activities of pharmacists at local, state, and national levels in the nineteenth and twentieth centuries; includes a list of pharmacists who served in Congress and cartoons depicting political leaders as pharmacists.

822. Griffenhagen, George. "Professional Organizations. Their Impact on the Delivery of Pharmaceutical Service." In *Perspectives on Medicines in Society*. eds. Albert I. Wertheimer, and Patricia J. Bush, pp. 386-413. Hamilton, IL: Drug Intelligence Publications, 1977.

Concise coverage of the growth of professional organizations from medieval guilds to the present, concentrating on America, where the rise of professional societies from the local to the national level is detailed (retail, manufacturing, and proprietary associations, even unions, are included).

823. Griffenhagen, George, and William Felter. *The Oregon Trail of Pharmacy*. Madison, WI: American Institute of the History of Pharmacy, 1952. 54 pp., illus., append., index.

Short history of drugstores, literature, education, and organization of pharmacy practice in Oregon.

824. Hall, Marie. "Apothecaries and Chemists in the Seventeenth Century." *Pharmaceutical Journal* 199 (1967): 433-36.

Discussion of the role of Paracelsian chemical remedies in the professionalization of pharmacy, the necessity of mastering new chemical methods encouraging higher educational and professional standards.

825. Hamarneh, Sami. "The Climax of Medieval Arabic Professional Pharmacy." *Bulletin of the History of Medicine* 42 (1968): 450-61.

Coverage of organization, standards of practice, ethics, and literature of Islamic pharmacy in the period of the 800s to the

1200s; concentrates on the content and significance of the thirteenth-century text *Minaj al-Dukkan*.

826. Hamarneh, Sami. "The Rise of Professional Pharmacy in Islam." *Medical History* 6 (1962): 59-66.

    Short but helpful overview of the separation of pharmacy into a distinct profession in the ninth-century Middle East.

827. Higby, Gregory J. "Professionalism and the Nineteenth-Century American Pharmacist." *Pharmacy in History* 28 (1986): 115-24.

    A reinterpretation of the early professionalization of American pharmacy. Developments in professional organization, education, and legislation are evaluated in the light of evolving views of pharmacists themselves on what constituted professionalism.

828. Higby, Gregory J., and Teresa C. Gallagher. "Pharmacists." In *Women, Health, and Medicine in America: A Historical Handbook*. ed. Rima D. Apple, pp. 497-516. New York: Garland Publishing, 1990.

    This chapter reviews the small number of articles that have been written about women in American pharmacy. Full citations are provided. Areas for future research are suggested.

829. Holloway, S. W. F. "The Apothecaries' Act, 1815: A Reinterpretation." *Medical History* 10 (1966): 107-29; 221-36.

    A detailed analysis of the origins and consequences of this important piece of legislation regulating the practice of apothecaries throughout England and Wales. The article challenges older interpretations of the Act as a professional triumph for apothecaries, suggesting that in fact it was detrimental to their professional status.

830. Kaufman, K. L. "Pharmaceutical Ethics." *American Journal of Pharmaceutical Education* 23 (1959): 213-18.

General outline of the development of ethical codes relating to the practice of pharmacy, from antiquity to the twentieth century. Much of the discussion is given to the ethics of the medical profession as a model for pharmacy.

831. Kinsey, Raymond, George Archambault, and Thomas Foster. "Pharmacy in the U. S. Public Health Service." *Journal of the American Pharmaceutical Association, Practical Pharmacy Edition* 9 (1948): 345-47, 376-84.

A review of the evolution of the duties of pharmacists attached to the Public Health Service, this article emphasizes the twentieth century and offers interesting details on the variety of demands made upon pharmaceutical appointees.

832. Kredel, F. E., and J. Hampton Hoch. "Early Relation of Pharmacy and Medicine in the United States." *Journal of the American Pharmaceutical Association* 28 (1939): 702-7.

Overview of the beginnings of the separation of pharmacy from medical practice during the 1700s, with emphasis given to the influence of John Morgan.

833. Lawall, Charles H. "Pharmaceutical Ethics." *Journal of the American Pharmaceutical Association* 10 (1921): 895-910.

Historical review of codes of ethics formulated to govern the practice of pharmacy from the sixteenth to the twentieth century. Codes are quoted at length, and include those of the Philadelphia College of Pharmacy and the American Pharmaceutical Association.

834. Lewis, Edward R. Jr. *Prairie State Pharmacy*. Chicago: Illinois Pharmacists Association, 1980. 163 pp., illus.

A model treatment of the history of the pharmacy profession in a particular state. Coverage includes state and local associations, pharmaceutical education, women and minorities in pharmacy, and pharmacists' contributions to public service.

835. Marland, Hilary. "The Medical Activities of Mid-Nineteenth-Century Chemists and Druggists, with Special Reference to Wakefield and Huddersfield." *Medical History* 31 (1987): 415-39.

    Study of English chemists and druggists as a medically ambiguous group—part professional, part fringe practitioners; richly detailed account of their circumstances and activities, relations with physicians and apothecaries, and patronage by the public.

836. Matthews, Leslie G. *The Pepperers, Spicers and Apothecaries of London During the Thirteenth and Fourteenth Centuries.* London: Society of Apothecaries of London, 1980. 63 pp., illus.

    A booklet that examines the activities of the three trade groups from which English pharmacy would evolve as a separate profession (with the founding of The Worshipful Society of Apothecaries, in 1617).

837. Matthews, Leslie G. *Pharmacists in the Wider World.* Hounslow, England: Merrill Pharmaceuticals, Ltd., 1981. 40 pp., illus.

    A booklet presenting short biographies of a number of pharmacists who made important or interesting contributions (everything from matches to Worcestershire sauce) to society outside their profession.

838. Matthews, Leslie G. *The Royal Apothecaries.* London: Wellcome Historical Medical Library, 1967. 191 pp., index.

    Full account of apothecaries to the English crown from the early 1200s to the present, including interesting information on the services expected in addition to the dispensing of medicines.

839. Matthews, Leslie G. "The Spicers and Apothecaries of Norwich." *Pharmaceutical Journal* 198 (1967): 5-9.

Study of professional development of English pharmacy, from the thirteenth to the eighteenth century, tracing "the line of descent" of chemists and druggists at the local level of a major provincial city.

840. Oddis, Joseph. "The Evolving Program of the American Society of Hospital Pharmacists." *Drug Intelligence and Clinical Pharmacy* 6 (1972): 435-40.

Straightforward account of the first 30 years of the American Society of Hospital Pharmacists, concentrating on economic aspects of the organization's development.

841. Orr, Jack, and Allen White. *A Century of Service to Pharmacy. The Washington State Pharmacists Association, 1890-1990.* Renton, WA: Washington State Pharmacists Association, 1990. 269 pp., illus. append., index.

Detailed account of the contributions of the state association to the professionalization of pharmacy in Washington with unusually thorough attention to the social context of pharmacy's development. [not seen].

842. Roberts, R. S. "The Apothecary in the Seventeenth Century." *Pharmaceutical Journal* 189 (1962): 505-9.

Survey of the transformation of the English apothecary from grocer to general practitioner, providing information on the training and work of apothecaries outside London, and the influence of social and economic forces.

843. Shannon, Sam. "The Army Pharmacist: A Historical Review." *Military Medicine* 143 (1978): 542-45.

Account of the role of the pharmacist in the U. S. Army from the Revolution through the Vietnam conflict. Coverage focuses on the expansion of the military pharmacist's duties, particularly in the twentieth century.

844. Urdang, George, et al. "The Sections of the American Pharmaceutical Association." *American Journal of Pharmaceutical Education* 17 (1953): 334-400.

An introduction and six articles, each by a different author, discussing the history of the several sections of American pharmacy's chief professional organization. The sections included are the Scientific Section, the Women's Section, Pharmaceutical Economics, Practical Pharmacy, Education and Legislation, and Historical Pharmacy.

845. Urdang, George. "Development of Modern Pharmacy in the United States." *Merck Report* 56, no. 4 (October, 1947): 4-10.

Coverage of pharmacy's growth from the post-Civil War period to the mid-twentieth century, including education and literature, and emphasizing the influence of John Maisch and William Proctor.

846. Urdang, George. "The First Century of the Pharmaceutical Society of Great Britain." *Journal of the American Pharmaceutical Association, Practical Pharmacy Edition* 3 (1942): 420-27.

This outline of the history of Britain's Pharmaceutical Society focuses on the influence of the Society on the fledgling American Pharmaceutical Association and subsequent interactions between the two organizations. The growth of each is interpreted in light of the political context of its home country.

847. Urdang, George. "Pharmacy in the United States Prior to the Civil War." *Merck Report* 56 (July, 1947): 18-23.

Outline of the emergence of a profession of pharmacy between the late 1700s and the 1860s with discussion of organization, education, literature, and regulation.

848. Virginia Pharmaceutical Association. *A Century of Virginia Pharmacy*. Richmond: Virginia Pharmaceutical Association, 1981. 179 pp.

   A good survey of the first century's developments in all areas of professional pharmacy in Virginia.

849. Wall, Cecil, H. Charles Cameron, and E. Ashworth Underwood. *A History of the Worshipful Society of Apothecaries of London*. London: Oxford University Press, 1963. 424 pp., illus., index.

   Detailed investigation of the first two centuries of London's Worshipful Society; based on extensive research in the Society's archives, it clarifies the changing role and professional status of the English apothecary during this period. Extensive notes by Underwood flesh out the main text by Wall and Cameron.

850. Whittet, T. Douglas. "The Apothecary in Provincial Guilds." *Medical History* 8 (1964): 245-73.

   A survey to complement the histories of London apothecaries, providing information on the guild associations of apothecaries in a number of British cities from the late Middle Ages through the eighteenth century.

851. Whittet, T. Douglas. "Pepperers, Spicers and Grocers— Forerunners of the Apothecaries." *Proceedings of the Royal Society of Medicine* 61 (1968): 801-6.

   Informative summary of the activities of pepperers and spicers in late medieval London, describing contributions both to their guild and to London civic life.

852. Whittet, T. Douglas. "The Transition from Apothecary to Pharmacist in British Hospitals." *American Journal of Hospital Pharmacy* 36 (1979): 492-97.

Review of the professional transition from hospital apothecaries (going back as far as twelfth-century monastic infirmaries) to modern hospital pharmacists. Particular attention is given to three hospitals—St. Thomas's, St. Bartholomew's, and Bethlehem.

853. Williams, William H. "Pharmacists at America's First Hospital, 1752-1841." *American Journal of Hospital Pharmacy* 33 (1976): 804-7.

General discussion of the evolving role of the pharmacist at the Pennsylvania Hospital, from its founding into the mid-nineteenth century. Attention is given to the pharmacist's duties, and relations with the medical staff.

2g—Economic and Business Aspects

854. Boussel, Patrice, Henri Bonnemain, and Frank J. Bové. *History of Pharmacy and the Pharmaceutical Industry*. Trans. by Desmond Newell and Frank J. Bové. Paris: Asklepios Press, 1983. 285 pp., bibl., illus.

A broad overview of developments of pharmacy from the time of the Sumarians. Contains company histories, superb illustrations, and a list of works in French.

855. Burkill, I. H. *A Dictionary of the Economic Products of the Malay Peninsula*. 2 vols. London: 1935. 2402 pp., index.

This is still a useful work for identifying products of commerce between China and the Malay Peninsula.

856. Chien, Robert I., ed. *Issues in Pharmaceutical Economics.* Lexington, MA: Lexington Books, 1979. vii + 247 pp., bibl., index.

   A useful collection of papers originally presented in seminars at UCLA and Northwestern that exhibit diverse perspectives. Several of the papers have an historical orientation.

857. Comanor, W. S. "The Drug Industry and Medical Research: The Economics of the Kefauver Committee Investigations." *Journal of Business* 39 (January 1966): 12-18.

   Assesses a central point of contention in the Kefauver Hearings: the nature and importance of industry-based pharmaceutical research, and the costs and benefits of compulsory patent licensing.

858. Comanor, William S. "The Political Economy of the Pharmaceutical Industry." *Journal of Economic Literature* 24 (September 1986): 1178-1217.

   The essential guide to the economics of the pharmaceutical industry. Much more than a bibliographic source, this paper provides incisive critiques of economic models and delineates a framework for further research.

859. Comanor, W. S. "Research and Competitive Product Differentiation in the Pharmaceutical Industry in the United States." *Economica* 31 (November 1964): 372-84.

   Based on the author's dissertation, this article argued that research by pharmaceutical companies was aimed at differentiating a product, rather than toward discovery of fundamentally new entities.

860. Conference on the History of Medicinal Drug Control (1968: National Library of Medicine). *Safeguarding the Public: Historical Aspects of Medicinal Drug Control.* ed. John Blake. Baltimore: Johns Hopkins Press, 1970. vii + 200 pp., index.

Many of the twelve papers presented at this conference relate to the development of institutions to assure the safety, purity, and eventually, efficacy, of drugs in Britain, France, and the U.S. Participants included distinguished scholars from varied backgrounds.

861. Cooper, Michael. *Prices and Profits in the Pharmaceutical Industry*. Oxford: Pergamon Press, 1966. xi + 274 pp., index.

   Contains data on the industry in Great Britain in the early 1960s. Presents position of pharmaceutical manufacturers.

862. Cowen, David L. "The Role of the Pharmaceutical Industry." In *Safeguarding the Public: Historical Aspects of Medicinal Drug Control*. ed. John B. Blake, pp. 72-82. Baltimore: Johns Hopkins Press, 1970.

   This article traces technological progress in the pharmaceutical industry and investigates the relationship between the profit motive and the public interest.

863. Cruttenden, Joseph. *Atlantic Merchant-Apothecary: Letters of Joseph Cruttenden 1710-1717*. ed. I. K. Steele. Toronto: University of Toronto Press, 1977. xxv + 135 pp., index.

   Joseph Cruttenden shipped drugs to apothecaries and other merchants in New England and the Barbados. These letters provide insights into the nature and size of the transatlantic trade.

864. Davis, Lee Niedringhaus. *The Corporate Alchemists: Profit Takers and Problem Makers in the Chemical Industry*. New York: William Morrow and Co., 1984. viii + 330 pp., index.

   Davis looks at the problem of external costs associated with the chemical industry. Chapter 7 deals with the drug industry, and contains a detailed, global, history of the thalidomide incident.

865. Egan, John W., Harlow N. Higenbotham, and J. Fred Weston. *Economics of the Pharmaceutical Industry*. Praeger Studies in Select Basic Industries. New York: Praeger, 1982. vii + 205 pp., illus., bibl., index.

   A lucid extensive critical review of the literature on the economics of the U.S. pharmaceutical manufacturing, by proponents of laissez faire.

866. Fischbaum, Marvin. "Drugs." In *Manufacturing: A Historical and Bibliographical Guide*. ed. David O. Whitten, pp. 146-60. Handbook of American Business History, 1. New York: Greenwood Press, 1990.

   Provides a brief general introduction to the economic and business history of the American pharmaceutical industry.

867. Gill, Harold B., Jr. *The Apothecary in Colonial Virginia*. Williamsburg, VA; Charlottesville: The Colonial Williamsburg Foundation, 1972. vii + 127 pp., illus., bibl., index.

   This small book on colonial pharmacy concentrates on practice in the broad sense, including therapeutics. The author includes inventories of shops, which provide insights into practice. Although a few dated secondary sources are relied on heavily, the author also used several manuscript sources largely untouched by other historians.

868. Grabowski, Henry, and John Vernon. "A New Look at the Returns and Risks to Pharmaceutical R&D." *Management Science* 36 (July 1990): 804-21.

   The authors found that firms earned below normal returns on investments in R&D in the first half of the 1970s but normal to above normal returns after 1975.

869. Johns Hopkins University, Conference on Drugs in Our Society, 1963. *Drugs in Our Society*. ed., Paul Talalay. Baltimore: Johns Hopkins, 1964. vii + 311 pp., index.

Several papers in this conference dealt with the interplay between research, competition, and the public weal. Others evaluated pharmaceutical advertising.

870. Keats, Charles. *Magnificent Masquerade: The Strange Case of Dr. Coster and Mr. Musica.* New York: Funk and Wagnalls, 1964. 275 pp., illus., index.

An entertaining tale of how a crook and imposter gained control of an old line drug distributor, McKesson & Robbins, and made it grow.

871. Liebenau, Jonathan. *Medical Science and Medical Industry: The Formation of the American Pharmaceutical Industry.* Baltimore: Johns Hopkins University Press, 1987. ix + 207 pp., bibl., index.

A scholarly investigation of the motivation behind earliest research laboratories. The study concentrates on H. K. Mulford, Smith Kline and French, and Parke Davis and Company.

872. Liebenau, Jonathan. "Ethical Business: The Formation of the Pharmaceutical Industry in Britain, Germany, and the United States before 1914." *Business History* 30 (January 1988): 116-29.

The author compares responses in the three countries towards: sponsorship of research, government quality regulation, and, attitude toward cartelization.

873. Liebenau, Jonathan. "Industrial R and D in Pharmaceutical Firms in the Early Twentieth Century." *Business History* 26 (November 1984): 329-46.

Liebenau compares drug company attitudes toward sponsored research and company laboratories, in Britain, German, and the United States during the 1890s.

874. Liebenau, Jonathan, Gregory J. Higby, and Elaine C. Stroud (eds.). *Pill Peddlers: Essays on the History of Pharmaceutical Industry*. Madison, WI: American Institute of the History of Pharmacy, 1990. vii + 133 pp. illus.

An important collection of six essays that covers the industries in England, the U.S., Switzerland, and France. Of uniform high quality, but the paper on the French industry by Robson focuses most clearly on economic and business issues.

875. Mahoney, Tom. *The Merchants of Life: An Account of the American Pharmaceutical Industry*. New York: Harper & Row, 1959. x + 278 pp., index.

A lively entrepreneurial history of a dozen American firms, with brief accounts of a half-dozen German and Swiss firms.

876. Meadsday, Walter S. "The Pharmaceutical Industry." In *The Structure of American Industry*. ed. Walter Adams, pp. 250-84. 5th ed. New York: Macmillan, 1977.

The classic presentation of the argument that drug companies exercise monopoly power to the detriment of the public interest. More recent assessments of the industry have been rather more positive.

877. National Research Council. *The Competitive Status of the U.S. Pharmaceutical Industry: The Influences of Technology in Determining International Industrial Competitive Advantage*. Washington: National Academy Press, 1983. x + 102 pp., index.

This study assembled much useful data on the industry for the period 1960-1980.

878. Numbers, Ronald L., ed. *Medicine in the New World: New Spain, New France and New England*. Knoxville: University of Tennessee Press, 1987. 175 pp., illus. bibl.

Traces European roots of early American medical practice. The chapter by Christianson contains information on colonial apothecary shops and wholesale druggists.

879. Nutton, Vivian. "The Drug Trade in Antiquity." *Journal of the Royal Society of Medicine* 78 (1985): 138-45.

    Expands the traditional view of ancient drug trade to extend beyond only Rome or Alexandria, and to various levels of society. Links societal levels with the style of drug trade.

880. Okun, Mitchell. *Fair Play in the Marketplace: The First Battle for Pure Food and Drugs*. DeKalb, IL: Northern Illinois Press, 1986. xvi + 345 pp., bibl. index.

    Okun related the story of the first battle for pure food and drug laws which took place in state legislatures prior to 1890.

881. Pearson, Michael. *The Million Dollar Bugs*. New York: G. P. Putnam's Sons, 1969. 291 pp., index.

    Although journalistic, this book provides fascinating insights into entrepreneurial decisions in the pharmaceutical industry following the discovery of sulfa drugs and penicillin. The main focus is on Lederle, and interconnections between the Kefauver Hearings, the tetracycline antitrust cases, and a case against thieves of proprietary information.

882. Pekkanen, John. *The American Connection: Profiteering and Politicking in the "Ethical" Drug Industry*. Chicago: Follett, 1973. 348 pp., index.

    Written in the form of an exposé, Pekkanen related events leading up to the Drug Abuse Control Amendments of 1965. This book takes a dim view of the morality of the pharmaceutical companies.

883. Poynter, F. N. L., ed. *The Evolution of Pharmacy in Britain*. London: Pitman Medical Publishing Co., 1965. 240 pp., index.

This collection of nine essays includes: "The Early History of the Import of Drugs in Britain" by R. S. Roberts, and "Some Eighteenth-Century Trading Accounts" by G. M. Watson.

884. Pradhan, Suresh B. *International Pharmaceutical Marketing*. Westport, CT: Quorum Books, 1983. xxiii + 281 pp., bibl., index.

Part III contains descriptions, with brief histories, of the pharmaceutical industries in seventeen countries. Government regulations and health insurance schemes are detailed.

885. Rabin, David L., and Patricia J. Bush. "The Use of Medicines: Historical Trends and International Comparisons." *International Journal of Health Services* 4 (January 1974): 61-87.

This article compares levels of drug use both within and between countries during the 1960s and relates usage to demand factors. Part of an issue devoted to pharmaceuticals in this Marxian-oriented journal.

886. Rorem, C. Rufus, and Robert P. Fischelis. *The Costs of Medicines: The Manufacture and Distribution of Drugs and Medicines in the United States and the Services of Pharmacy in Medical Care*. Publications of the Committee on the Costs of Medical Care, no. 14. Chicago: University of Chicago Press, 1932. xi + 250 pp.

A leading exponent of health insurance teamed up with a distinguished pharmacist to provide a comprehensive picture of the market for medicines ca.1930. Budget studies provide a view of the demand side, while the business aspects of pharmacy and pharmaceutical manufacturing are explored.

887. Schafer, Edward H. *The Golden Peaches of Samarkand. A Study of T'ang Exotics.* Berkeley: University of California Press, 1963. 399 pp., bibl., index.

   A marvelous book conveying the sense of wonder about objects from foreign lands during an important period in Chinese history, the T'ang dynasty (618-906). It contains the identification and descriptions of many aromatics and rare drugs as well as a useful bibliography of international commerce of this period.

888. Schwartzman, David. *Innovation in the Pharmaceutical Industry.* Baltimore: Johns Hopkins University Press, 1976. xvi + 399 pp., index.

   Schwartzman argues that the pharmaceutical industry is dynamically competitive; that profits are not excessive when adjusted for correct depreciation of R&D, and of risk; and that promotional expenditures aid rather than hinder competition.

889. Sevigny, David C. *Ethical Pharmaceutical Industry and Some of its Economic Aspects: An Annotated Bibliography.* Addiction Research Foundation, Bibliographic Series, edited by R. J. Hall, vol. 13. Toronto: Addiction Research Foundation, 1977. iv + 521 pp., index.

   Provides detailed abstracts for approximately 150 of the 576 citations. Emphasis is on works written in English between 1960 and 1974.

890. Silverman, Milton, and Philip R. Lee. *Pills, Profits, and Politics.* Berkeley: University of California Press, 1974. xviii + 403 pp., index.

   The authors were the staff director and the chairman of the Task Force on Prescription Drugs of the Department of Health, Education, and Welfare, in the Johnson Administration. The book supports the positions of Senators Kefauver and Nelson and criticizes the pharmaceutical industry and the medical establishment.

891. Sonnedecker, Glenn. "The Rise of Drug Manufacture in America." *Emory University Quarterly* 21 (1965): 73-87.

   Traces the evolution of pharmacies into pharmaceutical manufacturers in the United States and also in Germany and France. Emphasis is on scientific and technological developments.

892. Stage, Sarah. *Female Complaints: Lydia Pinkham and the Business of Women's Medicine*. New York: Norton, 1979. 304 pp., illus., bibl., index.

   While primarily a social history, this book provides fascinating insights into the marketing and cost structure of a successful patent medicine.

893. Starr, Paul. *The Social Transformation of American Medicine*. New York: Basic Books, 1982. xi + 514 pp., index.

   A winner of the Pulitzer Prize, this is the best general introduction to the social and economic history of medicine in the United States. It places the role of pharmacy in a broader perspective.

894. Swann, John P. *Academic Scientists and the Pharmaceutical Industry: Cooperative Research in Twentieth-Century America*. Baltimore: Johns Hopkins University Press, 1988. xi + 249 pp., illus., index.

   Between the two World Wars several distinguished academics disregarded the taboo against providing counsel to pharmaceutical manufacturers. Extensive case studies carefully document their contributions.

895. Temin, Peter. *Taking Your Medicine: Drug Regulation in the United States*. Cambridge: Harvard University Press, 1980. xi + 274 pp., bibl., index.

A history of drug regulation in the United States presented and evaluated in relation to such factors as medical practice, the introduction of new drugs, the impact on the pharmaceutical industry, and governmental policy making.

896. Trease, George Edward. *Pharmacy in History.* London: Ballière, Tindall and Cox, 1964. vii + 264 pp., illus., index.

The role of the purveyors of drugs in England is placed within a broader historical context. The book provides detailed coverage of the thirteenth through eighteenth centuries, with relatively summary treatment of more recent events.

897. United States Department of Commerce, International Trade Administration. *A Competitive Assessment of the U.S. Pharmaceutical Industry.* Washington: G.P.O., 1984. xii + 113 pp., bibl.

This is a good source of data on the industry for the period from 1950-1982. It presents an overview of the structure and performance of the U.S. pharmaceutical industry along with brief characterizations of the industry in the U.K., West Germany, and Japan.

898. United States Senate, Committee on the Judiciary, Subcommittee on Antitrust and Monopoly. *Hearings on Administered Prices, 86th Congress, First Session, Parts 14-26.* Washington: G. P. O., 1960-61.

Kefauver Committee hearings aimed at determining degree of monopoly power in the U. S. pharmaceutical industry.

899. United States Senate, Select Committee on Small Business, Subcommittee on Monopoly. *Hearings on Present Status of Competition in the Pharmaceutical Industry, 90th Congress, First and Second Sessions, Parts 1-21.* Washington: G. P. O., 1967-71.

Nelson Committee hearings: emphasis was on costs and benefits of patents, and brand names, and the possibility of mandatory licensing.

900. Walker, Hugh D. *Market Power and Price Levels in the Ethical Drug Industry.* Bloomington: Indiana University Press, 1971. xiii + 246 pp., bibl., index.

Based largely on evidence submitted to the Kefauver committee, analyzes the structure and performance of the industry in the period ending in 1960.

901. Wiggins, Steven N. "The Pharmaceutical Research and Development Decision Process." In *Drugs and Health: Economic Issues and Policy Objectives.* ed. Robert B. Helms, pp. 55-83. Washington: American Enterprise Institute for Public Policy Research, 1981.

Wiggins investigates the process by which pharmaceutical firms made decisions regarding the funding of R & D. He argues that in the late 1960s that process changed from being science driven to being dominated by expected profitability.

902. Wood, Donna J. *Strategic Uses of Public Policy: Business and Government in the Progressive Era.* Pitman Series in Business and Public Policy. Marshfield, MA: Pitman Publishing, 1986. xiii + 258 pp., bibl., index.

Analyses the events, debates, and processes, that led to passage of the Pure Food and Drugs Act. The treatment of the conflict between the manufacturers of ethical and proprietary drugs is of interest. Food and drug businesses are given the main attention.

903. Young, James Harvey. *Pure Food: Securing the Federal Food and Drugs Act of 1906.* Princeton: Princeton University Press, 1989. xiii + 312 pp., illus., index, bibliographic essay.

The culmination of years of study, this is the definitive history of the struggle for passage of the act. Pharmaceutical issues play a surprisingly small role in the story.

904. Young, James Harvey. *The Toadstool Millionaires: A Social History of Patent Medicines in America Before Federal Regulation.* Princeton, NJ: Princeton University Press, 1961. xii + 282 pp., illus.

The definitive history of patent medicines in the United States from colonial times to the beginning of the twentieth century. Informative and enjoyable reading. Includes a bibliographic essay.

2h—Education

905. Adam, Linda, and Ernst W. Stieb. "Women in Ontario Pharmacy, 1927-1952." *On Continuing Practice* 17, no. 3 (1990): 23-26.

Covers period form first required two-year term Phm. B. degree program to graduation of first four-year B.Sc.Phm. class. Continuation of Stieb, Coulas, and Ferguson paper for 1867-1927 (citation #992).

906. *American Journal of Pharmaceutical Education* .

A primary source with cumulative indices for the periods 1937-49, 1950-56, 1957-66 and then every 10 years. Prior to the founding of the journal, the Proceedings of the American Conference of Pharmaceutical Faculties (1900-1925) and its successor, the American Association of Colleges of Pharmacy (1925 on) provide a wealth of detail about the state of pharmaceutical education of the period.

907. Autio, D. E. "Development of Radiopharmacy Education in America—A Brief Survey." *Pharmacy in History* 18 (1976): 13-16.

Education 223

An interesting, well-documented account.

908. Bardell, Eunice Bonow. *Wisconsin Show Globe: The Wisconsin Pharmaceutical Association, 1880-1980.* Madison, WI: Wisconsin Pharmaceutical Association, 1983. 294 pp., illus., index.

There are sections on pharmaceutical education: pp. 15-23, 71-77, 93-99, 143-44, 164-74, 204-12.

909. Bardell, Eunice Bonow. "America's Only School of Pharmacy for Women." *Pharmacy in History* 26 (1984): 127-33.

An interesting, well-documented account of the Louisville School of Pharmacy for Women (1884-ca. 1895).

910. Blauch, Lloyd E., and George L. Webster. *The Pharmaceutical Curriculum.* Washington, D.C.: American Council on Education, [1952]. xvi + 257 pp.

The offshoot of the *Pharmaceutical Survey* of 1946-49, this work represents a detailed look at American pharmaceutical education of the time. Chapter 2, "A half-century of progress," surveys the period 1900-50, while other historical references appear from time to time throughout. Although it supports the recommendation of the *Survey* for a six-year program, it is somewhat more pragmatic in suggesting that a five-year program might be necessary as an intermediary step.

911. Blockstein, William L. "The Continuing Influence of the Survey During the 1960s, 70s, and Early 80s—A Personal Look." *Pharmacy in History* 30 (1988): 142-50.

Well-documented study of the important Pharmaceutical Survey of 1946-49, which helped shape American pharmaceutical education and practice in the twentieth century.

912. Bonow, Eunice R. "The History of Professional Pharmaceutical Fraternities for Women." *American Journal of Pharmaceutical Education* 18 (1954): 409-12.

   A good, documented basis for a more comprehensive study.

913. Bonow-Bardell, Eunice. *Into the Second Century of the College of Pharmacy at the University of Kentucky, 1970-1985.* Lexington, Kentucky: University of Kentucky, 1992.

   Sequel to Wrobel's *The First Hundred Years . . . 1870-1970* (1972). [not seen].

914. Bowers, Roy A., and David L. Cowen. *The Rutgers University College of Pharmacy: A Centennial History.* New Brunswick, New Jersey: Rutgers University Press, 1991. 175 pp., illus.

   This excellent school history is a model in form and content. Organized chronologically by the tenures of major deans, the book contains a good balance of detail and discussion.

915. Bowers, Roy A., and David L. Cowen. *The Rho Chi Society: The Development of the Honor Society of American Pharmacy.* Fourth ed. Columbus, Ohio: The Rho Chi Society, 1972. xxvi + 57 pp., illus., index.

   Fiftieth anniversary edition. A fine example of how institutional histories should be written.

916. Brodie, Donald C., Roger A. Benson, Donald E. Francke, Harvey A. K. Whitney, and Christopher A. Rodowskas. "Clinical Pharmacy in Historical Perspective." *Drug Intelligence and Clinical Pharmacy* 10 (1976): 505-27.

   Series of papers from an invitational symposium on the subject sponsored by the American Institute of the History of Pharmacy at the 1975 meeting of the American Pharmaceutical Association in San Francisco.

917. Bunnell, Kevin P. *Liberal Education and American Pharmacy*. New York: Institute of Higher Education, Teachers College, Columbia University, [1958?]. 43 pp. of typescript.

   Contains a general and historical discussion of the place of liberal education in American pharmacy.

918. "Catalogue of Books Belonging to the Library of the Philadelphia College of Pharmacy." *American Journal of Pharmacy* 31 (1859): 291-98.

   The Philadelphia College of Pharmacy, founded in 1821, was the first permanent English-speaking association and school of pharmacy in the world.

919. Charters, W. W., A. B. Lemon, and Leon M. Monell. *Basic Material for a Pharmaceutical Curriculum*. New York: McGraw-Hill, 1927. 358 pp. + index.

   The first comprehensive survey of pharmaceutical education in the USA. Devoted mostly to the curriculum by subject areas as it existed and was projected in the 1920s.

920. Cocolas, George H. "From West to East and Beyond." *American Journal of Pharmaceutical Education* 50 (1986): 290-91.

   A short summary of the author's experiences as editor (1980 on) of the *American Journal of Pharmaceutical Education*, on the occasion of its 50th anniversary.

921. "Colleges of Pharmacy." *Journal of the American Pharmaceutical Association, Practical Pharmacy Edition* 17 (1956): 646-58.

   Capsule histories of the 75 schools of pharmacy then accredited by the American Council on Pharmaceutical Education, with portraits of deans. Undocumented.

922. Cowen, David L. "Notes on Pharmaceutical Training in New Jersey before 1900." *American Journal of Pharmaceutical Education* 12 (1948): 302-14.

Covers period 1870-1900, from time of founding of the New Jersey Pharmaceutical Association. Well documented.

923. Culp, Robert W. "The Education, Career Opportunities and Status of American Women Pharmacists to 1900, Including a Directory." *Transactions and Studies of the College of Physicians of Philadelphia* 41 (1974): 211-27.

Most of this short article is taken up by a directory of 243 women pharmacists before 1900. The author's approach is that of a social historian.

924. Culp, Robert W. "A Multiplicity of American Pharmacy Schools from 1870 to 1900, Including a Directory." *Transactions and Studies of the College of Physicians of Philadelphia* 40, July (1972): 64-72.

Table of 64 American schools of pharmacy (1870-1900), showing date of establishment and name changes. The author discusses the difficulty in agreeing on which schools should be included on the list.

925. DeSalvo, Robert J., Robert W. Hammel, Joseph D. McEvilla, and Robert V. Evanson. *A History of the Discipline of Pharmacy Administration*. Kansas City, Missouri: Marion Laboratories, Inc., 1985. vii + 179 pp.

A special report commissioned by the Section of Teachers of Pharmacy Administration of the American Association of College of Pharmacy on the development of the field in USA. Well-documented with some useful tables and appendices.

926. Diaz, Luis Torres. "Pharmaceutical Education in Puerto Rico, 1512-1957." *Journal of the American Pharmaceutical*

Association, Practical Pharmacy Edition 18 (1957): 598-600. illus.

A quick overview with a short bibliography.

927. Duff, J. Gordon. "A Brief History of Pharmaceutical Education in the Maritimes." *Canadian Pharmaceutical Journal* 98 (1965): 6-8, 24.

Covers period from 1908 on. Written by then dean of College of Pharmacy, Dalhousie University; the College succeeded the Maritime College of Pharmacy, an association school (1911-1961).

928. Earles, Melvin P. "Pharmacy and its Relation to Scientific Education in Nineteenth-Century Britain." *Pharmacy in History* 11 (1969): 43-49.

A documented account of the efforts of the Pharmaceutical Society of Great Britain in relation to the school it established in 1841.

929. Earles, Melvin P. "The Pharmacy Schools of the Nineteenth Century." In *The Evolution of Pharmacy in Britain*. ed. F. N. L. Poynter, pp. 79-95. London: Pitman Medical Publishing Co., 1965.

Succinct, yet thorough, documented account.

930. Eckles, Robert B. *Purdue Pharmacy, The First Century*. West Lafayette, IN: Purdue University, 1979. x + 106 pp., illus.

Published in anticipation of the centennial in 1984 of the Purdue University School of Pharmacy and Pharmacal Sciences, this book covers the period 1884 to 1979. Highlights the evolution of the School in terms of faculty, particularly the deans, the undergraduate program, and graduate studies and research. Undocumented text, but select bibliography of sources.

931. "Education." *The Badger Pharmacist* (1900): 93-213.

> Undocumented. Pages 93-110 are mainly about the University of Wisconsin School of Pharmacy as a whole; 142-213, biographical sketches and portraits of alumni.

932. Elliott, Edward C. *The General Report of the Pharmaceutical Survey, 1946-49*. Washington, D.C.: American Council on Education, 1950. xix + 240 + i pp.

> The crux of this comprehensive survey of American pharmacy was the role that education would play in improving pharmacy practice. Among the recommendations is the suggestion that the American Association of Colleges of Pharmacy and American Council on Pharmaceutical Education proceed to the establishment of a six-year doctor of pharmacy program.

933. England, Joseph W., ed. *The First Century of the Philadelphia College of Pharmacy, 1821-1921*. Philadelphia: Philadelphia College of Pharmacy and Science, 1922. 728 pp., illus., index.

> Also three decennial supplements, edited by John E. Kramer, for 1921-31, 1931-41, and 1941-51 (see Kramer citation #949). More a reference book than a connected history. Largely a chronological approach with detours here and there to look at the development of pharmacy, the evolution of the *U. S. Pharmacopoeia*, etc. Biographical sketches interspersed about founders, staff, editors of the *American Journal of Pharmacy*, and alumni. Heavily illustrated. See also Osol [citation #967] for update to 1971.

934. Francke, Gloria N. "Evolution of Clinical Pharmacy." In *Perspectives in Clinical Pharmacy*. pp. 26-36. Hamilton, IL: Drug Intelligence Press, 1972.

> Good, documented overview from the 1940s to the 1970s. [not seen].

935. Freking, Harold C. "Gleanings from the Early History of the Cincinnati College of Pharmacy." *American Journal of Pharmaceutical Education* 12 (1948): 412-24.

Undocumented, chronological approach, 1850-99.

936. Gramling, L. G. "Pharmaceutical Education in Florida." In *A History of Pharmacy in Florida*. ed. L. G. Gramling, pp. 134-76. Gainesville, Florida: Ewing Printing, Inc., 1973.

Covers period from about 1895 to 1971; topical approach.

937. Granberg, C. Boyd. "Twenty-Five to Fifty." *American Journal of Pharmaceutical Education* 50 (1986): 286-87.

Some of the author's personal experiences and philosophies as editor (1961-74) of the *American Journal of Pharmaceutical Education*.

938. Harris, Robin S. *A History of Higher Education in Canada, 1663-1960*. Toronto: University of Toronto Press, 1976. xxiv + 715 pp., bibl., index.

Contains material relating to pharmaceutical education on pages 117, 176-78, 214, 291-92, 409-10, 477, 483, 486, 487, 539, 616-19, 676-77. Integrates sections and references concerning pharmaceutical education from about 1860-1960, within the context of higher education generally and professional education specifically. One in a series of publications, Studies in the History of Higher Education in Canada, sponsored by the Association of Universities and Colleges of Canada, with support from the Carnegie Corporation.

939. Harrod, D. C., and E. J. Shellard. *Pharmacy at Chelsea, 1919-1979*. London: Chelsea College of Science and Technology, 1979. vi + 36 pp., illus.

Chronological approach; no documentation.

940. Henderson, Metta Lou, and Tammy Lynn Keeney. "Women in Pharmacy Education: The Pioneers." *American Pharmacy* NS28, no. 5 (1988): 24-27.

   This brief overview contains several excellent photographs of early women educators in pharmacy.

941. Henderson, Metta Lou, and Tammy Lynn Kenney. "Women Pharmacy Faculty: Changing the Face of Pharmacy Education." *American Pharmacy* NS 28, no. 5 (1988): 18-22.

   Primarily historical treatment of subject but tied to contemporary situation.

942. Hoch, J. Hampton. "Pharmaceutical Education at the Medical College, Charleston." In *The History of Pharmacy in South Carolina*. J. Hampton Hoch, pp. 49-60. Charleston, South Carolina: Nelson's Printing Co., 1951.

   General references only.

943. Hoch, J. Hampton. "A Survey of the Development of Materia Medica in American Schools and Colleges of Pharmacy from 1821 to 1900." *American Journal of Pharmaceutical Education* 12 (1948): 148-61.

   Essentially a study of how materia medica became fragmented over the nineteenth century, with at least 15 courses eventually arising from the discipline by the end of the century, including pharmacy, botany, toxicology, pharmacognosy, physiology, bacteriology, and pharmacology.

944. Hughes, F. Norman. "The Faculty of Pharmacy—A Retrospective Look." *On Continuing Practice* 7, no. 3 (1980): 3-8.

   Insightful account from the perspective of the dean, 1953-73. Short list of references.

945. Hughes, F. Norman. "One Hundred Years of Pharmaceutical Education in Ontario, 1871-1971." *Bulletin of the Ontario College of Pharmacy* 20 (1971): 92-99.

Written on the occasion of the centennial of the Ontario College of Pharmacy. Hughes was the last dean (1952-53) when the school became the Faculty of Pharmacy of the University of Toronto in 1953. [not seen].

946. Hynson, Henry P. "Historical Notes on Degrees in Pharmacy." *Druggists Circular* 51 (1907): 79-81.

Deals with various diplomas and degrees in the USA during the nineteenth century.

947. Keiner, B. "Cornell—A Short-Lived School of Pharmacy." *Pharmacy in History* 14 (1973): 147-48.

A brief but interesting account about an institution of equally brief existence (1887-1890).

948. Knapp, David A. "Experiments in Pharmaceutical Education." *American Journal of Pharmaceutical Education* 30 (1966): 736-45.

An articulate plea for schools of pharmacy to be more adventuresome in planning for the future in their roles *vis-à-vis* practice.

949. Kramer, John E., ed. *First Decennial Supplement to the "First Century of the Philadelphia College of Pharmacy," 1921-1931; Second Decennial Supplement . . . 1931-1941; Third Decennial Supplement . . . 1941-1951*. Philadelphia: Philadelphia College of Pharmacy and Science,, 1934; 1942; 1952. 189 pp., illus.; 144 pp., illus.; 156 pp., illus.

Continuation of original publication edited by Joseph W. England (citation #933). See also Osol (citation #967) for update to 1971.

950. Kremers, Edward. "The Teaching of Pharmacy During the Past Fifty Years." *Druggists Circular* 51 (1907): 61-79.

Comprehensive, documented survey from 1821 to 1906 by key periods of developments. Portraits.

951. Little, Ernest. "A History of the American Foundation for Pharmaceutical Education." *American Journal of Pharmaceutical Education* 15 (1951): 367-88.

Fairly detailed account for period 1939-51. Not referenced but quotations tied to Board minutes.

952. Lynn, E. V. "A Century of Research in Pharmaceutical Chemistry in Schools of Pharmacy in the United States." *American Journal of Pharmaceutical Education* 17 (1953): 183-93.

A discussion not so much of the research itself as where the research was coming from; little research was actually being done at this time. This addresses APHA's query system as a means of stimulating research in the nineteenth century and mentions several of the leaders in research by the late nineteenth century. Finally, the article discusses the disappointment with productivity from pharmacy schools and how this might be alleviated. Undocumented.

953. Malone, Marvin H. "The Journal, 1975-1979: A Former Editor's Perspective." *American Journal of Pharmaceutical Education* 50 (1986): 287-89.

The writer's personal account of his period as editor of the *American Journal of Pharmaceutical Education* on the occasion of its 50th anniversary.

954. Manasse, Henry R. Jr. "Innovation, Confrontation, and Perseverence: Albert B. Prescott's Legacy to Pharmaceutical Education in America." *Pharmacy in History* 15 (1973): 22-28.

    Prescott (1832-1905) headed the first university-based school of pharmacy (Michigan, starting in 1869), thus marking a major turning point in the progress of pharmaceutical education in the USA.

955. Manners, Steven. "AFPC and ADPC: Upholding Standards of Pharmacy Education." *Canadian Pharmaceutical Journal* 120 (1987): 388-90.

    A brief history of the Association of Faculties of Pharmacy of Canada and the Association of Deans of Pharmacy of Canada. Undocumented.

956. Matthews, A. Whitney. "The Initial Impact." *Canadian Pharmaceutical Journal* 117 (1984): 578, 582-83.

    Explores the early (1944-51) influence of the Canadian Conference of Pharmaceutical Faculties, predecessor to the present Association of Faculties of Pharmacy of Canada.

957. Matthews, Leslie G. "The Pharmacist—His Education, Training, and Public Service." In *History of Pharmacy in Britain*. Leslie G. Matthews, pp. 157-207. London: E. & S. Livingstone Ltd., 1962.

    Covers the period from 1842 to about 1950.

958. Moir, J. Glen. "Pharmaceutical Education in B. C.: The Struggle for a College of Pharmacy." *Canadian Pharmaceutical Journal* 90 (1957): 780, 798, and 800.

    Covers period 1905-46, when the present Faculty of Pharmaceutical Sciences, University of British Columbia began. Documented.

959. Moran, Bruce T. *Chemical Pharmacy Enters the University: Johannes Hartmann and the Didactic Care of Chymiatria in the Early Seventeenth Century.* Madison, WI: American Institute of the History of Pharmacy, 1991.

Hartmann offered laboratory courses in the preparation of chemical medicines at Marburg until 1621, and the laboratory notebook presented here gives a detailed view of the techniques and goals of chemical medicine in the seventeenth century.

960. Mrtek, Robert G. "Pharmaceutical Education in These United States—An Interpretive Historical Essay of the Twentieth Century." *American Journal of Pharmaceutical Education* 40 (1976): 339-65.

Written to mark the Bicentennial of the United States of America. A masterful, interpretive, brief history of pharmaceutical education in the USA. Meticulously documented.

961. Mrtek, Robert G. "The Pharmaceutical Survey Revisited." *Pharmacy in History* 30 (1988): 129-41.

Well-documented look at the important Pharmaceutical Survey of 1946-49, which helped shape pharmacy education and practice in the USA in the second half of the twentieth century.

962. Mrtek, Robert G., and Charles D. King. *One Hundred and Twenty-Five Years of Pharmaceutical Education, The University of Illinois at Chicago.* Chicago, IL: University of Illinois at Chicago College of Pharmacy, [1984]. 32 pp., illus.

Imaginatively written and produced brief history. [not seen].

963. Netz, Charles V. *History of the University of Minnesota College of Pharmacy, 1892-1970.* Minneapolis, MN: University of Minnesota College of Pharmacy, [1971]. xiv + 259 pp., illus.

A chronological approach by chapter.

964. Newcomer, James, Kevin P. Bunnell, and Earl J. McGrath. *Liberal Education and Pharmacy*. New York: Institute of Higher Education, Teachers College, Columbia University, 1960. x + 125 pp.

A small section is historical. "Liberal Education and American Pharmacy" (pp. 20-35), and "The Pharmacy Curriculum: The Four-Year Program" (p. 36-48).

965. Noble, Alice. *The School of Pharmacy of the University of North Carolina: A History*. Chapel Hill: University of North Carolina Press, 1961. viii + 237 pp., illus., index.

Essentially a chronological approach.

966. Osborne, George E. "David Stewart, M.D., First American Professor of Pharmacy [1813-1899]." *American Journal of Pharmaceutical Education* 23 (1959): 219-230.

An interesting study of the various activities of pharmacist-physician Stewart, including his short stint (1844-1846) as first professor of pharmacy in USA at University of Maryland.

967. Osol, Arthur, Charles E. Welch Jr., and John E. Kramer (eds.). *A Sesquicentennial of Service, 1821-1971, of the Philadelphia College of Pharmacy and Science*. Philadelphia: Philadelphia College of Pharmacy and Science, 1971. x + 208 + v pp., illus., index.

Updates the earlier volumes edited by Joseph W. England, for 1821-1921, and three decennial supplements edited by John E. Kramer, for 1921-51. The present work concentrates on the period 1951-71, primarily from the point of teaching, research, public service, and publications. An interesting chronology of some of the more important events for the period 1821-1971. Appendices cover officials, faculty, awards, and so forth. Unfortunately, it is undocumented.

968. Parascandola, John, and John P. Swann. "Development of Pharmacology in American Schools of Pharmacy." *Pharmacy in History* 25 (1983): 95-115.

   A well-documented study beginning with the European foundations.

969. Paterson, G. R. "The Canadian Conference of Pharmaceutical Faculties." *American Journal of Pharmaceutical Education* 22 (1958): 201-209.

   Brief history of the chief organization since 1944 of Canadian schools of pharmacy, known since 1969 as the Association of Faculties of Pharmacy of Canada. Also some discussion of various earlier activities from 1907 on.

970. Paterson, G. R. "Pharmaceutical Education—1867-1967: Educators Win Tough Battles for Pharmacy." *Drug Merchandising* 48, no. 7 (1967): 21-22, 26-27, 43.

   Capsule histories of pharmaceutical education in provinces of Canada as well as concerning the Canadian Conference of Pharmaceutical Faculties and the Pharmacy Examining Board of Canada. Undocumented. [not seen].

971. Picchioni, Albert L., and George A. Bender. *A History of the College of Pharmacy at the University of Arizona*. Tucson: University of Arizona College of Pharmacy, 1985.

   Covers period from founding in 1947.

972. Redman, Kenneth. *History of the South Dakota State University, College of Pharmacy, 1975-1982: A Chronology*. Brookings, SD: K. Redman, 1983. xi + 94 pp.

A chronological update of Clark Eidsmoe book, *History of Pharmacy at South Dakota State University, 1887-1974* for the centennial of South Dakota State University.

973. Reif, Edward Clarence, and Thelma Reif. *A Contribution to Western Pennsylvania Pharmacy*. Pittsburgh: University of Pittsburgh Press, 1959. 396 pp., illus.

    History of the Pittsburgh College of Pharmacy, 1878-1958.

974. Riedel, Bernard E. "The UBC Faculty of Pharmaceutical Science: The Last 17 Years." *Canadian Pharmaceutical Journal* 117 (1984): 529-33.

    Told from the perspective of the dean of the faculty, 1967-1985.

975. Rodowskas, Christopher A. "A Matter of Degrees." *Drug Intelligence and Clinical Pharmacy* 16 (1982): 607-612.

    A general overview of the degrees offered and required at various times in USA, finishing with some detail regarding the Pharm.D. vs. the B.Sc.

976. Rowe, Tom D., and Nancy J. (eds.) Moncrief. *Centennial Celebration Proceedings. College of Pharmacy, The University of Michigan, 1876-1976*. Ann Arbor: College of Pharmacy, the University of Michigan, 1977. viii + 119 pp.

    Proceedings of a symposium, "Pharmacy in the Twenty-First Century." Wide-ranging subject, with only one strictly historical paper, by Robert A. Thom, "History and Highlights of the Founding of the College of Pharmacy" (pp. 9-19).

977. Schmitz, Rudolf. *Die deutschen pharmazeutisch-chemischen Hochschulinstitute; Ihre Entstehung und Entwicklung in Vergangenheit und Gegenwart*. Ingelheim am Rhein: C. H. Boehringer Sohn, 1969. 371 pp., illus., index.

Pharmaceutical education in Germany.

978. Sonnedecker, Glenn. "American Pharmaceutical Education before 1900." 752 pp. : Ph.D. dissertation, University of Wisconsin, 1952.

   A comprehensive history; never published.

979. Sonnedecker, Glenn. "The Conference of Schools of Pharmacy—A Period of Frustration." *American Journal of Pharmaceutical Education* 18 (1954): 389-401.

   A good account of the forerunner (1870-1884) of the American Conference of Pharmaceutical Faculties (1900-1925) and the American Association of Colleges of Pharmacy (1925-).

980. Sonnedecker, Glenn, ed. "The Development of Education and Appendix 4: Schools of Pharmacy in the United States." In *Kremers and Urdang's History of Pharmacy*. ed. Glenn Sonnedecker, pp. 226-54 and 383-86. 4th ed. Philadelphia: J. Lippincott, 1976; repr. 1986, by American Institute of the History of Pharmacy.

   A well-documented look at the development of pharmaceutical education in the United States. Also discussion concerning education in the chapters on France, Germany, and Britain.

981. Sonnedecker, Glenn. "Experimental Work Associated with American Pharmaceutical Education in the 19th Century." In *Medizingeschichte in unserer Zeit. Festgabe für Edith Heischkel-Artelt und Walter Artelt zum 65. Geburtstag*. eds. Hans-Heinz Eulner, et al., pp. 384-92. Stuttgart, 1971.

   The small amount of experimental work in pharmacy done in pharmacy schools in the nineteenth century was done with little academic support. The author examines the origins of experimental work associated with schools of pharmacy, although not done within the schools.

982. Sonnedecker, Glenn. "The Founding." *American Journal of Pharmaceutical Education* 50 (1986): 491-95.

Well-documented account centers around the remarkable founding editor (1937-55) of the *American Journal of Pharmaceutical Education*, Rufus Lyman, on the occasion of the 50th anniversary of the publication.

983. Sonnedecker, Glenn. "Pharmaceutical Education, 1867 and 1967." In *One Hundred Years of Pharmacy in Canada, 1867-1967.* pp. 1-10. Toronto: Canadian Academy of the History of Pharmacy, 1969.

Written from the author's perspective as an acknowledged expert on the history of pharmaceutical education in the USA. Some interesting contrasts and parallels.

984. Sonnedecker, Glenn. "Science in American Pharmaceutical Education of the 19th Century." *American Journal of Pharmaceutical Education* 15 (1951): 185-217.

A good, well-documented study. Examines the lag in introducing science into pharmacy education, and the role of physicians. After tracing the growth of some basic sciences in pharmacy schools, especially chemistry, it assesses the contributions of the University of Michigan and the University of Wisconsin as leaders in the movement to put pharmacy education on a scientific foundation.

985. Sonnedecker, Glenn. "The Scientific Background of Chemistry Teachers in Representative Pharmacy Schools of the United States during the 19th Century." *Chymia* 4 (1953): 171-200.

A comprehensive, well-documented account.

986. Sonnedecker, Glenn. "The Section on Education and Legislation of the American Pharmaceutical Association." *American Journal of Pharmaceutical Education* 17 (1953): 362-83.

A comprehensive, well-documented account of an interesting development.

987. Sonnedecker, Glenn. "Teaching Pharmacy in 19th-Century America—Some Aims and Issues." *American Journal of Pharmaceutical Education* 35 (1971): 379-90.

   A good overview prepared for the journal's sesquicentennial in 1971 of American pharmaceutical education.

988. Sonnedecker, Glenn. "Women as Pharmacy Students in 19th-Century America." *Veröffentlichungen der Internationalen Gesellschaft für Geschichte der Pharmazie e.V.* 40 (1973): 135-41.

   A short, balanced look at the difficulties faced by women pharmacy students in the 1800s. Comparisons are made with other American professions and with pharmacy abroad.

989. Stieb, Ernst W. "A Century of Formal Education in Ontario." *Canadian Pharmaceutical Journal* 116 (1983): 104-107.

   Written from the perspective of the deans of the school for the period 1882 to 1983.

990. Stieb, Ernst W. "Edward Buckingham Shuttleworth, 1841-1934." *Pharmacy in History* 12 (1970): 91-116.

   Shuttleworth was the first dean (1882-1892) of the school established by the Ontario College of Pharmacy; since 1953, the Faculty of Pharmacy of the University of Toronto.

991. Stieb, Ernst W. "Pharmaceutical Education in Ontario, Prelude and Beginnings." *Pharmacy in History* 16 (1974): 64-71.

Examines the first decade of the school of the Ontario College of Pharmacy, established in 1882, as well as ad hoc arrangements made from 1867 onward.

992. Stieb, Ernst W., Gail Coulas, and Joyce A. Ferguson. "Women in Ontario Pharmacy." *Pharmacy in History* 28 (1986): 125-34. Reprinted in Marianne Ainley, ed. *Despite the Odds: Essays on Canadian Women and Science.* Montreal, Canada: Véhicule Press, 1990. pp. 121-33, 403-406.

Covers the period from the first record of women in early pharmacy organizations (1867) and in the first school (1883) to the beginning of a required degree program.

993. Swann, John P. *Academic Scientists and the Pharmaceutical Industry: Cooperative Research in Twentieth-Century America.* Baltimore: Johns Hopkins University Press, 1988. xiv + 249 pp.

A well-documented study of cooperative biomedical research between universities and industry in the USA from the 1920s to the 1980s.

994. Taylor, H. L."Schools and Colleges of Pharmacy." *Pharmaceutical Era* 45 (1912): 177-81, 261-64, 333-36, 389-92, 459-61, 520-24, 575-78, 641-44, 707, 731-32, 767-71.

A wide-ranging series, topically arranged, covering American schools, mostly for the 25-year period 1887-1912. Although there are a number of illustrations of schools of pharmacy from around the world scattered through the account, the international theme is not reflected in the text. Many portraits and other illustrations.

995. The Massachusetts College of Pharmacy. *The Massachusetts College of Pharmacy, 1823-1973, An Informal History.* ed. David A. Fedo, Boston, Massachusetts: The Massachusetts College of Pharmacy, 1973. Special issue of its *Bulletin* 62(No. 5, Fall 1973): 1-83 + ofc and ifc.

Robert A. Walsh is the author of the major portion (pp. 5-59) of this issue, under the title: "The Massachusetts College of Pharmacy, 1823-1973." The rest constitutes letters of congratulations, reminiscences, and brief commentaries by various officials, faculty, and representatives of alumni and students. Walsh and Fedo emphasize (p. 5) that the work represents only "an *informal* and *highly selective* history; there has yet been no official history of the College."

996. Urdang, George. "College of Pharmacy Association." *American Journal of Pharmaceutical Education* 8 (1944):333-39.

    Deals with the educational role of various American organizations of pharmacy in nineteenth-century USA.

997. Urdang, George. "The Development of the Pharmaceutical Textbook, A Synopsis." *American Journal of Pharmaceutical Education* 8 (1944): 328-33.

    Covers period from Dioscorides's *De Materia medica* (1st century AD) to Joseph Remington's *The Practice of Pharmacy*(1885).

998. Urdang, George. "Edward Kremers (1865-1941): Reformer of American Pharmaceutical Education." *American Journal of Pharmaceutical Education* 11 (1947): 631-58.

    A major force in American pharmaceutical education. This is a broad biographical sketch, intent less on detail than sketching influences and contributions.

999. Urdang, George. "The Part of Doctors of Medicine in [U.S.A.] Pharmaceutical Education." *American Journal of Pharmaceutical Education* 14 (1950): 546-56.

    Well-documented study, mainly of the period 1821-1908.

Education 243

1000. Weinstein, Marvin, Marsha B. Mrtek, and Robert G. Mrtek. "Factors Leading to the Formation of the Chicago College of Pharmacy." *Pharmacy in History* 14 (1972): 3-17.

   An interesting study of the conditions in pharmacy leading up to the establishment of the College in 1859.

1001. Wilson, Robert Cummings. "Pharmaceutical Education." In *Drugs and Pharmacy in the Life of Georgia, 1733-1959*. Robert Cummings Wilson, pp. 267-78. Atlanta, Georgia: Foote & Davies, 1959.

   Undocumented and unindexed.

1002. Wimmer, Curt P. *The College of Pharmacy of the City of New York . . . A History*. [New York: Columbia University], 1929. viii + pp. 7-347, illus.

   Partly chronological, partly topical approach. Much biographical information.

1003. Winkelmann, John P. *History of the St. Louis College of Pharmacy*. [St. Louis: John P. Winkelmann], 1964. iv + 175 pp., illus.

   After a few introductory pages, arranged chronologically, 1865-1964, followed by brief biographical sketches of the founders, deans, and "Prominent Personalities of the Past." Mostly undocumented.

1004. Wrobel, Sylvia. *The First Hundred Years of the University of Kentucky College of Pharmacy, 1870-1970*. Lexington, KY: College of Pharmacy, University of Kentucky, 1972. 207 pp., illus.

   Chronological approach. Bonow-Bardell, *Into the Second Century* (citation # 913) continues the history of this school up to 1985.

1005. Zalai, K. "Pharmaceutical Education in Central Europe, A Historical Review." *Pharmacy in History* 28 (1986): 138-45.

> Wide-ranging but succinct survey from the twelfth century to the present, with some useful tables and comparisons with members of the European Economic Community; bibliography.

1006. Zopf, Louis C. "Pharmaceutical Education." In *Iowa Pharmacy— A Century of Service. A Chronology of the Iowa Pharmacists Association 1880-1980.* pp. 227-56. Des Moines, Iowa: Iowa Pharmacists Association, 1980.

> Although mainly a chronological history of the Iowa Pharmacists Association, education is one of the other facets well covered.

2i—Manufacturing (not including company histories)

1007. Aftalion, Fred. *History of the International Chemical Industry.* transl. Otto Theodor Benfy: 1991. xxiv + 411 pp., illus., index.

> A concise history of the chemical industry but with little on pharmaceuticals. Most of the emphasis is on the period 1939-89.

1008. Alcer, G. "Zur Entwicklung der Pharmaceutischen Industrie in Berlin." *Pharmazie* 42 (1987): 774-80.

> An overview of changes in the industry from the late eighteenth to the mid-twentieth centuries.

1009. Becker, Louis A. "The Soda Fountain Industry." *Pharmaceutical Era* 46 (1913): 63-66;124-27;185-88;243-46;303-305

> A good, contemporary overview of the history and state of the soda fountain industry in the United States in the beginning of

the twentieth century. Discusses the history of soda water, the development of the modern fountain, the responsibilities of manufacturers, the utensils and supplies used, and the soda fountain as a business builder in American drug stores.

1010. Beer, John J. "Coal Tar Dye Manufacture and the Origins of the Modern Industrial Research Laboratory." *Isis* 49 (1958): 123-31.

Initiation of research as a recognized function in the synthetic coal tar dye industry as seen principally through Bayer. Beer looks at the gradual shift from employing scientists strictly for routine control work to their use in new product development. In the late 1880s and early 1890s, the success of this venture led to a more independent research portion of the firm, but the nature of the work remained applied until World War I, with little if any consideration of theoretical principles.

1011. Comanor, W. S. "The Political Economy of the Pharmaceutical Industry." *Journal of Economic Literature* 24 (September 1986): 1178-1217.

A survey of post-Kefauver views about the drug industry by economists, with respect to competitiveness within the industry, the economics of R & D, the impact of advertising, and regulation and performance by the drug industry.

1012. Cowen, David L. "The Role of the Pharmaceutical Industry." In *Safeguarding the Public: Historical Aspects of Medicinal Drug Control*. ed. John B. Blake, pp. 72-82. Baltimore: Johns Hopkins Press, 1970.

Includes discussion of the history of quality control in the drug industry.

1013. Davis, A. B., and M. S. Dreyfuss. *The Finest Instruments Ever Made: A Bibliography of Medical, Dental, Optical, and Pharmaceutical Company Trade Literature; 1700-1939*. Arlington, MA: Medical History Publishing Associates I, 1986. vii, 448 p., illus., index.

With respect to literature (specifically, price lists and catalogues) from the pharmaceutical industry, this is best used as a supplement to the fine collection in the Edward Kremers Reference Files, University of Wisconsin School of Pharmacy, Madison, WI (as this book mentions briefly toward the end).

1014. Duckworth, Allan. "Rise of the Pharmaceutical Industry." *Chemist and Druggist* 100, no. (Special Centenary Number) (1959): 127-139.

This well-illustrated but undocumented article chronicles the British industry.

1015. England, Joseph W. "Pioneer Drug Milling in the United States." *American Journal of Pharmacy* 103 (1931): 389-98.

A short history of the origins of drug milling in the United States with special emphasis on the mill of Charles V. Hagner of Philadelphia. Last page of the article lists some of the other major drug millers of the nineteenth and early twentieth centuries. With six illustrations of various kinds of drug mills.

1016. Foote, Perry A. "Tablets. I. The Evolution of the Tablet Machine, II. A Bibliography on Tablets." *Bulletin of the University of Wisconsin* Serial No. 1566, General Series No. 1340 (1928): 164 pp.

A Master's thesis consisting of two parts: the evolution of the tablet machine from 1843 to 1914 with a line drawing or photograph and short description of each machine (about sixty machines described) together with a description of the process of manufacturing tablets, and an annotated bibliography on tablets from 1844 to 1926. Author and subject indexes. Good source for the history of tablet making.

1017. Forbes, R. J. *A Short History of the Art of Distillation: From the Beginnings to the Death of Cellier Blumenthal.* 1948; rpt., Leiden: E. J. Brill, 1970. 405 pp., illus., bibl., index.

An extremely valuable source on techniques, equipment, and theories behind distillation of therapeutic and other products from antiquity to the early modern period. Its coverage includes China and the Middle East, and the 200-plus woodcuts, drawings, and photos are immensely helpful.

1018. Guay, Y. "Internationalization of Industrial Research: The Pharmaceutical Industry, 1965-1979." *Scientometrics* 13 (1988): 189-213.

A comparison of research output as suggested by publications among firms in the U. S., Europe, and Japan. Concludes that fundamental research increased during this period, and dominance of U. S.-based firms decreased.

1019. Haber, Ludwig Fritz. *The Chemical Industry During the Nineteenth Century: A Study of the Economic Aspect of Applied Chemistry in Europe and North America.* Oxford: Clarenden Press, 1958. 292 pp., bibl., index.

Discussion of methods and economics that were relevant to the pharmaceutical industry.

1020. Helfand, William H., and David L. Cowen. "Evolution of Pharmaceutical Oral Dosage Forms." *Pharmacy in History* 25 (1983): 3-18.

The first half of the article describes the dosage forms introduced in the nineteenth century, such as cachets and gelatin capsules, and the enteric coating of medicines. The second half deals with the development of a variety of timed-release dosage forms in the twentieth century, bringing the history of oral dosage forms up to the 1980s.

1021. Hickel, Erika. "Die industrielle Arzneimittelforschung am Ende des 19. Jahrhunderts und die Durchsetzung einer reduktionistischen Biologie." In *Materialistische*

Wissenschaftsgeschichte. pp. 132-54. Argument-Sonderband AS 54. Berlin: Argument-Verlag, 1981.

The period 1870-1905 sees the development of a pharmaceutical industry in Germany characterized by the priority of pharmacology, experimentation, and studies of basic chemical structure. There are links between biochemistry and pharmacy, academic institutions, and industry as shown in the text and accompanying tables.

1022. Liebenau, Jonathan. *Medical Science and Medical Industry: The Formation of the American Pharmaceutical Industry.* Baltimore: Johns Hopkins University Press, 1987. ix + 207 pp., bibl., index.

Actually, a history of the early industry in Philadelphia in the late nineteenth and early twentieth centuries. He includes discussion of how some of these Philadelphia firms adopted science, and how they used this knowledge. Though virtually no attention is given to companies—well-established companies—outside of Philadelphia, this contributes to our understanding of the beginnings of the drug industry in this country.

1023. Liebenau, Jonathan. "Scientific Ambitions: The Pharmaceutical Industry, 1900-1920." *Pharmacy in History* 27 (1985): 3-11.

Author looks at three pharmaceutical firms—two in Philadelphia and one in New York—to compare how each used science. One company used science rhetorically, principally to sell products. The two others used it more for quality control and modest product expansion.

1024. Liebenau, Jonathan, Gregory J. Higby, and Elaine C. Stroud, eds. *Pill Peddlers: Essays on the History of Pharmaceutical Industry.* Madison, WI: American Institute of the History of Pharmacy, 1990. vii + 133 pp. illus.

Seven papers presented at a symposium: "The rise of the English drugs industry," "The American Society for Pharmacology and Experimental Therapeutics' ban on industrial pharmacologists,"

"A brief history of the pharmaceutical industry in Basel," "Universities, industry, and the rise of biomedical collaboration in America," "The early history of the Wellcome Research Laboratories," "The French pharmaceutical industry, 1919-39," "The twentieth-century British pharmaceutical industry in international context."

1025. Little, Arthur, and K. A. Mitchell. *Tablet Making*. Liverpool: The Northern Publishing Co., Ltd., 1949. 121 pp., illus.

Not a history but a very good description of the process of tablet making (by hand and machine) in the mid-twentieth century, of tablet-making machines, and the coating and coloring of tablets together with some representative formulas. Forty nice illustrations of primarily British tablet machines, coating pans, mixers, compact presses, drying ovens, and other equipment.

1026. Madison, James H. *Eli Lilly: A Life, 1885-1977*. Indianapolis: Indiana Historical Society, 1989. 342 pp., notes, illus., index.

Includes a detailed study of scientific management methods at one of the major drug companies in America, a unique contribution to the literature.

1027. Meyer-Thurow, George. "The Industrialization of Invention: A Case Study from the German Chemical Industry." *Isis* 73 (1982): 363-81.

Focuses on Bayer to explore the slow institutionalization of research in the (therapeutically significant) synthetic dye industry, how research was organized, and the actual contribution of the industrial research program to the success of Bayer. Complements Beer's article (citation #1010) quite well.

1028. Parascandola, John. "Industrial Research Comes of Age: The American Pharmaceutical Industry, 1920-40." *Pharmacy in History* 27 (1985): 12-21.

Examines several indicators of the growth of research in the drug industry, including laboratories, personnel, attention to fundamental research, publications, and collaborative work and recognition by academic scientists.

1029. Paterson, G. R. "Relationships Between Synthetic Dyes and Drug Entities." *Bulletin Canadien d'Histoire de la Medicine* 1, no. 2 (1984): 1-23.

Identifies three revolutionary developments in the evolution of drug manufacturing: isolation of alkaloids, the rise of dye manufacture, and the development of sulfonamides. [not seen].

1030. Porter, Roy, and D. Porter. "The Rise of the English Drugs Industry: The Role of Thomas Corbyn." *Medical History* 33 (1989): 277-95.

Also reprinted in *Pill Peddlers*, ed. Jonathan Liebenau, Gregory J. Higby, Elaine C. Stroud (citation #1024). Describes transition from dispensing chemists shop to the emerging business of large-scale pharmaceutical trading.

1031. Puerto Sarmiento, F. Javier, ed. *Farmacia e industrialización: Libro homenaje al Doctor Guillermo Folch Jou*. Madrid: Sociedad Española de Historia de la Farmacia, 1985. 246 pp.

Articles on the evolution of the pharmaceutical industry in a dozen countries in Europe, South America, and North America.

1032. Riley, John J. *A History of the American Soft Drink Industry*. Washington, DC: American Bottlers of Carbonated Beverages, 1958; repr. Arno Press Inca.: New York, 1972. xii + 302 pp., illus., index.

A very good history of bottled carbonated beverages in the United States from 1807 to 1957. Major sections on the evolution of American soft drinks, the early years of the soda fountain, and the commercial and mechanical development of the carbonated beverage industry in the United States in the nineteenth and twentieth centuries. Very useful chronology of the industry from 1807 to 1957 and lists of well-known bottling companies during the 1920s as well as alphabetical lists of major brands and manufacturers in 1957. Photos interspersed throughout the text of early and contemporary bottling equipment, labeling machines, syrup-making equipment, carbonators, filters, fillers, bottle washing equipment, bottle caps and stoppers, and soda fountains. Good source of information for an important part of drugstore history.

1033. Schreiner, Oswald. *History of the Art of Distillation and of Distilling Apparatus*. Milwaukee, WI: Pharmaceutical Review Publishing Co., 1901. 59 pp., illus.

An excellent historical overview of the history of distillation and distilling apparatus from ancient times to the twentieth century with greater emphasis on the pre-eighteenth century period. 65 excellent illustrations, many quite rare, of distilling apparatus.

1034. Sigvard, Jacqueline. *L'industrie du médicament*. Paris: Calman-Lévy, 1975. 333 pp., index.

Economic analysis of French industry, focussing on the 1960s but with some historical background. Business aspects of the drug market, and regulation.

1035. Sonnedecker, Glenn. "The Rise of Drug Manufacture in America." *Emory University Quarterly* 21 (1965): 73-87.

Begins by discussing the roots of pharmaceutical manufacturing in European pharmacies of the eighteenth and nineteenth centuries, and compares the American experience in the same era. Looks at changes in post bellum America, especially the impact of the Industrial Revolution. Finally, examines the rise of the American pharmaceutical industry vis-á-vis changes in practical therapeutics from the late nineteenth to the mid-twentieth centuries.

1036. Sonnedecker, Glenn, and George Griffenhagen. "A History of Sugar Coated Pills and Tablets." *Journal of the American Pharmaceutical Association, Practical Pharmacy Edition* 18 (1957): 486-88, 553-55.

The first part of this article presents a history of pills and tablets and their coatings from antiquity through the nineteenth century. The second part deals with the methods and equipment for coating pills and tablets. Black-and-white photographs of three pill coating devices, and very useful footnotes with citations to United States, British, and French patents for pill coating apparatus.

1037. Southern, Walter. "Sources of Drug Market Data." *Drug and Cosmetic Industry* 73 (1953): 328-29, 417-21.

A useful, annotated bibliography on production, distribution, pricing, inventory, and other data relevant to the economic history of pharmaceutical manufacturing.

1038. Swann, John P. *Academic Scientists and the Pharmaceutical Industry: Cooperative Research in Twentieth-Century America.* Baltimore: Johns Hopkins University Press, 1988. xiv + 249 pp.

Traces resistance to a facilitation of collaborative and contractual research between some of the major American pharmaceutical manufacturers and biomedical scientists in American universities between the two World Wars, and the impact of this union in terms of practical therapeutics, support of academics, and the scientific image of companies.

1039. Swintosky, Joseph V. "Personal Adventures in Biopharmaceutical Research During the 1953-1984 Years." *Drug Intelligence and Clinical Pharmacy* 19 (1985): 265-76.

An interesting perspective by a pharmaceutics researcher working in a firm (Smith Kline and French) at the leading edge of this field, during the 1950s.

1040. Taylor, Frank Sherwood. *A History of Industrial Chemistry*. New York: Abelard-Schuman, 1957. 467 pp., illus., index.

Useful on techniques and other pertinent information relevant to drug manufacturing. Has a good discussion of the synthetic dye industry.

1041. Urdang, George. "Retail Pharmacy as the Nucleus of the Pharmaceutical Industry." *Bulletin of the History of Medicine* Supp. No. 3 (1944): 325-46.

Traces the differences and similarities, from the seventeenth to the twentieth centuries, in the evolution of pharmaceutical manufacturing from retail pharmacy in Germany, France, England, and the United States. Presents many examples of particular establishments in each country to illustrate his points.

1042. Vershofen, Wilhelm. *Die Anfänge der Chemische-Pharmazeutischen Industrie: Eine Wirtschafthistorische Studie*. 3 vols. Berlin: Deutscher Betriebswirte-Verlag, 1949 (vol. 1); Aulendorf im Württ.: Editio Cantor, 1952 (vol. 2); Aulendorf im Württ.: Editio Cantor, 1958 (vol. 3). 151 pp., (vol. 1), 120 pp., (vol. 2), 155 pp. (vol. 3). index.

Title of volume 3 is *Wirtschaftgeschichte der Chemische-Pharmazeutischen Industrie*. Volume one covers to 1834, volume 2 to 1870, and volume 3 to 1914. A valuable work on the economic history of the German pharmaceutical industry.

1043. Wood, Joseph Remington. *Tablet Manufacture, Its History, Pharmacy and Practice*. Philadelphia: Lippincott, 1906. 224 pp., illus.

The first chapter is on the history of compressed tablets, followed by chapters on triturating, mixing, granulating, coloring, formulas, and a formulary. Emphasis is on American equipment and techniques. 23 illustrations of mixers, mills, sieves, dryers, punches and dies, and tablet machines. Good contemporary source.

1044. Woodruff, H. Boyd. "A Soil Microbiologist's Odyssey." *Annual Review of Microbiology* 35 (1981): 1-28.

A first-hand account of what it was like to be a researcher for a major drug manufacturer. This includes information on Merck's experience with antibiotic production.

2j—Equipment and Museology

1045. Andersen, Dannesboe. *Gammelt Dansk Apoteksinventar*. Copenhagen: Ejnar Munksgaard, 1944. 415 pp., illus., bibl., index.

A heavily illustrated catalog of objects and furnishings from Danish pharmacies organized by object category. Large sections on drug containers and mortars are included, with over 200 black-and-white photographs. No English text, this book is recommended for its illustrations.

1046. Arnold-Forster, Kate. "The Museum of the Royal Pharmaceutical Society of Great Britain." *Pharmacy in History* 33 (1991): 11-18.

A very good history of the museum and its collections together with an interesting description of their collections management and current activities, including publications. 4 illustrations. Useful notes and references.

1047. Baldwin, Joseph K. *A Collector's Guide to Patent and Proprietary Medicine Bottles of the Nineteenth Century*. Nashville: Thomas Nelson, Inc., 1973. 540 pp., illus.

A guide to 4,385 American patent or proprietary medicine bottles of the nineteenth century together with about 600 line drawings of bottles. Entries are organized alphabetically by product name and include information about the product's use, the proprietor's name and address, and the name and year of the publication in which the earliest found advertisement for that product appeared. Physical descriptions are also given when known. No index or bibliography.

1048. Bender, George A., and John Parascandola (eds.). *Historical Hobbies for the Pharmacist*. Madison: American Institute of the History of Pharmacy, 1974. repr.1980. 57 pp.

Papers by six knowledgeable pharmacists on the collecting of pharmaceutical stamps, artifacts, ephemera, and books. John Crellin writes on glass pharmacy containers, Michael R. Harris on American pharmaceutical artifacts. Harris's paper has a very useful bibliography on the conservation of antique objects in general and by different materials, such as ceramics and glass, metals, leather, paper, and wood. Reprinted with amendments.

1049. Bennion, Elisabeth. *Antique Medical Instruments*. Berkeley and Los Angeles: University of California Press, 1979. xii + 355 pp., index, illus.

Useful guide to primarily British and European medical instruments. Descriptions of pharmacy-related objects can be found in the chapters on medicine receptacles, infant and invalid feeding utensils, articles of medical association, and toilet articles. Heavily illustrated with large black-and-white and color photographs. Limited, unannotated bibliography.

1050. Bergevin, Al. *Drugstore Tins and Their Prices*. Radnor, PA: Wallace-Homestead Book Company, 1990. 284 pp., illus.

An illustrated catalog of over 750 nineteenth- and early twentieth-century tins sold primarily in pharmacies. The tins are organized according to the following categories: cosmetics, cough drop tins, dental hygiene, foot care, hair products, laxative tins, medical/curative tins, prophylactic tins, samplers, shaving products, shoe care, sundries, and talcum tins. Within each category the objects are arranged alphabetically by name of product. For each tin there is a photograph, 30 in color; a very brief description that includes size, shape, and composition; and a price. No historical information about the products or their manufacturers. No index and no bibliography. [not seen].

1051. Bethman, David. *The Pioneer Drug Store: A History of Washington State Drug Stores and Their Artifacts.* Ferndale, WA: David Bethman, 1991. 910 pp., illus.

A very valuable in-depth study of the history of pharmacies and their artifacts in one geographical area, Washington state, from the late 1850 to about 1920. Separate smaller sections on pharmacy labels, prescription forms, advertising trade cards, dose glasses, redware pots, and bottle producers and manufacturers. A comprehensive listing, together with histories, of all known drugstores and druggists in Washington state in alphabetical order by city or town. A large section on embossed glass medicine bottles, with a drawing of each bottle, and a history of the drugstore, medicine manufacturer, or wholesale drug firm that used each particular bottle. A chronological listing of Washington's oldest drugstores, a list of research sources, and an index to the embossed bottles.

1052. Blasi, Betty. *A Bit About Balsams: A Chapter in the History of Nineteenth Century Medicine.* Louisville, Kentucky: Farley-Goepper Printing Co., 1974. 175 pp., illus., index.

A catalog and guide to over 500 medicine bottles known as Balsams (containing resin gathered from the Balsam trees of South and Central America). Physical descriptions of the objects arranged in alphabetical order by product name, historical and biographical information when known, many photographs of objects and illustration of advertising, a glossary, bibliography, and index.

1053. Bogard, Mary. "Colored Glass in Pharmacy." *Pharmacy in History* 26 (1984): 20-27.

A good overview of the history of the use of colored glass for pharmaceutical containers, primarily in the United States from the late eighteenth century to the 1920s but also mentions its use in Britain, France, Germany, and Denmark. Information gathered mostly from trade catalogs, patent documents, and journal literature. 8 color illustrations. Useful notes and references.

1054. Bogard, Mary O. "The Celebrated Glass Label." *Pharmacy in History* 28 (1986): 34-40.

The best history to date of glass labels on pharmaceutical glassware in Britain and the United States from their introduction in the mid-nineteenth century until the 1920s. Much useful patent information, good notes and references, and 4 illustrations.

1055. Brandel, I. W., and Edward Kremers. "The Balance." *Pharmaceutical Review* 23 (1905): 351-354; 384-88; 24 (1906): 49-60, 75-83, 105-11, 151-54, 166-74.

A detailed technical description of mostly nineteenth-century precision balances and their use in pharmacy. Forty-five line drawings of balances or their parts. Meant as a guide to practicing pharmacist or students, but now of historical interest.

1056. Burnett, John. "The Guistiniani Medicine Chest." *Medical History* 26 (1982): 325-33.

An in-depth description and history of a very large, ornate Italian prince's medical chest from the mid-sixteenth century. It has 126 drug containers, many with original labels and some with contents. An appendix includes a list of 95 labels that are legible in whole or in part. Four photographs.

1057. Conradi, Helmut Peter. *Apothekengläser im Wandel der Zeit.* Würzburg: Jal-Verlag, 1973. 199 pp., illus.

A survey history of the use of glass containers for pharmaceuticals and cosmetics beginning with the ancient Egyptians but concentrating primarily on Germany and German-speaking lands from the Middle Ages to the twentieth century. Physical descriptions and small photographs (half of them in color) of 118 glass containers. Footnotes and bibliography, but no index.

1058. Crellin, John K. *Medical Ceramics: A Catalogue of the English and Dutch Collections in the Museum of the Wellcome Institute of the History of Medicine.* London: Wellcome Institute of the History of Medicine, 1969.

A very good descriptive catalog, with extensive footnotes to the literature and a good bibliography, of about 500 English and Dutch ceramic objects from the Wellcome Collection of about 2,500 pieces of medical and pharmaceutical ceramics from many countries (now housed in the Science Museum in London). Descriptions primarily of drug jars, but also good sections on pharmacy tiles, mortars, invalid feeding cups and bottles, posset pots, spoons and measures, bed pans, eye baths, and inhalers. Black-and-white photographs of most of the objects.

1059. Crellin, John K. "Domestic Medicine Chests: Microcosms of 18th and 19th Century Medical Practice." *Pharmacy in History* 21 (1979): 122-31.

Discussion of how the commercially produced home medicine chests of the eighteenth and nineteenth centuries in Britain and the United States mirrored the orthodox medical practices of those times. Good notes and references.

1060. Crellin, John K. "Tiles, Pills and Boluses." *Medical History* 16 (1972): 81-85.

Short, but still very informative article on the history of British pharmaceutical tiles, commonly called "pill tiles," used to roll pills and to prepare boluses. Contains a list and physical descriptions of pill-making equipment in the Wellcome Collections, now at the Science Museum in London.

1061. Crellin, John K., and D. A. Hutton. "Comminution and English Bell-Metal Mortars c. 1300-1850." *Medical History* 17 (1973): 266-87.

An excellent history of the development and use of bell-metal mortars in England based on the Wellcome Collections now at the Science Museum in London. Very helpful charts and photographs of different mortar shapes and decorations as well as makers' marks. Physical descriptions of about 200 mortars and good reference notes. One of a very few substantive monographs on mortars.

1062. Crellin, John K., and J. R. Scott. *Glass and British Pharmacy 1600-1900: A Survey and Guide to the Wellcome Collection of British Glass*. London: Wellcome Institute of the History of Medicine, 1972. viii + 69 pp., illus., index.

A heavily illustrated catalogue (all black-and-white photographs) of the Wellcome Collection of about 1,200 pieces of British pharmaceutical glassware arranged by type of container. Nice introductory essay placing glass containers within the context of the changing nature of pharmacy window displays and pharmacy interiors. 119 helpful notes and references, and index.

1063. Crellin, John K., and J. R. Scott. "Drug Weighing in Britain, c. 1700-1900." *Medical History* 13 (1969): 51-67.

An important study of eighteenth- and nineteenth-century English scales and weights in the Wellcome Collections at the Science Museum in London. Good notes and references, 10 plates with black-and-white photographs of objects together with physical descriptions, and an appendix on hand scales.

1064. Crellin, John K., and J. R. Scott. "Fluid Medicines, Prescription Reform and Posology 1700-1900." *Medical History* 14 (1970): 132-53.

An article based on the study of nearly 700 British medicine vials and bottles, mostly green glass and pre-1850, in the Wellcome Collections, now at the Science Museum in London. These artifacts highlighted the growth in popularity of the multidose mixture at the expense of small-volume preparations.

Useful chart of some of the major bottle shapes. Good notes and reference sources. Posology is the science of dosage.

1065. Crellin, John K., and William Helfand. "Picture Postcards—A Resource for the Social History of Pharmacy." *Pharmacy in History* 25 (1983): 116-30.

These cards contain numerous images of pharmacy exteriors and interiors, equipment used, and products sold.

1066. Danforth, Ellen Zak. *Nesting Weights, Einsatzgewichte, and Piles a Godets*. Hamden, Connecticut: Archon Books. Published as *Transactions* of the Connecticut Academy of Arts and Sciences, vol. 50, March 1988, pp. 1-117, 1988. 115 pp., illus.

A catalog of 80 nested cup weights in the Edward Clark Streeter Collection of Weights and Measures at the Medical Historical Library of Yale University. Complete physical description and black-and-white photograph of every object. No specific mention of pharmaceutical or medical applications. Brief bibliography. Most useful when used in conjunction with the works of Kisch and Houben.

1067. Davis, Audrey B., and Mark S. Dreyfuss. *The Finest Instruments Ever Made: A Bibliography of Medical, Dental, Optical, and Pharmaceutical Company Trade Literature; 1700-1939*. Arlington, MA: Medical History Publishing Associates I, 1986. vii, 448 p., illus., index.

A bibliography of medical, dental, optical, and pharmaceutical company trade literature from 1700 to 1939. The most comprehensive catalog of medical trade catalogs available. Although not as strong for pharmaceutical trade literature as for medical and dental, most major manufacturers of pharmaceutical equipment from the late nineteenth and the first half of the twentieth centuries are represented.

1068. De Jonge, C. H. *Delft Ceramics*. New York: Praeger Publishers, Inc., 1969. 168 pp., illus., bibl., index.

A scholarly, yet popular, survey of Delft faience with no separate discussion of drug jars but important and informative mentions of them interspersed throughout the text. Very useful information about Delft potteries and ceramic marks. A general index as well as separate indices on museums, potteries, personal names, and marks.

1069. DeGrafft, John. *American Sarsaparilla Bottles*. East Greenville, PA: John Degrafft, 1980. 158 pp., illus., index.

A catalog of 234 embossed American sarsaparilla bottles. Sarsaparilla was a popular nineteenth-century medicine, often advertised as a "blood purifier." The catalog is organized alphabetically with complete physical descriptions of the objects but no dates or histories. Small sections on dose glasses, pot lids, and label only bottles. Reference guide to the different kinds of bottle mouths (p. 11) and index. Line drawings for most bottles.

1070. Delaveau, Pierre, et al. "The Museum of Materia Medica of Paris." *Pharmacy in History* 26 (1984): 143-45.

A brief history and description of the crude drug collection of about 22,000 specimens that form the core of the Materia Medica Museum in the Faculty of Pharmaceutical and Biological Sciences at the René Descartes University in Paris. Photographs of some of the display cases with thematic exhibits.

1071. Devner, Kay. *Patent Medicine Picture*. Tombstone, AZ: The Tombstone Epitaph, 1968. 106 pp., illus.

An alphabetical listing by product name of about 1500 patent medicines from the 1870s to the 1920s with date of advertising and advertised uses. Additional historical information for some products and manufacturers as well as small line drawings for a few. A glossary and bibliography (without complete references). No physical descriptions of the products and no index. [not seen].

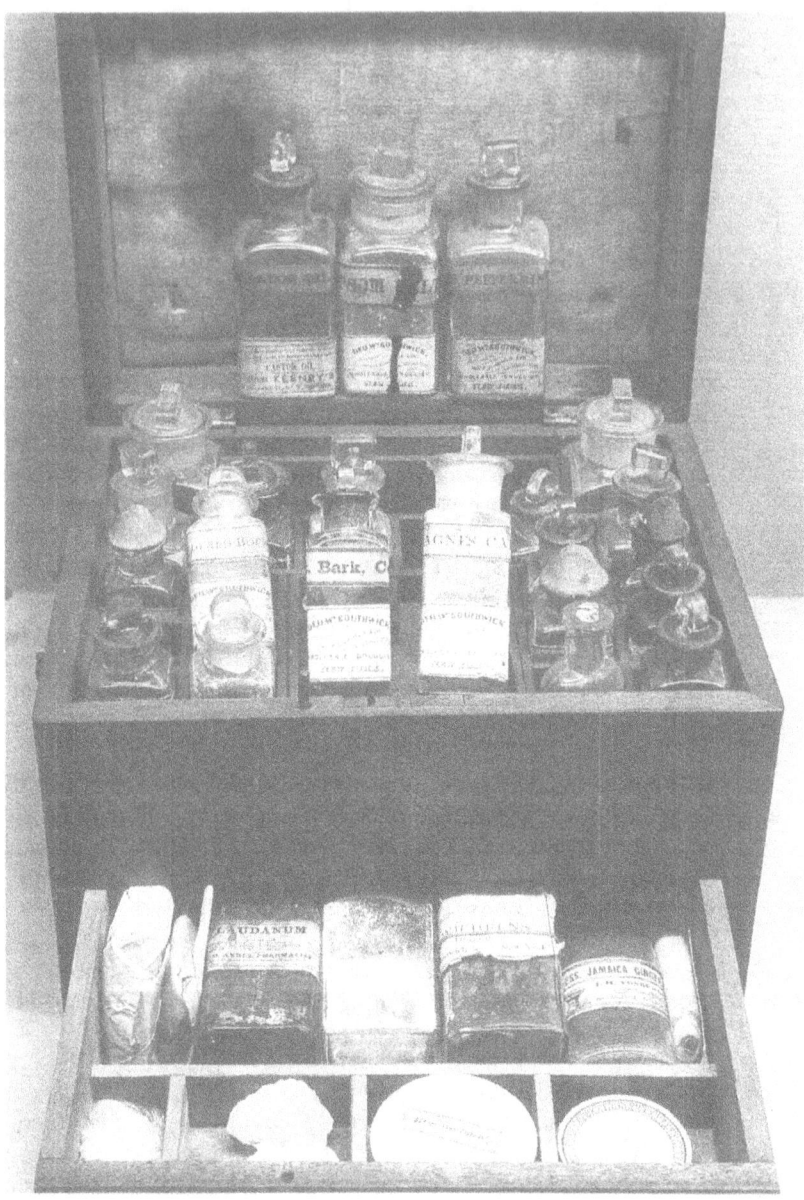

Marine medicine chests, such as the one shown above, were necessary to insure the well-being of passengers traveling by ship. The chests and their contents now provide pharmaceutical antique collectors with examples of eary American pharmacy.

1072. Drake, T. G. H. "Antiques of Interest to the Apothecary." *Journal of the History of Medicine and Allied Sciences* 1960 (15): 31-44.

An eclectic and superficial look, based on Drake's own collection, at the kinds of pharmaceutical objects that can be collected. There are descriptions of English delftware drug jars and pill tiles, mortars, coins, medicine spoons, medicine chests, medicine vials, ancient Egyptian and Roman specimens, and literature on quack practitioners. With 15 black-and-white illustrations.

1073. Drey, R. E. A. *Apothecary Jars: Pharmaceutical Pottery and Porcelain in Europe and the East 1150-1850*. London: Faber and Faber, 1978. 249 pp., illus.

The most definitive work to date in English on the history of drug jars. The chapters are organized according to country, beginning with the Near Eastern origins of the drug jar, but concentrating primarily on the history of the major production centers in Europe from the sixteenth to the eighteenth centuries, and ending with a description of the pharmaceutical ceramic wares from China. A 59-page glossary of the more important terms used in apothecary jar inscriptions is an invaluable guide to the mostly Latin drug names of the period and an important reference tool for researchers and keepers of collections. Excellent notes and bibliography organized by country. Eight full-page color illustrations and 96 black-and-white photographs. Translated into German (1980) and French (1984), and published in larger formats with some changes and additions.

1074. Eaches, Albert R. "Scales and Weighing Devices: An Aid to Identification." *History News* 27, no. 3 (March 1972): 12 pp., illus. American Association for State and Local History Technical Leaflet 59.

A useful guide for identifying and documenting early weighing devices. Describes the four basic types of mechanical scales (equal arm balances, unequal arm balances, spring balances, and pendulum balances) and how to differentiate between them.

Mentions pharmaceutical and medical applications. With 27 black-and-white object photographs.

1075. Ekiert, Leszek, and Anna Stabrawa. "New Exposition in the Museum of Pharmacy at the Medical Academy of Cracow." *Pharmacy in History* 34 (1992): 166-69.

A brief history of the pharmacy museum in Cracow, which houses the largest collection of pharmaceutical artifacts in Poland, and a floor-by-floor tour of the collections and period rooms on display in their new quarters, a restored fifteenth-century house. Photographs of three period rooms. A slightly more detailed article describing the collections, together with two photographs, was published earlier by Miroslawa Pabis-Braunstein: "Museum of Pharmacy at the Medical Academy of Cracow," *Pharmacy in History* 30 (1988): 39-42. Both articles have references to publications on the history of pharmacy and pharmaceutical artifacts in Poland (some in English).

1076. Fike, Richard E. *The Bottle Book: A Comprehensive Guide to Historic, Embossed Medicine Bottles.* Salt Lake City: Peregrine Smith Books, 1987. 293 pp., illus.

An excellent reference book and authoritative guide to about 4,000 patent medicine bottles. Numerous line drawings and color photographs; thorough physical descriptions; company history, marketing, and product advertising as background and context for nearly every product; very good user's guide and indices; and, an excellent, annotated bibliography. Chapter headings organized by commonly used product names or companies embossed within the glass and within each chapter, the bottles are listed alphabetically according to the actual name of the product or company. Highly recommended for museum workers, cultural historians, and collectors.

1077. Fourest, Henri-Pierre, and Pierre-Nicolas Sainte-Fare-Garnot. *Les Pots de Pharmacie.* 2 vols. Paris: Les Éditions Roger Dacosta, 1981-82. Vol. 1 *Paris et l'Ile-de-France* (229 pp., illus.). Vol 2. *Rouen et la Normandie la Picardie et la Bretagne* (230 pp., illus.).

Two large-format books, heavily illustrated with large color and black-and-white photographs of pharmaceutical ceramic ware from different regions in France. Physical descriptions and curatorial locations for each illustrated object (about 100 in each book). Running narrative throughout the texts discussing the history and evolution of drug jars and the variations in design and manufacture. No notes, select bibliographies, no English text. [not seen].

1078. Friedenwald, Julius, and Samuel Morrison. "The History of the Enema with Some Notes on Related Procedures." *Bulletin of the History of Medicine* 8 (1940): 68-114; 239-76.

A very broad and wide-ranging history of the enema as a therapeutic measure and of the development of enema apparatus from ancient times to the twentieth century in the Old World and the New World. Useful notes and 22 illustrations. The last part of the article describes the historical development of therapeutic procedures and instruments related to the enema such as colonic irrigations, rectal anesthesia, the speculum, and the endoscope.

1079. Griffenhagen, George. *Tools of the Apothecary.* Washington, DC: American Pharmaceutical Association, 1957. 30 pp., illus.

Reprinted from a series appearing in 1956 in the *Journal of the American Pharmaceutical Association, Practical Pharmacy Edition,* with monographs on the mortar and pestle, pharmaceutical balances, pharmaceutical weights, suppository molds, pill tiles and spatulas, pill machines, filtration equipment, drug percolators, the drug mill, lozenges, capsules, and tablets. Each short monograph includes a number of small black-and-white illustrations of some of the equipment and a very useful selected bibliography of difficult to find primary and secondary sources describing the use and history of that equipment. Updated in 1975. A broad-ranging overview and indispensable guide to the different kinds of pharmaceutical equipment.

1080. Griffenhagen, George. *Private Die Proprietary Medicine Stamps.* Milwaukee, WI: American Topical Association, 1969; second ed., 1991.

Summarizes the proprietary medicine company histories prepared by Holcombe (see entry no. 1156) and expands upon the product descriptions, especially their compositions and uses. Many of the 135 entries, listed alphabetically by company name, cite additional reference sources to those in Holcombe. *Scott's Catalogue* descriptions of the tax stamps are listed in each entry. Appendix material includes an index of the proprietary medicines mentioned throughout the text and check list of facsimile labels of U.S. private die proprietary medicine stamps prepared by Henry Holcombe.

1081. Griffenhagen, George. "Dose: One Spoonful." *Journal of the American Pharmaceutical Association, Practical Pharmacy Edition* 20 (1959): 202-5.

A short history of the medical spoon from the time of the ancient Egyptians to the debates over the standard pharmacopeial teaspoon in the mid-twentieth century. Useful references and six illustrations showing different kinds of medicine spoons.

1082. Griffenhagen, George. "The Evolution of the Medicine Chest." *The Antiques Dealer* 26 (Oct. 1974): 32-35 and (Nov., 1974): 37-39.

A short survey history of medicine chests from ancient times to the twentieth century with emphasis on military and naval chests. Second part of the article contains listing of the titles of US medicine chest manuals from 1792 to 1839. 10 illustrations. [not seen].

1083. Griffenhagen, George. "A History and Evolution of the Suppository Mold." *American Journal of Pharmacy* 125 (1953): 135-42.

A suppository is an easily fusible medicated mass that is introduced into an orifice of the body. A suppository mold is a piece of equipment that shapes that mass into form. This monograph is still the best general history of the suppository mold, illustrated with photographs of objects in the medical collections at the Smithsonian Institution's National Museum of American History. Useful notes and references to the early literature.

1084. Griffenhagen, George. "The Lost Art of Plaster Spreading." *American Professional Pharmacist* 23 (1957): 139-43.

Plasters, usually paste-like medicated substances spread directly on the skin or spread on materials such as muslin or linen and then adhered to the skin, have been used since ancient times. This article summarizes this history both chronologically and by types of plasters: Diachylon, leather, linen, Court, adhesive, porous, machine-made, and Burgandy pitch. There is also a section on plaster manufacturers and black-and-white photographs of plaster machines and spreaders.

1085. Griffenhagen, George. "Poison Bottles and Safety Closures." *Journal of the American Pharmaceutical Association* NS1 (1961): 563-66.

A short, informative article on the history of poison bottles and safety closures, primarily in the United States and Britain in the nineteenth century. Nine illustrations.

1086. Griffenhagen, George. "The Show Globe—A Symbol of Pharmacy." *Journal of the American Pharmaceutical Association, Practical Pharmacy Edition* 19 (1958): 233-35.

Author summarizes previous hypotheses about the origins of the show globe, including that of Urdang, and argues that the show globe as a generally recognized symbol of pharmacy by the public did not appear in pharmacies until the second half of the eighteenth century and that its appearance was intimately associated with the development of vessels known as "show carboys" in England. Five illustrations.

1087. Griffenhagen, George. "Signs and Signboards of the Pharmacy." *International Pharmacy Journal* 3, no. 1 (1989): 25-31.

A good overview of the signs and symbols that have been used on signboards to identify pharmacies throughout the world from the fifteenth century until the present. A French translation follows the English text. Illustrations of 28 signs used by pharmacies worldwide.

1088. Griffenhagen, George, and Lawrence B. Romaine. "Early U. S. Pharmaceutical Catalogues." *American Journal of Pharmacy* 131 (1959): 14-33.

An informative overview of the early history of pharmaceutical trade literature in the United States, followed by a check list of pharmaceutical catalogs dating from 1760 to 1890. Trade catalogs are important sources of information for identifying and dating pharmaceutical equipment as well as for determining the period of use, the manufacturer, and distributor.

1089. Griffenhagen, George, and Ernst W. Stieb. *Tools of the Apothecary: A Select Bibliography.* Madison: American Institute of the History of Pharmacy, 1975. 13 pp., mimeographed.

An updated bibliography of sources, primarily in English, to accompany Griffenhagen's selected bibliographies after each equipment group described in *The Tools of the Apothecary* (citation #1079). List of sources divided topically as in the original publication but with new sections added on drug jars and containers, show globes, medicine spoons, miscellaneous equipment, and general references that provide information about more than one pharmaceutical artifact. Can be used alone as a bibliographic guide but more useful in tandem with *Tools*, especially for those just starting to learn about pharmaceutical equipment.

1090. Griffenhagen, George, and Ernst W. Stieb. *Pharmacy Museums and Historical Collections in the United States and Canada.* Madison, WI: American Institute of the History of Pharmacy, 1988. 92 pp., illus.., index.

Updated and revised edition of the 1981 museum guide by Hamarneh and Stieb (citation #1095), but without the bibliographic guide. Museums and historical collections in the United States are described in alphabetical order by state (including the District of Columbia and Puerto Rico) and by city. These are followed by descriptions of Canadian museums in alphabetical order by province and city. An annotated list of 11 markers dedicated by the American Institute of the History of Pharmacy at historical sites from 1963 through 1983 also included.

1091. Häfliger, Josef Anton. *Pharmazeutische Altertumskunde und die Schweizerische Sammlung für Historisches Apothekenwesen an der Universität Basel*. Zurich: Buchdruckerei zur Alten Universität, 1931. 203+ pp., illus.

Primarily a guide to the rich pharmaceutical object collections in Switzerland, with a particular focus on the collections at the University of Basel. Physical and historical descriptions are organized according to object categories with extensive, albeit now dated, references. Fifty-three clear black-and-white photographs of individual objects and object collections. No English text.

1092. Hamarneh, Sami. *Temples of the Muses and a History of Pharmacy Museums*. Tokyo: The Naito Foundation, 1972. x + 146 pp., illus., index.

Musings on the history of museums interspersed with personal reminiscences. Most useful are the chapters on the history of pharmacy museums and the Naito Museum of Pharmaceutical Pharmacy and Industry in Japan, which have some nice illustrations and descriptions of Japanese pharmaceutical equipment.

1093. Hamarneh, Sami. *History of the Division of Medical Sciences [in the Museum of History and Technology]*. Contributions from the Museum of History and Technology, paper 43. Washington, DC: Smithsonian Institution, 1964.

The most comprehensive description to date of the early history of the national collections related to the history of the health sciences at the Smithsonian Institution from their beginnings in the Section of Materia Medica in 1881 through 1964. Good descriptions of the collections, the collectors, and their changing institutional setting. Extensive bibliography and 24 photographs. A later article by S. Hamarneh (*Pharmacy in History* 21(1979):163-76) summarizes some of this material, focuses more on the pharmacy and public health collections, and brings the story up to 1979. For the most recent description of the national collections, see Audrey B. Davis, "The history of the health sciences at the National Museum of American History," *Caduceus* 4 (1988):58-71. [not seen].

1094. Hamarneh, Sami, and Henry A. Awad. "Arabic Glass Seals on Early Eighteenth-Century Containers for Materia Medica." *Pharmacy in History* 18 (1976): 95-102.

Description of glass seals excavated from sites in old Cairo, Egypt, which were affixed to vessels containing crude drugs and which usually carried the names of the officials who ordered their manufacture or use, and the names of the drugs in the containers. These are some of the earliest known seals of this kind. The article provides some historical context and information about their manufacture. More detailed physical, historical, and pharmacological descriptions are given of the 13 most commonly used vegetable drugs mentioned on the seals. Four illustrations and extensive references.

1095. Hamarneh, Sami, and Ernst W. Stieb. *Pharmacy Museums and Historical Collections on Public View in the United States and Canada*. Madison, WI: American Institute of the History of Pharmacy in cooperation with the National Museum of American History, Smithsonian Institution, Washington, D.C., 1981. 144 pp., illus.., bibl.

Although the listing of pharmacy museums has been superseded by a later edition of this work [Pharmacy Museums and Historical Collections in the United States and Canada, by George Griffenhagen and Ernst W. Stieb. AIHP, 1988, citation

#1090], the partly annotated bibliographic note (pp. 128-44) is useful for topics in museology, the history of pharmacy, its tools, and related arts and antiques. Earlier edition by Hamarneh in 1972.

1096. Hein, Wolfgang-Hagen, and Dirk A. Wittop Koning. *Deutsche Apotheken-Fayencen*. Frankfurt am Main: Govi-Verlag, 1977. 160 pp., illus.

An overview of the development of drug jars in German presented through the physical and historical descriptions of about 70 containers and organized by geographic regions. Full-page black-and-white or color illustrations of the object on the right-hand side of the page accompanied by about a half-page description on the left together with notes. Introductory section contains table with 30 maker's marks. No English text.

1097. Hill, C. R., and R. E. A. Drey. *Drug Jars*. University of Oxford, Museum of the History of Science, catalogue 3. Oxford: Seacourt Press Ltd., 1980. vi + 41 pp., illus., bibl., index.

A catalog describing and illustrating each of the 73 items in the drug jar collection in the Museum of the History of Science at the University of Oxford. Entries are grouped chronologically under geographical headings (Italy, the Low Countries, France, England, and Spain). Good introductory sections setting the containers in their pharmaceutical and ceramic context. Short select bibliography and index.

1098. Hömberg, Wolfgang. *Der Norddeutsche Bronzemörser im Zeitalter von Gotik und Renaissance*. Quellen und Studien zur Geschichte der Pharmazie, vol. 23. Stuttgart: Deutscher Apotheker Verlag, 1983. 366 pp., illus.

A comprehensive work on North German bronze mortars from about the fourteenth to the seventeenth centuries. Much information on the making of mortars, together with line drawings. Very good descriptions of the different styles of mortars and what various parts of the mortar are called. Several short chapters on the pestle, including one on fake pestles. 153

black-and-white photographs of mortars and pestles with extended physical descriptions. Extensive bibliography and index.

1099. Houben, Gerard M. M. *2000 Years of Nested Cup-Weights*. Zwolle, the Netherlands: G. M. M. Houben, 1984. 81 pp., illus.

Fourth in a series of monographs by G. Houben on weights and scales which include: *European Coin-weights for English Coins* (1978), *Muntgewichten voor Munten van de Nederlanden* (1981), and *The Weighing of Money* (1982). This work on the richly ornamented nested weights used by pharmacists primarily from the sixteenth to the nineteenth centuries is an excellent reference guide. It contains the most thoroughly documented information to date about the manufacture and use of these weights—materials used, design and decoration, maker's marks, standards and denominations, as well as a section on counterfeits and a useful glossary of terms in English, French, German, and Dutch. Nearly 200 black-and-white photographs. [not seen].

1100. Howard-Jones, Norman. "A Critical Study of the Origins and Early Development of Hypodermic Medication." *Journal of the History of Medicine and Allied Sciences* 2 (1947): 201-49.

To date, still the best and most comprehensive study of the history of hypodermic medication and syringes. Excellent references and 15 illustrations. A shorter, condensed version of this article entitled "The Origins of Hypodermic Medication" was published later in *Scientific American* 224 (1971): 96-102.

1101. Jackson, W. A. *The Victorian Chemist and Druggist*. Aylesbury, Bucks, England: 1981. 32 pp., illus.

Brief, but useful, overview of British pharmaceutical equipment with chapters on furnishings, storage containers, dispensing equipment, and sundries. Numerous black-and-white photographs of groupings of objects. No detailed bibliography. Reprinted 1984, 1987, and 1989.

1102. Kallinich, Günter. *Schöne Alte Apotheken*. Munich: Verlag Georg D. W. Callwey, 1975. 251 pp., illus.

A large, beautifully illustrated book about old European pharmacies with nearly 500 black-and-white as well as color (many full-page) photos of pharmacy interiors and exteriors, together with pharmaceutical dispensing equipment and shelfware. No English text but a French translation from the German appeared in 1976 (entry #1211).

1103. Kebler, L. F. "The Tablet Industry—Its Evolution and Present Status—The Composition of Tablets and Methods of Analysis." *Journal of the American Pharmaceutical Association* 3 (1914): 820-48, 937-58, 1062-99.

Still the best single source history of tablet making, primarily in the United States. A comprehensive, historical discussion of the methods of tablet manufacture and the various resulting products, such as compressed tablets, tablet triturates, and hypodermic tablets. Particular emphasis on the equipment used in tablet making, with numerous illustrations. The last section devoted to the tabulation of results of product analyses of numerous tablets on the market around 1913.

1104. Kirsis, Janis. "The Homeopathic Drugstore of Riga." *Pharmacy in History* 33 (1991): 76-79.

A detailed description and history of the first homeopathic drugstore in Riga, Latvia, which opened in 1833 and his been in continual use since then, providing medicines and services for the whole Baltic region as well as vast areas in Russia. The article describes the staff, pharmacy routine, and equipment, and give a glimpse into the history of homeopathy in the Baltic region. Photographs of the pharmacy exterior, machines for ointments and liquid preparations, and storage of bulk supplies for liquid medications.

1105. Kisch, Bruno. *Scales and Weights: A Historical Outline*. New Haven: Yale University Press, 1965. xxi + 297 pp., illus.

A good introduction to an overview of the history of scales and weights, with a separate section on pharmaceutical weights (pp. 140-45). Very useful charts of mastersigns and symbols, tables of weights, good bibliography and indices, and about 100 black-and-white photographs.

1106. Krüger, Mechthild. *Zur Geschichte der Elixiere, Essenzen und Tinkturen*. Veröffentlichung aus dem Pharmaziegeschichtlichen Seminar der Technischen Hochschule Braunschweig. Bd. 10. Braunschweig, Germany: 1968. 323 pp., bibl., index

A history of elixirs, essences, and tinctures primarily in Germany from the sixteenth to the twentieth centuries. Information and formulas gathered from German pharmacopeias. Results from modern chemical analyses of some of the formulas. An extensive bibliography (pp. 291-303), subject, and name indices.

1107. Levy, Bernard. "Pharmacy Graduates in Use from 1880 to 1920." *Pharmacy in History* 26 (1984): 150-54.

One of a very few articles documenting the history of pharmaceutical laboratory utensils. Describes the design, production, and use of glass graduates as measuring devices in the United States. Study based primarily on information in trade literature and patent documents. Thirteen black-and-white photographs of glass graduates in the author's personal collection. Good reference source.

1108. Lipp, Martin R. *Medical Landmarks USA: A Travel Guide to Historic Sites, Architectural Gems, Remarkable Museums and Libraries, and Other Places of Health-Related Interest*. New York: McGraw-Hill, Inc., 1991. xiii + 550 pp., illus., bibl.

An interesting travel guide to historic places, architectural landmarks, museums and libraries, and other places of health-related interest, including those related to pharmacy. Provides broader medical context to the pharmacy museum guidebooks. Includes bibliographical references and index.

1109. Matthews, Leslie G. *Antiques of the Pharmacy*. London: G. Bell & Sons, 1971. 120 pp., illus., index.

A brief overview of British pharmaceutical equipment from about the seventeenth to the twentieth century organized primarily according to the materials from which the objects were made, e.g., ceramics, metals, glass, wood, and paper. Separate chapters on medicine chests and proprietary medicines. Select bibliography and about 90 black-and-white photographs.

1110. Matthews, Leslie G. "Apothecaries' Pill Tiles." *English Ceramic Circle Transactions* 7 (1970): 200-209 + plates.

A description of 110 pill tiles bearing the arms of the Worshipful Society of Apothecaries of London and exhibited by freemen of that Society. These armorial pill tiles dating from the seventeenth to the nineteenth centuries and primarily used for display seem to be a purely English product. They are grouped according to their style of decoration. Eighteen illustrations. [not seen].

1111. McEwen, Alan. *Collecting "Quack Cures."* Southampton, Great Britain: Southern Collectors Publications, 1977. 67 pp., illus.

A compendium of about 60 Victorian era medicine bottles embossed with the word "CURE" or variations thereof to be found in Great Britain. Physical description for each item, histories for many, about a dozen black-and-white photographs, no index.

1112. Müller-Jahncke, Wolf-Dieter. "Sammeln und Bewahren: Pharmaziehistorische Museen in der Bundesrepublik Deutschland und der Deutschen Demokratischen Republik." *Pharmazie in unserer Zeit* 19 (1990): 56-60.

Short but informative article describing the histories and current status of pharmacy history museums in the former West and East Germanies. Ten illustrations.

1113. Noël Hume, Ivor. *A Guide to Artifacts of Colonial America.* New York: Alfred A. Knopf, 1970. xviii + 323 pp., + vi, illus., index.

An archeological guide to artifacts of Colonial America organized alphabetically into sections by artifact type. Two sections devoted exclusively to early American pharmaceutical artifacts: pharmaceutical glass bottles (pp. 72-76) and drug pots, jars, and pill tiles (pp. 203-210). Each section has a few illustrations and short bibliographies. Artifact index.

1114. Putnam, P. A. *Bottled Before 1865.* Los Angeles: Rapid Blue Print Co., 1968. 100 pp., illus.

A compilation from English language newspapers and magazines printed before 1865 of names of bottled products and their uses— mainly, but not exclusively, medicinal products. Product names and advertising excerpts are listed chronologically from 1708 through 1864. Sketches of some of the products. A chapter on the history of glass making in the United States organized by state. An index by product type. Helpful for dating early medicine bottles.

1115. Rainwater, Dorothy T., and Donna H. Felger. *American Spoons: Souvenir and Historical.* Camden, N.J.: T. Nelson, 1968. 416 pp., illus.

Chapter titled "Open Wide," is devoted to medical spoons. Not as much historical material as in the Griffenhagen article on medical spoons but many more illustrations (56) and more patent information.

1116. Richardson, Lillian C., and Charles G. Richardson. *The Pill Rollers: Apothecary Antiques and Drug Store Collectibles.* 2nd ed. Harrisonburg, VA: Old Fort Press, 1992. iii + 177 pp., illus.

Very useful guide for museum workers, collectors, and those interested in a broader and more in-depth description of the objects associated with the practice of pharmacy and the drugstore trade in the nineteenth and twentieth centuries. Major sections on: glass and ceramic containers, including patent medicines: pharmacy equipment, such as, pill makers and rug mills; home health care products, like medicine chests, and quack devices; fixtures, including tins and soda fountain items; and, labels and prescriptions. Appendix contains lists of pharmaceutical companies, bottle markings, drug jar inscriptions, diseases and symptoms, dosage forms, therapeutic classifications, a bibliography, and index. Very heavily illustrated throughout with black-and-white images, primarily from trade catalogs and photographs. Much information about different styles, shapes, and models of objects as well as dates when objects appeared in the trade literature, patent information, approximate sizes, and construction material.

1117. Ring, Carlyn. *For Bitters Only*. Boston: The Nimrod Press Inc., 1980. 543 pp., illus.

A large, comprehensive guide to about 3,000 bitters bottles. Complete physical description for each item as well as historical and label data and references, when known. Heavily illustrated with line drawings and 8 pages of color photographs, geographical index, and rarity index. Many auction houses and major glass dealers use "Ring numbers" as references. An 116-page *Up-Date and Price Guide* published by C. Ring in 1984.

1118. Rocchietta, Sergio. *Antichi vasi di farmacia italiani*. Milan: L'Ariete, 1986. 171 pp., illus.

A large format, beautifully illustrated reference guide to Italian pharmaceutical containers. Organized by region, then by city and holder, such as a museum, library, pharmacy, or private collector. Short bibliography after each section. Hundreds of illustrations, many in color. Physical descriptions for illustrated drug jars, including the names of the holders. Good index.

1119. Rouse-Ostrander, Diane. *A Guide to American Nursing Bottles: The Big Beautiful Book of Baby Bottles*. Willoughby, OH: Will-O-Graf Publications, 1984. 196 pp., illus.

A good catalog of American nursing bottles, which were an important part of the drugstore trade. Introductory materials include a bibliography, a classification system consisting of 16 categories and a very useful guide to nomenclature, and a list of the numerous trade catalogs used for reference. The body of the text consists of 678 individual bottle entries in alphabetical order giving very detailed physical descriptions, advertising and patent information, when available, and illustrations for many.

1120. Schmitz, Rudolf. *Mörser, Kolben und Phiolen aus der Welt der Pharmazie*. Stuttgart: Franckh'sche Verlagshandlung, 1966. 208 pp., illus.

Beautiful color plates document 600 years of pharmacy. Art works, pharmaceutical title pages, photographs of pharmaceutical glassware, and other artifacts show many facets of pharmacy through history.

1121. Schmitz, Rudolf. "The Pomander." *Pharmacy in History* 31 (1989): 86-90.

The pomander often is a very ornate and highly decorative receptacle for scented or fragrant substances, which have been used as both medicaments and perfumes. This article briefly presents the definition, function, and origin of the pomander as well as its historical background, medical uses, and decorative function as jewelry. Few pomanders are preserved in museums or private collections. This study is based in part on a private collection of 150 objects. Seven illustrations and a bibliographic note.

1122. Segers, E. G., and Dirk A. Wittop Koning. *Apothicaireries anciennes en Benelux*. Devente: Davo, 1958. 50 pp., illus.

Equipment and Museology 279

Describes pharmacies and their contents in Belgium and Holland, from the thirteenth to the nineteenth century. Focus is on drug containers. Text in French and Dutch.

1123. Shimko, Phyllis. *Sarsaparilla Bottle Encyclopedia*. Aurora, OR: Andrew & Phyllis Shimko, 1969. 200 pp., illus.

An illustrated, descriptive guide to 554 sarsaparilla bottles. Well-documented chronologies and company histories. Numerous line drawings of products and excerpts from the advertising literature. Useful bibliography and index.

1124. Sonnedecker, Glenn, and Gregory J. Higby. *Bibliography on the History of Dosage Forms*. Madison, WI: American Institute of the History of Pharmacy, n.d. (ca. 1983). 10 pp., mimeographed.

A partial, annotated bibliography of mostly English secondary sources on the history of the various kinds of dosage forms. Sources arranged topically with larger sections on ampuls and injections, enemas and clysters, pills and tablets, capsules, sprays and inhalants, and suppositories. Useful bibliographic guide to dosage forms and drug delivery systems.

1125. Spaulding, Mary, and Penny Welch. *Nurturing Yesterday's Child*. Philadelphia: B. C. Decker, Inc., 1991. xi + 338 pp., illus., bibl., index.

A beautifully designed and illustrated, large-format catalog of the T. G. H. Drake Collection of Pediatric History at the Academy of Medicine in Toronto, Canada. The collection consists of about 3000 artifacts, 1500 rare books, 1000 prints, 1000 coins and medals, and about 1000 album pages of child welfare stamps. The catalog is organized thematically with hundred of all-color photographs of objects and graphics together with physical descriptions. Numerous pharmacy-related objects such as infant feeders, pap boats, medicine spoons and bottles, drug jars and ointment pots, mortars, and medicine chests. Appendices include a listing of the museum catalog numbers for all the illustrated objects, an extensive bibliography, and an index.

1126. Stieb, Ernst W. "The Ortho Museum on the History of Contraception." *Pharmacy in History* 31 (1989): 182-83.

A brief history and description of the collections related to the history of contraception from ancient Egyptian times to the present, which are located in the entry hall of Ortho Pharmaceutical (Canada) Ltd. near Toronto, Canada. Items in the collection include vaginal sponges, cervical caps, diaphragms, intrauterine devices, condoms, crude drugs, and pharmaceuticals. 3 illustrations. Not listed in the Griffenhagen and Stieb guide to pharmacy museums.

1127. Swanson Jr., Ben Z., and William H. Helfand. "Cachous: Their Containers and Promotion." *Pharmacy in History* 33 (1991): 42-52.

Cachous are small but very strong tablets or pills that can be chewed or dissolved slowly in the mouth. Their main appeal has been to tobacco smokers and chewers. Excellent description of the different kinds of cachou containers, especially embossed boxes, and of the advertising associated with the selling of cachou products. Appended is a catalog with complete physical descriptions of 27 known embossed cachou boxes from Austria, France, Great Britain, and the United States. 17 illustrations. Good references.

1128. Tallis, Nigel, and Kate Arnold-Forster. *Pharmacy History: A Pictorial Record*. London: The Pharmaceutical Press, 1991. 92 pp., illus.

Second in a series of monographs describing the collections at the Museum of the Royal Pharmaceutical Society of Great Britain. The 153 black-and-white photographs reproduced in this catalog are grouped into the following chapters: the Society's house, portraits, Jacob Bell Memorial scholars, Benevolent Fund, pharmacy education and schools of pharmacy, conferences and meetings, pharmacy premises, social setting, and pharmacy raw materials and production. Illustrations index and photographer index.

1129. Thomas, K. Bryn. *The Development of Anaesthetic Apparatus: A History Based on the Charles King Collection of the Association of Anaesthetists of Great Britain and Ireland.* Oxford, Great Britain: Blackwell Scientific Publications, 1975. x + 268 pp., illus., index.

An excellent comprehensive survey of the development of anesthesia apparatus from the time of the first public demonstration of ether anesthesia in 1846 to 1940. Based on the Charles King Collection of the Association of Anaesthetists of Great Britain and Ireland at the Royal College of Surgeons of England in London. Over 230 illustrations and detailed descriptions of each piece of equipment with contemporary references and biographical information about its inventor. Includes sections on the development of apparatus for ether, chloroform, nitrous oxide, and mixed vapor anesthesia and analgesia.

1130. Turner, Helen. *Henry Wellcome: The Man, His Collection, and His Legacy.* London: The Wellcome Trust and Heinemann Educational Books, Ltd., 1980. 96 pp., illus.

The book is divided into 3 parts. The first is a brief biography of Henry Wellcome and of the pharmaceutical firm of Burroughs Wellcome & Co., which he helped to establish in 1880. The second part deals with the large collections he amassed, including nearly a half million medical artifacts. Since he was particularly interested in old pharmacies, pharmaceutical objects are well represented in those collections. The third part deals with The Wellcome Trust, the largest medical research charity in Britain. About 30 illustrations and an index.

1131. Urdang, George. "New Light on the Origin of Show Globes." *Journal of the American Pharmaceutical Association, Practical Pharmacy Edition* 10 (1949): 604-06, 640.

A short history of the origins of apothecary show globes, beginning with several earlier hypotheses that the author discounts, and then states his own: namely, that the show globe had its origins about 1550 in the shops of the "preparers of chemical medicines" in London, called the "chymists," and was later adopted by the apothecaries.

1132. Urdang, George, and F. W. Nitardy. *The Squibb Ancient Pharmacy*. New York, NY: E. R. Squibb and Sons, 1940. 190 pp., illus.

A very heavily illustrated (black-and-white photographs of over 1,000 objects) catalog of the Squibb European Pharmacy Collection, which is now part of the medical collections at the Smithsonian Institution's National Museum of American History. Detailed description of nearly 1,200 pre-nineteenth century European, primarily German, pharmaceutical artifacts, especially of glass, ceramic, and wooden containers, mortars and pestles, balances, utensils, and fixtures. Pharmacy books, documents, paintings, and graphic illustrations are also important parts of this collection and catalog.

1133. Vida, Maria. *Pharmacy Museums of Hungary*. Budapest: Hungarian Society for the History of Medicine and Semmelweis Institute, 1984. 48 pp., illus.

A very good guide and historical introduction to the very rich pharmaceutical heritage of Hungary. The introduction contains a nice summary of the history of pharmacy and pharmacies in Hungary as well as a brief description of national policies regarding historic preservation. The rest of the monograph describes in great detail the individual pharmacy museums and functioning pharmacies under protection, starting with those in Budapest and then proceeding by county and city through the rest of Hungary. Six color and 20 black-and-white plates, bibliography, and index of place names. Supplements an earlier work by Livia Nekam, *Old Hungarian Pharmacies* (Budapest: Cornvina Press, 1968), 65 pp. Nekam's monograph includes many more illustrations—40 in color and 15 black-and-white plates—but not as much detailed information about each pharmacy. [not seen].

1134. Watson, Richard. *Bitters Bottles*. New York: Thomas Nelson and Sons, 1965. 304 pp., illus.

Bitters was the name given to preparations of medicinal herbs, roots, or barks with a high alcohol content. This book provides a brief history of bitters and a guide to the physical description of the containers. The bulk of the work is a checklist of 379 known marked bitters bottles, with detailed physical descriptions for each, and line drawings for most. Separate listing by shape, and index. *Supplement to Bitters Bottles* published in 1968. Same format and organization as original book with 141 additional bottles described.

1135. Whitall, Tatum &. Co. *Whitall, Tatum & Co., 1880*. Facsimile Reproduction of Original Catalog by the American Historical Catalog Collection. Princeton, NJ: The Pyne Press, 1971. 80 pp., illus.

Whitall, Tatum & Co. was one of the major U.S. manufacturers of pharmaceutical glassware from the mid-nineteenth to the mid-twentieth century. This 1880 illustrated catalog features flint glassware, blue ware, perfume and cologne bottles, show bottles and globes, green glassware, stoppers, and druggists' sundries. A short history of the company and its products can be found in the historical introduction at the end of the catalog. The bibliography lists general books on glass, and glassmaking in the South Jersey area, and specific books on bottles. A short list of public collections of commercial glassware follows. A very useful reference and pictorial guide to pharmaceutical artifacts at the turn of the twentieth century.

1136. Wilson, Bill, and Betty Wilson. *19th-Century Medicine in Glass*. Amador City, CA: 19th Century Hobby and Publishing Co., 1971. 157 pp., illus., bibl., index.

A heavily illustrated collector's guide to nineteenth-century American patent or proprietary medicines. Useful introductory materials on bottle molds, including patent information.

Photographs and histories for over 800 products. Physical descriptions not very detailed. Short bibliography and index.

1137. Wittop Koning, Dirk A. *Delftse apothekerspotten*. Deventer: De Ijsel, 1954. 174 pp., illus.

   A catalogue and physical description of about 400 Delft drug jars in the collections of the Medical Pharmaceutical Museum of Amsterdam. 92 illustrations with captions in Dutch, English, French, and German. Brief descriptions of the designs and marks on the containers also in four languages. A chapter on marks and one on fakes.

1138. Wittop Koning, Dirk A. *Nederlandse vijsels*. Deventer, The Netherlands: Davo, 1953. 114 pp., illus., bibl., index.

   A good descriptive catalog of Dutch and Belgian mortars, primarily from the sixteenth to the eighteenth centuries, organized by maker or mortar founder. Very useful chronological lists of Dutch and Belgian mortar founders and illustrations of signed work by almost every Dutch maker. Good descriptions of various decorative motifs and inscriptions, bibliography, index, and English summary. [not seen].

1139. Wittop Koning, Dirk A. *Bronzemörser*. Frankfurt am Main: Govi-Verlag, 1975. 66 pp., illus.

   An illustrated catalog of primarily European bronze mortars from the fifteenth to the eighteenth centuries, though there are illustrations of a twelfth-century Persian mortar and a twentieth-century Dutch mortar. Twenty-seven full-page illustrations of mortars (mostly black and white) on the right side of the page with descriptive text on the left. The introduction includes a short history of the mortar as well as a discussion of manufacturing techniques and design.

1140. Young, Anne Mortimer. "Domestic Medicine Chests: Home Pharmacy in the Nineteenth Century." *Pharmaceutical Historian* 22, no. 3 (1992): 7-12.

Primary focus on British medical chests. Covers much of the same ground as Crellin's article on medicine chests but also discusses homeopathic medical chests and includes 5 large photographs.

1141. Zupko, Ronald Edward. *Revolution in Measurement: Western European Weights and Measures Since the Age of Science.* Philadelphia: The American Philosophical Society, 1990. xiii + 548 pp., illus., index.

A detailed history of weights and measures in Europe, especially Britain and France. Nearly 100 pages of notes with numerous references, including those to other important works by Zupko on this topic, and an index. No separate section or mention of pharmaceutical weights, but Appendix 2 (The Quantity Measures of Pre-metric Europe) and Appendix 3 (The Weights of Pre-metric Europe) provide information about medical and pharmaceutical applications.

1142. Zupko, Ronald Edward. "Medieval Apothecary Weights and Measures: The Principal Units of England and France." *Pharmacy in History* 32 (1990): 57-62.

Good descriptions of the weights and measures used by medieval apothecaries, alchemists, and physicians. Principal units divided into two categories: inexact and exact. 3 illustrations. Very good select bibliography of the most important metrological sources for medieval European pharmaceutical weights and measures.

2k—Patent Medicines and Quackery

1143. American Medical Association. *Nostrums and Quackery.* 3 vols. Chicago: AMA Press, 1911, 1921, 1936.

Articles on quack cures and nostrums reprinted from JAMA. Many labels from products are reproduced.

1144. Carson, Gerald. *One for a Man, Two for a Horse: A Pictorial History, Grave and Comic, of Patent Medicines.* Garden City, NY: Doubleday, 1961. 128 pp., illus., bibl., index.

   Entertaining social history of American patent medicine advertising. Heavily illustrated.

1145. Cook, James. *Remedies and Rackets: The Truth about Patent Medicines Today.* New York: W. W. Norton, 1958. 252 pp., bibl., index.

   A series of exposés from the *New York Post*.

1146. Dukes, M. N. G. *Patent Medicines and Autotherapy in Society.* The Hague: Drukkerij Pasmans, 1963. 191 pp.

   A comparison of the promotion, sale, and use of proprietary medicines in Britain and the Netherlands.

1147. Estes, J. Worth. "The Pharmacology of Nineteenth-Century Patent Medicines." *Pharmacy in History* 30 (1988): 3-18.

   An examination of the therapeutic claims, ingredients, and pharmacological properties of nineteenth-century American patent medicines by a pharmacologist-historian.

1148. Estes, J. Worth. "Public Pharmacology: Modes of Action of Nineteenth-Century 'Patent' Medicines." *Medical Heritage* 2 (1986): 218-28.

   This well-illustrated piece looks in brief at some of the supposed rationales for some popular American nostrums.

1149. Francesco, Grete de. *The Power of the Charlatan.* New Haven: Yale University Press, 1939. 288 pp., illus., bibl., index.

The history of medical quackery, including details on the careers of well-known charlatans, and containing 68 illustrations of prints, paintings, etc. The analysis of quackery focusses on early modern Europe.

1150. Griffenhagen, George, and James Harvey Young. "Old English Patent Medicines in America." In *Contributions from the Museum of History and Technology*. pp. 155-83. Washington: U. S. National Museum Bulletin 218, Smithsonian Institution, 1959. [reprinted in *Pharmacy in History* 34(1992):199-230].

The popularity of old English patent medicines in eighteenth-century America is evident in the advertising and imitation of these products when the supplies were cut short.

1151. Hambridge, Roger A. "'Empiricomany, or an Infatuation in Favour of Empiricism or Quackery': The Socio-Economics of Eighteenth-Century Quackery." In *Literature and Science and Medicine*. Serge Soupel, and Roger A. Hambridge, pp. 47-102. Los Angeles: William Andrews Clark Memorial Library, University of California, 1982.

Quackery in Western civilization seems to have peaked in the eighteenth century, as shown here. Taking an interdisciplinary approach, the author examines the reasons for its development during this period.

1152. Holcombe, Henry W. *Patent Medicine Tax Stamps: A History of the Firms Using Private Die Proprietary Medicine Tax Stamps*. Lawrence, MA: Quarterman Publications, 1979. 604 pp., illus. bibl., index.

A useful compilation of 137 brief histories of firms that used United States private die proprietary medicine tax stamps in the nineteenth century to help defray the costs of the Civil War. Information for the histories of these firms and their products was gathered from such diverse sources as city directories, medical almanacs, biographies, and newspaper advertisements. The histories are arranged alphabetically by name of firm; include numerous photographs of tax stamps, products, advertisements, and portraits; and are preceded by an informative foreword by George Griffenhagen. Appendices include a bibliography, an index of persons and firms, an index of products, and an index by the philatelic Scott number. An important reference source for the history of proprietary medicines in the United States.

1153. McNamara, Brooks. *Step Right Up*. New York: Doubleday, 1976. 233 pp., illus.

Articles that appeared in philatelic magazines collected by George Griffenhagen.

1154. Thompson, C. J. S. *The Quacks of Old London*. Worcester: The Trinity Press, 1929.

The main focus is the sixteenth through the eighteenth centuries.

1155. Young, James Harvey. *The Toadstool Millionaires: A Social History of Patent Medicines in America Before Federal Regulation*. Princeton, NJ: Princeton University Press, 1961. xii + 282 pp., illus.

Both lively and scholarly, this is the story of the marketing of patent medicines in the United States in the nineteenth century.

Part Three:
Pharmacy in the Arts

3a—Architecture and Interior Design

1156. "Chemist's House and Shop in Munster." *Deutsche Bauzeitschrift* 27, no. 8 (1979 Aug.): 1143-44.

    Includes plans, sections, photos. In German. Sebastian Apotheke in Munster, Germany. [not seen].

1157. de Gravelain, Frederique. "Sante Hospitals." *Architecture d'aujourd'hui* 256 (1988 Apr.): 1-50.

    Pharmacy in Belgium, p. 50. [not seen].

1158. Edwards, Tudor. "Treasure of the Hotels-Dieu: Some Old French Pharmacies." *Country Life* 163, no. 4220 (1978 May 25): 1468-69.

    Dispensaries, France. Includes photos. [not seen].

1159. Frothingham, Alice Wilson. "Apothecaries' Shops in Spain." *Notes Hispanic* (NY: Hispanic Society of America, 1941): 101-24.

    Describes the design of pharmacies and drug jars in Spain from the thirteenth to the eighteenth centuries. Many illustrations.

1160. Heger, Hans. *Apothekenbilder von Nah und Fern.* 4 vols. Vienna: 1896-1908.

Illustrations of pharmacies from around the world, including some floor plans, photographs, and engravings. Text gives context for the illustrations.

1161. Hein, Wolfgang-Hagen, and Dirk A. Wittop Koning. *Bildkatalog zur Geschichte der Pharmazie*. Veröffentlichungen der Internationalen Gesellschaft für Geschichte der Pharmazie, Band 33. Stuttgart: Wissenschaftliche Verlagsgesellschaft MBH, 1969. 288+ pp., illus.

Group illustrations that appeared in pharmacy calendars, etc., by their subjects. These include pharmacy interiors, portraits, caricatures, and so forth.

1162. "Living Beneath Old Gables." *MD Moebel—interior design* 31, no. 4 (1985 Apr.): 26-31.

Text in English, German, French. Includes plans, photos. Creation of a dwelling in the roof space and first floor of a sixteenth-century house with ground floor pharmacy. [not seen].

1163. "Markus Luscher and Viktor Michel: Business Premises." *Archithese* 14, no. 1 (1984 Jan/Feb): 40-42.

Text in German, English (p.3). Pharmacy with flat above. Chemists shop in Switzerland. [not seen].

1164. Miller, Nory. "Immaculate Distillation: Central Pharmacy, Karlsruhe." *Progressive Architecture* 61, no. 9 (1980 Sep): 148-50.

Includes plans, photos, axonometric views. [not seen].

1165. "Modern Chemist Under an Old Roof." *Architektur und Wohnwelt* 85, no. 6 (1977): 526-27.

Includes plans, sketches, photos. In German. Engel Apotheke in Aschaffenburg, Germany. [not seen].

1166. "Pharmacy in a Historic Setting." *AIT* 92, no. 3 (1984 Apr/May): 46-47.

   Text in German. Alterations include a new ground-floor facade. Apotheke Schneider, Kirchheim, Germany. [not seen].

1167. "Pharmacy in Lubbecke." *Deutsche Bauzeitung* 116, no. 1 (1982 Jan): 36-37.

   Text in German. English summary (p.11). Includes plans, sketches, photos. [not seen].

1168. Segers, E. G., and Dirk A. Wittop Koning. *Apothicaireries anciennes en Benelux. De oude apotheek in de Benelux.* Devente: Davo, 1958. 50 pp., illus.

   Describes pharmacies and their contents in Belgium and Holland, from the thirteenth to the nineteenth century. Focus is on drug containers. Text in French and Dutch.

1169. "Stadtapotheke in Kulsheim." *Baumeister* 87, no. 10 (1990 Oct): 46-49.

   Includes photos, plans, sections, sketches. Text in German. [not seen].

1170. "The Three Periods of Health." *Construction Moderne* no. 39 (1984 Sep): 7-14.

   Text in French. Pharmacy in Lille. [not seen].

1171. Vitta, Maurizio. "La farmacia di Richie." *Arca* no. 46 (1991 Feb.): 36-41.

Includes photo, plans, sections. Text in English, Italian—chemist's shop, France, Boves. [not seen].

1172. Wittop Koning, Dirk A., and Wolfgang-Hagen Hein. "Die Allegorische Apotheke des Kornelis Elzevier." *Beiträge zur Geschichte der Pharmazie* 40 (1988): 39-40.

Copperplate title page for "Lexicon galeno-chymico-pharmaceuticum universale" by Elsevier, eighteenth century.

1173. "The Zentral Apotheke in Karlsruhe." *Domus*, no. 594 (1979 May): 50-51.

Includes sketches, photos. Text in English, Italian, French. [not seen].

1174. Zwettler, Gerhardt. "Umbau einer alten Apotheke [Refurbishment of old pharmacy]." *Bauforum* 21, no. 130 (1988): 47.

Includes photos, plans. Text in German. Pharmacy in Austria. [not seen].

3b—Painting, Sculpture, Graphic Arts, and Photography

1175. Angenot, Jean-François. *La Pharmacie et l'art de Guerir au Pays de Liége des Origines a nos Jours.* Liége: Eugéne Wahle Editeur, 1983. 230 pp., illus.

Essentially a text on the history of pharmacy in the area surrounding Liége. The 219 illustrations include paintings, ceramics, antiques, medals, and caricatures, several in full color.

1176. Apple, Rima D., compiler. *Illustrated Catalogue of the Slide Archive of Historical Medical Photographs at Stony Brook, Center for Photographic Images of Medicine and Health Care,*

State University of New York at Stony Brook. Westport, Connecticut: Greenwood Press, 1984. 442 pp., bibl, illus.

Brief descriptions, sources, and small reproductions of 3171 images of medical and related subject. Includes 35 images of pharmacies and 17 of pharmacists (there is some duplication), indexes of personal names, institutions, photographers, and subjects, as well as a chronological list and a thorough bibliography.

1177. Arano, L. C. *The Medieval Health Handbook: Tacuinum Sanitatis*. transl. O. Ratti and A. Westbrook. New York: George Braziller, 1976. 153 pp.

This work includes 48 color plates, which reveal much about late medieval life. Plate 41, showing the sale of theriac, is an exquisite depiction of southern European pharmacy c. 1400. The book's text is primarily about the history of art.

1178. Arnold-Forster, Kate, and Nigel Tallis. *The Bruising Apothecary: Images of Pharmacy and Medicine in Caricature*. London: The Pharmaceutical Press, 1989. 84 pp., illus.

A catalogue of prints and drawings in the caricature collection at the Royal Pharmaceutical Society of Great Britain, listing 171 objects, with a title index and biographical notes. Containing 58 illustrations, 8 in color.

1179. Bardell, Eunice Bonow. "Pharmacists in Motion Pictures." *American Journal of Hospital Pharmacy* 45 (1988): 179-83.

Discusses films such as W. C. Fields' "It's the Old Army Game," (1926), his "The Pharmacist" (1933), "It's a Wonderful Life" (1946), etc. Four illustrations are included.

1180. Baudet, Jean. *Livre d'Or des apothicaireries de France*. St.-Mandé, France: Editions Thériaque, 1962. 225 pp., illus.

Antique ceramics, mortars, glassware, and other objects used in French pharmacies, with chapters devoted to geographical regions and the antiques indigenous to them.

1181. Bender, George A. *Great Moments in Pharmacy*. Detroit: Northwood Institute Press, 1966.

Contains 40 illustrations of significant events in the history of pharmacy by Robert A. Thom, commissioned by Parke-Davis & Co. for a series, "A History of Pharmacy in Pictures." Each of the paintings is reproduced in color, with commentary by George A. Bender.

1182. Bender, George A., and John Parascandola (eds.). *Historical Hobbies for the Pharmacist*. Madison: American Institute of the History of Pharmacy, 1974. repr.1980. 57 pp.

Chapters cover antiques, glassware, ephemera, philately, etc.

1183. Blunt, Wilfred, and Sandra Raphael. *The Illustrated Herbal*. New York: Metropolitan Museum of Art, 1979. 187 pp. + index.

With more than 150 illustrations, many in full color, this book conveys the artistry of the herbals. The illustrations are well documented and the book contains a short bibliography and index.

1184. Bosman-Jelgersma, Henriette A. *Poeders, Pillen en Patiënten*. Amsterdam: Sijthoff, 1983. 179 pp., illus.

The history of pharmacy in the Netherlands with illustrations in black and white and color of pharmacy interiors, facades, equipment, and antiques.

1185. Carroll Reece Museum. *Say Ah! Say Ah!* Johnson City, Tennessee: Carroll Reece Museum, 1968. 60 pp., illus.

Catalogue of an exhibition on the history of American pharmacy, describing 160 objects, with illustrations of 54 of them. The cover reproduces a number of trade cards advertising proprietary medicines.

1186. Crellin, John K. *Medical Ceramics: A Catalogue of the English and Dutch Collections in the Museum of the Wellcome Institute of the History of Medicine.* London: Wellcome Institute of the History of Medicine, 1969.

Includes 488 illustrations. The catalogue is organized by product use, and includes sections on pharmacy jars, tiles, mortars, nursing and hygiene, inhalers, eye baths, spittoons, chamber pots, urinals, bidets, phrenological heads, etc.

1187. Dillemann, Georges. "Die französische Pharmazie vom 3. Jahrhundert bis zur Gegenwart." In *Illustrierte Geschichte der Medizin.* ed. J. C. Sournia, M. Martiny, and J. Poulet, pp. vol. 3, 1669-1723. 6 vols. Salzburg: Andreas, 1980.

Color illustrations from pharmacy text or manuscripts in France. Not limited to French works. Covers the ancient through modern period.

1188. Dorveaux, Paul. *Les Pots de Pharmacie, Leur Historique suivi d'un Dictionnaire de leurs Inscriptions.* Toulouse: Librairie Marqueste, 1923. 89 pp., illus.

There are 36 pages of text and 46 of a useful dictionary listing French translations for abbreviations which appear on drug jars. With 14 black-and-white plates.

1189. Drake, T. G. H. "Antiques of Interest to the Apothecary." *Journal of the History of Medicine and Allied Sciences* 1960 (15): 31-44.

Describes Delftware, mortars, numismatics, ceramics, containers, nostrums, caricatures, etc. With 15 illustrations inserted into the text.

1190. Drake, T. G. H. "English Caricatures of Medical Interest, circa 1800." *Ciba Symposia* 6, no. 8 (1944): 1925-1932.

   Contains 11 reproductions of prints on quackery and other subjects, both social and political. The issue of the journal in which this article appeared contains two others on medical caricature, Wolfgang Born, "The Nature and History of Medical Caricature," and Curt Proskauer, "The Dentist in Caricature."

1191. Drey, R. E. A. *Apothecary Jars: Pharmaceutical Pottery and Porcelain in Europe and the East 1150-1850.* London: Faber and Faber, 1978. 249 pp., illus.

   A review of ceramics from the twelfth to nineteenth centuries, with 96 illustrations and a glossary of terms used in apothecary jar inscriptions.

1192. Fox, Daniel M., and Christopher Lawrence. *Photographing Medicine: Images and Power in Britain and America since 1840.* Westport, Conn.: Greenwood Press, 1988. 356 pp., illus., index.

   A study of photographic representation of medicine and related health professions in Great Britain and the United States since the 1840s. Includes several photographs in pharmaceutical settings at Bellevue Hospital, New York; St. Bartholomew's Hospital, London, and so forth.

1193. Hamarneh, Sami. "Pharmacy in Prints." *Journal of the American Pharmaceutical Association* NS 10, no. 4 (1970): 216-20.

   On Smithsonian exhibition of prints from the collection of William H. Helfand, including reproductions of ten of the objects on exhibit.

1194. Hein, Wolfgang-Hagen. *Die Deutsche Apotheke, Bilder aus Ihrer Geschichte.* Stuttgart: Deutsche Apotheker-Verlag, 1960. 231 pp., illus.

Contains 125 black-and-white reproductions of German paintings, prints, portraits, antiques, pharmacies, medals, etc., each with a descriptive text.

1195. Hein, Wolfgang-Hagen. *Die Pharmazie in der Karikatur/Pharmacy in Caricature*. Frankfurt am Main: Govi-Verlag, 1964. 222 pp., illus., index.

With 210 black-and-white illustrations and text in both English and German, subjects covered include both political and social caricature with examples from German, French, British, and American sources. There is an index of artists and an index of sources.

1196. Hein, Wolfgang-Hagen. *Emailmalereigläser aus Deutschen Apotheken* Monographien zur pharmazeutischen Kulturgeschichte, ed. Wolfgang-Hagen Hein and Dirk A. Wittop Koning, Band 1. Frankfurt am Main: Govi-Verlag, v.d., 1972. 61 pp., illus.

One of a series of monographs, each devoted to a specific pharmaceutical antique or other object of interest to collectors.

1197. Hein, Wolfgang-Hagen, and Dirk A. Wittop Koning. *Bildkatalog zur Geschichte der Pharmazie*. Veröffentlichungen der Internationalen Gesellschaft für Geschichte der Pharmazie, e.V., Bd. 33. Stuttgart: Wissenschaftliche Verlagsgesellschaft MBH, 1969. 288 pp., illus.

A listing of the illustrations, including paintings, prints, ceramics, antiques, etc., which have been published in the German and Dutch pharmaceutical-historical calendars as well as the publication *Zur Geschichte der Pharmazie* and its predecessor. Contains 32 illustrations, 4 in color.

1198. Helfand, William H. *Drugs and Pharmacy in Prints*. Toronto: n.p., [1967] 53 pp., illus.

Catalog of an exhibition of 120 prints, drawings, and pharmaceutical ephemera held in Toronto, with 16 black-and-white illustrations.

1199. Helfand, William H. *Medicine and Pharmacy in American Political Prints (1765-1870)*. Madison: American Institute of the History of Pharmacy, 1978. 84 pp., illus.

Describes 125 political prints published in the United States prior to 1871, with black-and-white illustrations of each. A chronological index is included.

1200. Helfand, William H. *Medicine and Pharmacy: 100 Years of Poster Art*. Albany: New York State Museum, 1981. 62 pp., illus.

Catalog of an exhibition of 60 posters for pharmaceutical products, pharmacies, and public health issues, with black-and-white illustrations for each.

1201. Helfand, William H. "Art and Medicine in Professional Communications." *Adler Museum Bulletin* April; June (1983): 13-20; 3-11.

Posters, "porcelain cards," trade cards, post cards, and other media advertising the professional activities of pharmacists, physicians, etc. With 35 black-and-white illustrations. [not seen].

1202. Helfand, William H. "Art in the Service of Public Health: The Illustrated Poster." *Caduceus* 6, no. 2 (1990): 1-37.

A review of posters designed for public health issues, with a checklist of 115 items. Includes 35 illustrations, of which 8 are in color.

1203. Helfand, William H. "The Pharmaceutical Poster." *Pharmacy in History* 15 (1973): 67-86.

Painting, Sculpture, Graphic Arts, and Photography 299

Reproduces 8 posters advertising proprietary products in color and includes a checklist of 69 European and American posters.

1204. Helfand, William H. "The Pharmacy in the Popular Arts." *Pharmacy in History* 28 (1986): 75-88.

Illustrations of pharmacy in postcards, trade cards, caricatures, playing cards, games, song sheets, and other popular media; with 18 black-and-white illustrations.

1205. Helfand, William H. "Pharmacy in L'Imagerie Populaire." *Pharmacy in History* 29 (1987): 116-24.

Illustrations of pharmacy and pharmacists in popular prints, largely French, with 10 black-and-white illustrations.

1206. Helfand, William H., and David L. Cowen. "American Pharmaceutical Posters." *Veröffentlichungen der Internationalen Gesellschaft für Geschichte der Pharmazie e.V.* 50 (1981): 207-19.

A study of the differences between American and European nineteenth century posters, with four black-and-white reproductions.

1207. Helfand, William H., and Sergio Rocchietta. *Medicina e Farmacia Nelle Caricature Politiche Italiane, 1848-1914.* Milan: Edizioni Scientifiche Internazionali, 1982. 183 pp., illus., bibl., index.

A collection of 151 Italian political caricatures on medical and pharmaceutical themes, including a brief text in English, French, and Italian, and reproductions of each of the prints along with explanatory captions.

1208. Holländer, Eugen. *Die Karikatur und Satire in der Medizin.* Stuttgart: Ferdinand Enke, 1905. 354 pp., illus.

A comprehensive survey of medical caricature, with many descriptions of pharmaceutical subjects.

1209. Jackson, W. A. *The Victorian Chemist and Druggist*. Aylesbury, Bucks, England: 1981. 32 pp., illus.

With 43 illustrations of pharmaceutical antiques, caricatures, and advertising trade cards.

1210. Julien, Pierre, and François Ledermann (eds.). *Saint Côme et Saint Damien, Culte et Iconographie*. Zurich: Juris Druck + Verlag, 1985. 127 pp., illus.

Thirteen papers dealing with the patron saints of pharmacy, with illustrations of statues, miniatures, paintings, and ephemera on which their effigy appears.

1211. Kallinich, Günter. *Pharmacies Anciennes*. Fribourg: Office du Livre; and Paris, Société Française du Livre, 1976. 252 pp., illus.

First published as *Schöne alte Apotheken* (Munich: Verlag George D. W. Calway, 1975). Contains 458 illustrations, in black and white and color, of pharmacy interiors. Reproduces sculptures, containers, equipment, and other pharmaceutical antiques. [not seen].

1212. Karp, Diane R., ed. *Ars Medica: Art, Medicine and the Human Condition*. Philadelphia: Philadelphia Museum of Art, 1985. 231 pp., illus., bibl., index.

Catalogue of an exhibition of prints, drawings, and photographs from the Ars Medica Collection. Includes several pharmaceutical subjects.

1213. Lewis, John. *Printed Ephemera*. Ipswich, Suffolk: W. S. Cowell, 1962.

The pioneering study of ephemera, based on the changing uses of type and letterforms in English and American printing. With 713 illustrations, many in color, and containing a number of labels and other examples of pharmaceutical interest.

1214. MacKinney, Loren. *Medical Illustrations in Medieval Manuscripts.* Berkeley and Los Angeles: University California Press, 1965. 263 pp., illus., index.

Reproduces 104 miniatures, 18 in color, showing medical and pharmaceutical scenes. Includes extensive review of medicines, pharmaceutical practices, etc., as illustrated in miniatures from European and American collections.

1215. Masino, Cristoforo, Angelo Schwarz, and Guiseppe Ostino. *Piemonte e Valle d'Aosta.* Per una storia della farmacia e del farmacista in Italia, ed. Angelo Schwarz, vol 1. Turin: Edizioni Skema v.d., 1980. 96 pp., illus.

Well-illustrated with antiques, paintings, statues, portraits, etc., from this region of Italy. For other regions, see citation #1229.

1216. Matthews, Leslie G. *Antiques of the Pharmacy.* London: G. Bell & Sons, 1971. 120 pp., illus., index.

Contains 89 illustrations. The text contains chapters on pottery, metals, glass, wooden objects, medicine chests, materia medica cabinets, prints, proprietary medicines, stamps and advertisements.

1217. Matthews, Leslie G. "Pharmacy in Song." *The Pharmaceutical Journal* 21 December, vol. 179 (1957): 480-81.

Includes reproductions of the covers of 5 songs in the Wellcome Library collection, Morison's Pills, The Quack Doctor, Medicine Jack, Doctor Compes Mentis, and The Quack's Song.

1218. Mez-Mangold, Lydia. *A History of Drugs*. Basel: F. Hoffmann-La Roche & Co., Ltd., 1971. 175 pp., illus., bibl., index.

Uses illustrations of objects in the collection of the Swiss Pharmaziehistorisches Museum, grouped by historical period, to trace the development of drugs through artifacts. There is a reprinted black-and-white edition (Totowa, NJ: Barnes & Noble Books, 1986) that includes references and an index.

1219. Mornand, Pierre, ed. "La Publicité Pharmaceutique." *Le Courrier Graphique* Paris, No. 15 (1938): 1-96.

An entire issue devoted to pharmaceutical advertising with articles on art and pharmacy, French pharmaceutical advertising since the fifteenth century, methods and trends in pharmaceutical advertising, books, albums, reviews, and packaging of pharmaceutical firms, etc. With many original advertisements included.

1220. Nékám, Livia. *Old Hungarian Pharmacies*. Budapest: Corvina Press, 1968. 65+ pp., illus.

The interiors and antiques of pharmacies in Hungary, with 15 black-and-white illustrations and 40 in color.

1221. Novotny, Ann, and Carter Smith. *Images of Healing*. New York: Macmillan Publishing Co., 1980. 144 pp., illus., bibl., index.

A portfolio of American medical and pharmaceutical practices from the eighteenth century, containing over 400 black-and-white and sepia prints, photographs, and documents.

1222. Olonetzky, Beny. *Die Sammlung*. Stuttgart: Georg Thieme Verlag, 1980. 123 + 115 + 127 pp., illus.

With contributions by Lydia Mez. A collection of illustrations of the antiques and other holdings at the Swiss Pharmaziehistorische Museum in Basel. Chapters are devoted to mortars, medals, weights, statues, glassware, clysters, and other antiques.

1223. Pedrazzini, Carlo. *La Farmacia Storica ed Artistica Italiana.* Milan: Edizioni Vittoria, 1934. 592 pp., illus.

Copiously illustrated, in sepia, with photographs of Italian pharmacies, their interiors, antiques, drug jars, etc. Paintings in which pharmacies appear are included.

1224. Peters, Hermann. *Pictorial History of Ancient Pharmacy.* 3rd ed. Chicago: G. P. Engelhard & Co., 1902. 210 pp., illus.

Contains chapters on pharmacy in the Middle Ages up to the eighteenth century, distillation, pharmacopoeias, etc., with 83 black-and-white illustrations.

1225. Power, Jed. *Drug Antiques: A Photographic Look at Old and Unusual Drug Artifacts and Rarities. With Current Values and an Introduction.* Peabody, Mass.: Cape Ann Antiques, 1986. 201 pp., illus.

Primarily devoted to those antiques which relate to narcotic and other psychoactive drugs, reproducing postcards, advertisements, paperback book covers, and packages.

1226. Richardson, Lillian C., and Charles G. Richardson. *The Pill Rollers: Apothecary Antiques and Drug Store Collectibles.* 1st ed. Fort Washington, Maryland: Old Fort Press, 1979. 170 pp., illus.

A catalogue of pharmacy antiques, with sections on glassware, labels, equipment, pill tiles, scales and weights, advertisements, etc. An appendix lists museums, American pharmaceutical firms, etc.

1227. Rickards, Maurice. *Collecting Printed Ephemera.* NY: Abbeville Press, 1988. 224 pp., illus.

A thorough review of the collecting, conservation, display, organization, sources, and values of ephemera. Contains 750 illustrations, 300 in color, largely from the collection of the author, including numerous examples of pharmaceutical ephemera.

1228. Rocchietta, Sergio. *Antichi Vasi di Farmacia Italiani.* Milan: L'Ariete Edizioni, 1986. 171 pp., illus.

A thorough study of Italian drug jars, organized by their place of origin, with present locations noted for each of the jars reproduced.

1229. Schwarz, Angelo, ed.. *Per una storia della farmacia e del farmacista in Italia.* Bologna: Edizione Skema v.d., 1980-, illus.

Vol. 1: Cristoforo Masino, Angelo Schwarz, and Guiseppe Ostino, *Farmacie e Farmacisti in Piemone e Valle d'Aosta,* 1980, 96 pp., with 137 illustrations in color and black and white. Vol. 2: Ruggiero Romano, Angelo Schwarz, *Venezia e Veneto,* 1981, 96 pp., with 175 illustrations in color and black and white. [not seen] Vol. 3: Cesare de Seta, Gianluigi Degli Esposti, and Cristoforo Masino, *Sicilia,* 1983, 95 pp., with 146 illustrations in color and black and white. Vol. 4: Ezio Raimondi, Luigi Guicciardi, and Cristoforo Masino, *Emilia-Romagna,* 1986, 135 pp. [not seen] Vol. 5: Cristoforo Masino, Pasquale Villani, Paolo Frascani, Andrea Russo, *Napolie Campania,* 1988, 95 pp. Vol. 6: Carlo Cipolla, Andrea Russo, Dante Zanetti, *Milano e Lombardia,* 1992, 111 pp.

In this series published by Schiapparelli, the Italian pharmaceutical manufacturing firm, each volume is well illustrated with antiques, paintings, statues, portraits, etc., from individual regions of Italy.

1230. Short, Agnes Lothian. "Englische pharmazeutische Karikaturen." *Zur Geschichte der Pharmazie* 1 (1961): 1-4.

Reproduces 12 social caricatures on Jenner's smallpox vaccine, Perkin's Metallic Tractors, Morison's Pills, etc.

1231. Stafski, Heinz. *Aus alten Apotheken*. Munich: Prestel Verlag, 1958. 48 + pages, illus.

Contains more than 75 illustrations, in color and black and white, or miniatures, portraits, caricatures, etc.

1232. Starks, Michael. *Cocaine Fiends and Reefer Madness*. New York: Cornwall Books, 1982. 242 pp., illus.

An illustrated history of drugs in the movies, describing films in which narcotics and psychoactive drugs play a role, such as the 1936 films "Marihuana," and "Reefer Madness," etc. Contains illustrations of posters, stills, on drug-related films.

1233. Steinbart, Hiltrud. *Arzt und Patient in der Geschichte, in der Anekdote, im Volksmund. Eine sittengeschichtliche Studie*. Stuttgart: Ferdinand Enke Verlag, 1970. viii + 340 pp., illus.

Includes a section on pharmacists as well as one on clysters. Among the 331 black-and-white illustrations are several of pharmacists and their clients.

1234. Stoeckle, John D., and George Abbott White. *Plain Pictures of Plain Doctoring*. Cambridge: MIT Press, 1985. xxiii + 250 pp., illus.

A review of "vernacular expression in New Deal medicine and photography," with 80 photographs from the Farm Security Administration. Advertisement for pharmaceuticals and other pharmaceutical images are included.

1235. Tait, H. P. "Medicine and Pharmacy in Caricature." *Pharmaceutical Journal* 23 March, vol. 190 (1963): 247-53.

Contains reproductions of 12 social caricatures on quacks, medicine, and pharmacy by British and French artists.

1236. Ulmer, Bruno, Thomas Plaichinger, and Charles Advenier. *A Votre Sante! Histoire de la publicité pharmaceutique et médicale*. Paris: Éditions Syros-Alternatives, n.d. [ca. 1989]. 148 pp., illus.

A study of medical and pharmaceutical advertising in France from the charlatans of medieval times to contemporary journal advertisements. Many of the 116 illustrations of posters, labels, signs, etc., 85 of which are in color, are rare and unfamiliar.

1237. Underwood, E. Ashworth, ed. *The History of Pharmacy*. Oxford: Oxford University Press, 1951. 61 pp., illus.

Catalogue of an exhibition at the Wellcome Historical Medical Museum, with sections on Alchemy and Pharmacy, Herbals, Pharmacology, Chemotherapy, Vessels for Pharmaceutical Preparations, Mortars and Pestles, etc. Contains 11 illustrations.

1238. Warthin, Aldred Scott. *The Physician of the Dance of Death*. New York: Paul B. Hoeber, Inc., 1931. 142 pp., illus., index.

A historical study of the evolution of myths concerning the Dance of Death in art. Contains 92 illustrations, several of which show Death in a pharmaceutical setting.

1239. Weber, A. *Tableau de la caricature médicale depuis les origines jusqu'à nos jours*. Paris: Editions Hippocrate, 1936. 143 pp., illus.

Primarily devoted to social caricature and containing about 130 illustrations.

1240. Wittop Koning, Dirk A. *Art and Pharmacy*. Deventer, Holland: The Ysel Press [vol. 6 published by Twist Productions, Haarle, Holland], v.d.; Vol. 1, 1957 [12 pp. + 42 plates with descriptions]; Vol. 2, 1958 [9 pp. + 42 plates with descriptions]; Vol. 3, 1964 [95 pp., incl. 42 plates with descriptions]; Vol. 4,

1976 [108 pp., incl. 42 plates with descriptions]; Vol. 5, 1980 (100 pp., incl. 42 plates with descriptions]; Vol. 6, 1986 [100 pp., incl. 42 plates with descriptions].

Color reproductions of illustrations of paintings, ceramics, statues, prints, and other works of art originally published by the author in an annual pharmaceutical-historical calendar.

1241. Wittop Koning, Dirk A. *De oude apotheek*. Bussum, Holland: C. A. J. Van Dishoeck, 1966. 112 pp., illus.

Reproduces prints, paintings, antiques, etc. from Dutch pharmacies. Includes 66 illustrations in color and black-and-white.

1242. Wittop Koning, Dirk A. *Pharmazeutische Münzen und Medaillen*. Monographien zur Pharmazeutischen Kulturgeschichte, ed. Wolfgang-Hagen Hein and Dirk A. Wittop Koning, Band 2. Frankfurt am Main: Govi-Verlag, 1972. 48 pp., illus.

A series of monographs, each devoted to a specific pharmaceutical antique or other object of interest to collectors.

1243. Wittop Koning, Dirk A. *De Farmacie in tekening en prent [The Pharmacy in Drawings and Prints]*. Amsterdam: Buijten & Schipperheijn/Repro-Holland, 1976. n.p., 81 illus.

Contains black-and-white illustrations of a variety of Dutch images: prints, posters, caricatures, bookplates, labels, portraits, imagerie populaire, etc.

1244. Wittop Koning, Dirk A. *Geneeskunde en farmacie in de Nederlandse politieke prent 1632-1932*. Haarlem, Netherlands: Merck Sharp and Dohme, B.V., 1979. 159 pp., illus.

Describes 188 political prints published in Holland prior to 1933, with illustrations for each. A brief text is printed in

Dutch and English; captions for each of the prints give further details.

1245. Wittop Koning, Dirk A. *Compendium voor de geschiedenis van de pharmacie van Nederland [Compendium of Dutch History of Pharmacy]*. 's-Gravenhage: Koninklijke Nederlandse Maatschappij ter Bevordering der Pharmazie, 1986. 314 pp., illus.

A comprehensive encyclopedic compilation of information on the history of pharmacy in Holland, reproducing documents, portraits, paintings, etc., with 249 illustrations in color and black and white and a thorough bibliography. [not seen].

1246. Zglinicki, Friedrich von. *Kallipygos und Askulap: das Klistier in der Geschichte der Medizin, Kunst und Literatur*. Baden-Baden: Verlag für angewandte Wissenschaften, 1972. 296 pp., illus.

The clyster in the history of medicine, art, and literature, with 186 black-and-white illustrations of paintings, caricatures, etc., in which this instrument appears.

1247. Zigrosser, Carl. *Medicine and the Artist*. 3rd ed. New York: Dover Publications, Inc., 1970. 177 pp., illus.

Prints from the Ars Medica collection at the Philadelphia Museum of Art, with 137 black-and-white illustrations. A later version of earlier catalogs published by the Museum in 1955 and 1959.

3c—Creative Literature

1248. Bardell, Eunice Bonow. "The Novels of the American Pharmacist, John Uri Lloyd." *Pharmacy in History* 29 (1987): 177-80.

A review of some of John Uri Lloyd's fiction and indications of the connections to details of his own life and career.

1249. Diehl, Digby. *Drug Themes in Fiction*. DHEW Publ. No. (ADM)75-191. Washington, D.C.: National Institute on Drug Abuse, Research Issues, 10, 1974. 40 pp.

Survey of selected works of fiction with drug-related themes.

1250. Hansen, Poul. *Apoteket og Farmaceuten i dansk Litteratur*. Copenhagen: 1947. 93 pp., illus.

This book, modeled after Urdang's *Der Apotheker im Spiegel der Literature*, examines the portrayal of pharmacy in Danish literature. (In Danish, with an index and short bibliography.).

1251. Poirer, S. "Ann Petry: From Pharmacist to Novelist." *Pharmacy in History* 28 (1986): 26-33.

The fiction of Ann Petry reflects her concern with maintaining personal (and professional) integrity in times of historical, moral, or social upheaval.

1252. Silverberg, Robert. *Drug Themes in Science Fiction*. National Institute on Drug Abuse, Research Issues, 9. Washington, D.C.: DHEW Publ. No. (ADM)75-191, 1974. 55 pp.

English-language short stories dealing with mind-altering drugs. Bibliography with abstracts.

1253. Urdang, George. *Der Apotheker als Subjekt und Objekt der Literatur*. Berlin: J. Springer, 1926. 181 pp., illus., index.

Classic study linking pharmacy and literature, with index to literature and authors cited. Old German type makes the reading slow going.

1254. Urdang, George. *Der Apotheker in Spiegel der Literatur*. Berlin: J. Springer, 1921. 157 pp., bibl.

Covers the representation of the pharmacist in well-known literature (mostly from the sixteenth century on), as well as music and other literary art forms.

3d—Music

1255. Friedrich, Christoph. ""Der Apotheker und der Doktor" Zum 200. Jubiläum der Uraufführung einer Oper." *Beiträge zur Geschichte der Pharmazie* 39 (1986): 285-89.

   Dittersdorf's "Der Apotheker und der Doktor" opened in Vienna in 1786. This article reviews the opera, Dittersdorf's biography, and the place of this opera in pharmaceutical literature, with documentation.

Author Index
Numbers in index refer to entry numbers

Ackerknecht, Erwin H., 482, 483
Adam, Linda, 905
Adams, David P., 582
Adams, Walter, 876
Adlung, Alfred, 137
Advenier, Charles, 1236
Aftalion, Fred, 1007
Albert, Adrien, 408
Alcer, G., 1008
Alderson, Wroe, 365
Ali, Mohammad, 103
Allen, D. G., 688
Andersen, Dannesboe, 1045
Anderson, Frank J., 769
Anderson, Lee, 795
Anderson, Oscar Edward, Jr., 691, 692
André-Pontier, L., 128
Andrews, Theodora, 1
Angenot, Jean-François, 1175
Antoine J. Balard (1802-1876), 239
Apple, Rima D., 828, 1176
Appleby, John H., 154
Arano, L. C., 1177
Araujo, Carlos da Silva, 112, 113
Arber, Agnes R., 770
Archambault, George, 831
Armstrong, James W., 211
Arnold-Forster, Kate, 1046, 1128, 1178
Artelt , Walter, 2
Austin, Robert B., 3
Autian, J., 409
Autio, D. E., 907
Avicenna (Ibn Sina), 749
Awad, Henry A., 1094
Ayd, Frank J., 584
Bachmann, C., 410
Bailey, Thomas A., 693

Baldwin, Joseph K., 1047
Ballard, Charles W., 796
Bardell, Eunice Bonow, 908, 909, 1179, 1248
Barkan, Ilyse D., 694
Bartels, Karl H., 695
Baudet, Jean, 1180
Baumé, Antoine, 750
Bäumler, Ernst, 261
Bautista, Teresa, 69
Beal, Harold M., 403
Beal, J. H., 696
Bearman, David, 411
Becker, Louis A., 1009
Beer, John J., 1010
Beguin, Jean, 751
Bell, Jacob, 114
Bell, W. J., 243
Bender, George A., 160, 337, 621, 797, 971, 1048, 1181, 1182
Bennion, Elisabeth, 1049
Benson, Roger A., 916
Berendes, Julius, 77, 78
Bergevin, Al, 1050
Berman, Alex, 60, 79, 80, 255, 356, 585, 586, 587, 588, 697, 798, 799, 800, 801
Bernsmann, W., 412, 698
Berridge, Virginia, 367, 589, 590
Bethman, David, 1051
Bett, W. R., 331
Bickel, Marcel H., 410, 418, 591
Bindra, Jasjit S., 592
Björkman, Edwin, 360
Blackwell, Barry, 584
Blais, Gerard D., Jr., 593
Blake, John B., 5, 6, 697, 699, 731, 741, 744, 862, 1012
Blasi, Betty, 1052

Blauch, Lloyd E., 910
Bliss, Michael, 242, 594
Blochman, Lawrence, 345
Blockstein, William L., 215, 911
Blunt, Wilfred., 771, 1183
Bobst, Elmer Holmes, 250
Bogard, Mary O., 1053, 1054
Bonnemain, Henri, 169, 231, 854
Bono, James, 802
Bonow, Eunice R., 912
Bonow-Bardell, Eunice, 913
Borell, Merriley, 595, 596
Bosman-Jelgersma, Henriette A., 1184
Boussel, Patrice, 169, 259, 854
Bouvet, Maurice, 7, 129
Bové, Frank J., 169, 597, 854
Bovet, Daniel, 598
Bowers, Roy A., 914, 915
Boxer, C. R., 315, 320
Boylan, James C., 372
Bradley, Theodore J., 273
Brandel, I. W., 1055
Bretschneider, Emile V., 123
Brewer, William A., 413
Brockbank, William, 368
Brodie, Donald C., 916
Bromell, John R., 369
Brown, Michael S., 192
Brown, P. S., 599
Brown, T. R., 708
Brown, William, 370
Bruinvels (eds.), J., 462, 510
Brunner, Theodore F., 527
Bruppacher-Cellier, Marianne, 252
Buerki, Robert A., 8, 371, 372
Bunnell, Kevin P., 917, 964
Bürgin, Alfred, 186
Burkholder, D. F., 358
Burkill, I. H., 855
Burlingham, Robert, 600
Burnby, Juanita G. L., 803
Burnett, John, 1056
Burt, Joseph B., 299
Bush, Patricia J., 657, 822, 885
Butler, T. C., 414
Bynum, William F., 688, 804
Caldwell, Anne E., 601

Callisen, Adolf Carl Peter, 10
Cameron, H. Charles, 849
Campbell, Leslie Caine, 805
Carl S. N. Hallberg, 1856-1910, 272
Carlisle, Robert D. B., 212
Carlson, D. G., 102
Carpenter, Kenneth J., 602
Carroll, Edward J., 373, 374
Carson, Gerald, 1144
Cash, Philip, 619
Caspari, Charles, Jr., 375
Cassar, Paul, 149
Cavers, David B., 699
Chadwick, Alena F., 519
Chapman-Huston, Desmond, 180
Charters, W. W., 376, 919
Chen, K. K., 416
Chien, Robert I., 856
Christianson, Eric H., 619
Cignoli, Francisco, 105
Cocolas, George H., 920
Colapinto, Leonardo, 700
Colebrook, L., 258
Coley, Noel G., 603
Comanor, W. S., 857, 858, 859, 1011
Combes, Reg, 152
Conci, Giulio, 81
Connors, Kenneth A., 417
Conradi, Helmut Peter, 1057
Conroy, Mary Schaeffer, 155
Conti, A., 418
Cook, E. Fullerton, 377
Cook, Harold, 701, 806
Cook, James, 1145
Cook, Roy Bird, 294, 378
Cooper, Michael, 861
Cooper, Norman, 115
Cooper, William C., 528
Copeman, W. S. C., 807
Cordasco, Francesco, 11
Cordus, Valerius, 752
Coulas, Gail, 992
Coulter, Harris L., 604
Cowen, David L., 12, 82, 83, 84, 161, 379, 391, 419, 420, 421, 439, 484, 605, 606, 607, 702, 703, 704, 705, 772, 773, 774,

Index

775, 776, 808, 809, 862, 914, 915, 922, 1012, 1020, 1206
Craker, Lyle E., 519
Cray, William C., 198
Crellin, John K., 380, 608, 609, 810, 811, 812, 813, 814, 1058, 1059, 1060, 1061, 1062, 1063, 1064, 1065, 1186
Cripps, Ernest C., 180, 232
Croll, Oswald, 753
Cruttenden, Joseph, 863
Cruz, Martin de la, 529, 754
Culp, Robert W., 923, 924
Curtis, Robert I., 530
Danforth, Ellen Zak, 1066
Dann, Georg Edmund, 14, 138, 256, 283, 605
Dannenfeldt, Karl H., 485
Davenport-Hines, R. P. T., 187
Davis, Audrey B., 610, 1013, 1067
Davis, Lee Niedringhaus, 864
Davy, René, 245

De Jonge, C. H., 1068
Debus, Allen G., 85, 86, 87, 130, 422, 423, 486, 487, 531, 578
DeGrafft, John, 1069
Delaveau, Pierre, 1070
Delépine, M., 424
Delgado, Frank A., 381, 382
DeSalvo, Robert J., 925
Deshler, Charles D., 393
Devner, Kay, 1071
Diaz, Luis Torres, 926
Diehl, Digby, 1249
Dillemann, Georges, 132, 324, 706, 1187
Dioscorides, 755, 756, 757
Dorveaux, Paul, 1188
Dowling, Harry F., 383, 611
Doyle, Paul A., 88
Drake, T. G. H., 1072, 1189, 1190
Drey, R. E. A., 1073, 1097, 1191
Dreyfuss, Mark S., 1013, 1067
Duckworth, Allan, 1014
Duff, J. Gordon, 927
Dukes, M. N. G., 1146
Dulieu, Louis, 131

Dunglison, Robley, 15
Durling, Richard J., 16
Dymock, William, 488
Eaches, Albert R., 1074
Earles, Melvin P., 89, 425, 426, 427, 928, 929
Eckhardt, Shohreh B., 646
Eckles, Robert B., 930
Edsall, John T., 411
Edwards, Griffith, 590
Edwards, Tudor, 1158
Efron, Daniel H., 489
Egan, John W., 865
Einbeck, Arthur, 815
Eisner, D. A., 688
Ekiert, Leszek, 1075
Elferink, Jan G. R., 150
El-Gammal, Samir Yahia, 127
Elliott, Edward C., 932
Ellis, Frank, 816
Engel, Leonard, 213
Engelmann, W., 17
England, Joseph W., 1015
England, Joseph W. , ed., 933
Erichsen-Brown, Charlotte, 612
Erlen, Jonathon, 18
Erni, Paul, 184
Estes, J. Worth, 428, 429, 430, 431, 432, 433, 434, 490, 532, 613, 614, 615, 619, 1147, 1148
Eulner, Hans-Heinz, 981
Evanson, Robert V., 925
Fabre, R., 132
Fantus, Bernard, 384
Farber, Eduard, 435
Fedo, David A., 995
Feehan, H. V., 106
Fehlmann, Hans-Rudolf, 101, 159
Feldmann, Edward G., 777
Felger, Donna H., 1115
Felter, Harvey Wickes, 281
Felter, William, 823
Ferchl, Fritz, 216
Ferguson, John, 19
Ferguson, Joyce A., 992
Ferguson, Thomas, 817
Figurovskii, N. A., 313
Fike, Richard E., 1076

Fischbaum, Marvin, 866
Fischelis, Robert P., 707, 886
Flanagan, Sabina, 276
Florey, H. W., et al., 616
Florey, K., 170
Florkin, Marcel, 533
Flückiger, Friedrich A., 617
Folch Jou, Guillermo, 20, 21, 156
Foote, Perry A., 1016
Forbes, R. J., 1017
Forbes, Thomas, 818
Foster, Thomas, 831
Fourest, Henri-Pierre, 1077
Fourneau, Jean-Pierre, 268
Foust, Clifford M., 491
Fox, Daniel M., 1192
Frampton, John, 758
Francesco, Grete de, 1149
Francis, Anne, 248
Francis, John W., 310
Francke, Donald E., 385, 801, 916
Francke, Gloria N., 385, 934
Freedley, Edwin T., 386
Freking, Harold C., 935
French, R. K., 145
Friedenwald, Julius, 1078
Friedrich, C., 436
Friedrich, Christoph, 1255
Frothingham, Alice Wilson, 1159
Fruton, Joseph S., 437
Fye, W. Bruce, 618
Galambos, Louis, 192
Galen, 759
Gallagher, Teresa C., 828
Ganzinger, Kurt, 90, 110, 219
García Hernández, Manuel, 126
Garcia Serrano, Rafael, 70
Garrison, Fielding H., 23
Gathercoal, E. N., 387
Gaude, Werner, 91
Geissler, Ewald, 24
Geoffroy, Etienne-François, 760
Gibson, Melvin R., 249
Gicklhorn, Renée, 148
Gifford, George E., 619
Gill, Harold B., Jr., 867
Gillispie, Charles C., 255, 291
Gillispie, Charles Coulston, 220

Gilman, Alfred, 438
Ginzburg, Isaiah, 388
Gohlman, William E., 237
Goldstein, Avram, 285
Goldstein, Joseph L., 192
Goldwater, Leonard J., 620
Goltz, Dietlinde, 534, 778
Goodman, Louis S., 438
Goris, Albert, 293
Götz, Wolfgang, 349
Grabowski, Henry, 868
Gramling, L. G., 936
Granberg, C. Boyd, 215, 937
Grapes, Z. T., 708
de Gravelain, Frederique, 1157
Grier, James, 92
Griffenhagen, George, 163, 389,
    621, 819, 820, 821, 822, 823,
    1036, 1079, 1080, 1081, 1082,
    1083, 1084, 1085, 1086, 1087,
    1088, 1089, 1090, 1150
Griffith, Ivor, 327
Grover, Kathryn, 631
Guay, Y., 1018
Guerra, Francisco, 25, 316, 492, 493
Guislain, André, 111, 709
Guitard, Eugène Humbert, 26, 27
Gwei-Djen, Lu, 652
Haber, Ludwig Fritz, 1019
Habermann, Ernst R., 253
Haffner, Gerald O., 390
Häfliger, Josef Anton, 221, 1091
Hagen, Karl G., 761
Haggis, A. W., 622
Haines, Gregory, 107, 108
Hale, Hobart Amory, 362
Hall, Courtney Robert, 311
Hall, Marie, 824
Haller, John S., Jr., 494, 623, 624,
    625, 626, 627, 628
Hamarneh, Sami, 28, 104, 495, 535,
    536, 779, 780, 825, 826, 1092,
    1093, 1094, 1095, 1193
Hambridge, Roger A., 1151
Hameed, Hakeem Abdul, ed., 537
Hammel, Robert W., 925
Hammond, Daniel J., 655
Hanbury, Daniel, 617

Index

Hansen, Poul, 1250
Hare, Ronald, 629, 630
Harper, Donald J., 538
Harré, R., 274
Harris, Michael R., 631
Harris, Richard, 710
Harris, Robin S., 938
Harrison, R. K., 539
Harrod, D. C., 939
Hartmeier-Sutter Cora, 101
Hartwell, Jonathan L., 496
Haug, Thomas, 264
Haynes, William, 171, 214
Hedges, Henry T., 29
Heger, Hans, 1160
Hein, Wolfgang-Hagen, 222, 223, 279, 280, 497, 711, 712, 713, 1096, 1161, 1173, 1194, 1195, 1196, 1197
Helfand, William H., 84, 391, 439, 809, 814, 1020, 1127, 1061, 1198, 1199, 1200, 1201, 1202, 1203, 1204, 1205, 1206, 1207
Helms, Robert B., 901
Henderson, Metta Lou, 940, 941
Hershenson, Benjamin R., 632
Hickel, Erika, 139, 440, 498, 1021
Higby, Gregory J., 14, 61, 62, 329, 372, 499, 777, 781, 789, 827, 828, 874, 1024, 1124
Higenbotham, Harlow N., 865
Hill, C. R., 1097
Hirsch, Rudolf, 30
Ho, Norman F. H., 385
Hobby, Gladys L., 633
Hoch, J. Hampton, 441, 832, 942, 943
Holcombe, Henry W., 1152
Holländer, Eugen, 1208
Holloway, S. W. F., 714, 829
Holmstedt, Bo, 442, 489
Hömberg, Wolfgang, 1098
Hooper, David, 488
Houben, Gerard M. M., 1099
Howard-Jones, Norman, 1100
Hu, Shiu-ying, 500
Hügel, Herbert, 31, 32
Hughes, F. Norman, 944, 945

Hughes, R. Elwyn, 501
Hutton, D. A., 1062
Hynson, Henry P., 946
Ihde, Aaron J., 634
Ince, Joseph, 332
Issekutz, Béla, 635
Jack, D. B., 172
Jackson, Charles O., 715
Jackson, W. A., 1101, 1209
James, Robert, 35
Janssen, Wallace F., 716
Jarcho, Saul, 636
Jasensky, Ronald, 460
Jayawardene, S. A., 36
Jeanjean, Jean-Félix, 240
Johnson, F. Neil, 637
Julien, Pierre, 37, 241, 246, 247, 266, 1210
Just, Theodor, 42
Kahn, Ely Jacques, Jr., 190
Kallinich, Günter, 1102, 1211
Kalman, Samuel H., 392
Karnick, C. R., 540
Karp, Diane R., 1212
Kaufman, K. L., 830
Kawakita, Yosio, 502
Keating, Peter, 638
Keats, Charles, 870
Kebler, Lyman F., 312, 717, 1103
Keeney, Elizabeth, 51
Keeney, Tammy Lynn, 940, 941
Keiner, B., 948
Kendall, Edward C., 639
Kerner, Dieter, 322
Kersaint, G., 267
Keys, Thomas E., 443
Khan, S. Y., 525
Kilmer, F. B., 393
Kimball, Arthur A., 381, 382
King, Charles D., 962
King, Louis, 379
King, Nydia, 164
Kinsey, Raymond, 831
Kirsis, Janis, 1104
Kisch, Bruno, 1105
Kline, Nathan S., 489
Klinkenberg, Norbert, 640
Knapp, David A., 948

Knightley, Phillip, 641
Koch-Weser, Jan, 444
Kogan, Herman, 177
Kohler, Robert E., 445
Kondratas, Ramunas A., 718
Kraemer, Henry, 446
Kramer, John E., 949, 967
Kredel, F. E., 832
Kremers, Edward, 244, 265, 950, 1055
Krivatsy, Peter, 38, 39
Krömeke, Franz, 341
Kronick, David A., 40
Krüger, Mechthild, 1106
Kuhnke, Laverne, 433
Kuschinsky, Gustav, 447
Kuznicka, Barbara, 541
Laar, J., 173
Lakey, Roland T., 347
Lamb, Ruth deForest, 719
Lasagna, Louis, 739
Lasserre, François, 564
Latiolais, Clifton J., 385
Laurent, Jean, 133
LaWall, Charles H., 165, 238, 254, 377, 833
Lawrence, C., 688
Lawrence, Christopher, 1192
Leake, Chauncey D., 289, 448, 449, 542
Ledermann, François, 41, 1210
Lednicer, Daniel, 592
Lee, Philip R., 890
LeFebvre, Nicaise, 762
Leicester, Henry M., 450
Lémery, Nicolas, 763, 764, 765
Lemon, A. B., 376, 919
Lesch, John, 451
Levey, Martin, 543, 544, 545, 782
Levy, Bernard, 1107
Lewis, Edward R. Jr., 834
Lewis, John, 1213
Li, Yu-t'ien, 512, 513
Liebenau, Jonathan, 642, 643, 871, 872, 873, 874, 1022, 1023, 1024
Liljestrand, G., 442
Lim, Beda, 581

Liot, Andre, 134
Lipan, Visile I., 153
Lipp, Martin R., 1108
Little, Arthur, 1025
Little, Ernest, 951
Livesay, Harold, 399
Lloyd, Alistair, 109
Lloyd, John Uri, 42, 348, 503
Lonie, I. M., 145
Lord, R. A., 343
Lordi, Nicholas, 379
Lucia, Salvatore P., 504
Lutz, Alfons, 783
Lyman, Rufus A. 394
Lynn, E. V., 452, 952
MacEwan, Peter, 395
MacFarlane, Gwyn, 262
MacGillivray, Helen, 257
MacGregor, Alasdair B., 505
MacKinney, Loren, 1214
Madison, James H., 292, 1026
Mahoney, Tom, 174, 875
Malone, Marvin H., 953
Manasse, Henry R. Jr., 954
Manliis, Joannes Jacobus de, 766
Mann, Gunter (ed.), 43
Mann, Ronald D., 644
Manners, Steven, 955
Manniche, Lise, 546
Marchetti, Marcello, 700
Marcum, James A., 645
Marion, John Francis, 209
Marland, Hilary, 835
Marquet, Louis, 241
Marshall, E. K., 229
Marti-Ibañez, Felix, 740
Martin, Richard T., 506
Martinez-Fortun y Foyo, Susana, 126
Martiny, M., 1187
Martius, E. Wilhelm, 305
Masino, Cristoforo, 1215
Mason, N.P., 172
Matthews, A. Whitney, 956
Matthews, Leslie G., 93, 116, 784, 836, 837, 838, 839, 957, 1109, 1110, 1216, 1217
Maxwell, Robert A., 646
McCormick, G. E., 288

McDougall, D., 118
McEvilla, Joseph D., 925
McEwen, Alan, 1111
McFadyen, Richard E., 647
McGrath, Earl J., 964
McIntyre, A. R., 648
McKearin, Helen, 260
McNamara, Brooks, 1153
McTavish, Jan R., 649, 650
McVaugh, Michael, 547, 548, 549, 550
Meadsday, Walter S., 876
Mepham, J., 274
Merlin, Mark David, 551
Meserole, W. H., 365
Meyer, A. C., 195
Meyer, Minnie, 44
Meyerhof, M., 552
Meyer-Thurow, George, 1027
Mez-Mangold, Lydia, 1218
Miller, Genevieve, 45
Miller, Nory, 1164
Millman, Morton M., 233
Mines, Samuel, 203
Mitchell, K. A., 1025
Moeller, Josef, 24, 65
Moeller, R., 357
Moir, J. Glen, 958
Möller, Rudolf, 271
Monardes, 767
Moncrief, Nancy J., 976
Monell, Leon M., 376, 919
Montaña, Ma. Teresa, 69
Moran, Bruce T., 959
Mornand Pierre, 1219
Morrison, Samuel, 1078
Morsingh, Francis, 581
Morton, Julia F., 651
Mrtek, Marsha B., 234, 1000
Mrtek, Robert G., 960, 961, 962, 1000
Mudry, Philippe, 564
Müller-Jahncke, Wolf-Dieter, 1112
Multhauf, Robert P., 46, 507. 553, 554
Muñoz Calvo, Sagrario, 20, 21, 720, 721
Musto, David F., 722

Nakayama, Shigeru, 528
Needham, Joseph, 94, 652
Neill, John R., 653
Nékám, Livia, 1220
Nelson, Gary L., 175
Netz, Charles V., 963
Neu, John, 48
Newcomer, James, 964
Niemeyer, Gloria, 801
Nitardy, F. W., 1132
Noble, Alice, 965
Noel, H. S., 397
Noël Hume, Ivor, 1113
Nordenskiöld, A. E., 338
Norman, Jeremy M., 49
Novotny, Ann, 1221
Numbers, Ronald L., 420, 878
Núñez Varela, Victoria, 21
Nutton, Vivian, 688, 879
Oddis, Joseph, 840
O'Hara-May, Jane, 508
Okazaki, Kanzo, 147
Okun, Mitchell, 880
Olmsted, J. M. D., 301
Olonetzky, Beny, 1222
O'Mara, J., 380
Orr, Jack, 841
Orta, Garcia da, 768
Ortiz de Montello, Bernard R., 509
Osborne, George E., 593, 966
Osol, Arthur, 967
Ostino, Guiseppe, 1215
Otsuka, Yasuo, 502
Pagel, Walter, 275, 323
Pak, C., 514
Palliser, Susan M., 654
Palmer, R., 144, 145
Palmieri, Anthony, III, 655
Panem, Sandra, 656
Parascandola, John, 51, 160, 230, 454, 455, 456, 457, 458, 459, 460, 461, 621, 657, 659, 658, 968, 1028, 1048, 1182
Parish, H. J., 660
Parke, D. V., 481
Parnham, M. J., 462, 510
Parrish, Dillwyn, 304
Parrish, Edward, 398

Paterson, G. R., 723, 969, 970, 1029
Pearson, Michael, 881
Peck, F. H., 210
Pedrazzini, Carlo, 1223
Pekkanen, John, 882
Pelner, Louis, 321
Penn, R. G., 724
Pérez Romero, José A., 523, 794
Perez, Valentin Islas, 151
Peters, Hermann, 1224
Peumery, Jean-Jacques, 287
Phillippe, A., 135
Phillips, Joel L., 511
Phillips, Max, 328
Philpott, Jane, 609
Picchioni, Albert L., 971
Plaichinger, Thomas, 1236
Plumpe, Gottfried, 182
Poggendorff, Johann Christian, 53
Poirer, S., 1251
Porter, D., 1030
Porter, Glenn, 399
Porter, Roy, 661, 1030
Poulet, J., 1187
Power, Jed, 1225
Poynter, F. N. L., 652, 784, 883, 929
Pradhan, Suresh B., 884
Pratt, Edmund, 204
Pratt, William D., 178
Prevet, François, 136
Puerto Sarmiento, F. Javier, 736, 1031
Pugsley, L. I., 725
Putnam, P. A., 1114
Qadry, J. S., 103
Quance, Elizabeth J., 734
Quincy, John, 54
Rabin, David L., 885
Rainwater, Dorothey T, 1115
Raison, Arnold, 120
Raphael, Sandra., 771, 1183
Raubenheimer, Otto, 270, 352
Read, Bernard E., 512, 513, 514
Redman, Kenneth, 972
Redwood, Theophilus, 114
Reif, Edward Clarence, 973
Reif, Thelma, 973

Remington, Joseph P., 235
Richardson, Charles G., 1116, 1226
Richardson, Lillian C., 1116, 1226
Rickards, Maurice, 1227
Riddle, John M., 555, 556, 557, 558, 559, 560
Riedel, Bernard E., 974
Riley, John J., 1032
Ring, Carlyn, 1117
Risse, Guenter B., 614, 662
Rivier, L., 515
Roberts, R. S., 842
Rocchietta, Sergio, 1118, 1207, 1228
Rodowskas, Christopher A., 916, 975
Roeske, Wojciech, 95, 298
Roldan y Guerrero, Rafael, 225
Romaine, Lawrence B., 1088
Roos, Charles, 6
Rorem, C. Rufus, 886
Rosenberg, Charles E., 463, 464, 663
Roth, George B., 363
Röthlisberger, Paul, 330
Rouse-Ostrander, Diane, 1119
Rowe, Tom D., 976
Rubiola, Carlo, 146
Ruiz, Juan Francisco Sanchez, 151
Sadek, M. M., 561
Sainte-Fare-Garnot, Pierre-Nicolas, 1077
Sakai, Shizu, 502
Sakula, Alex, 664
Sappert, Kurt, 713, 726
Sarton, George, 55
Scarborough, John, 96, 516, 562, 563, 564, 565, 785
Schafer, Edward H., 887
Schecheter, Paul, 444
Schelenz, Hermann, 97
Schlegel, John F., 392
Schmidt, C. F., 335
Schmitt, Charles, 802
Schmitz, Rudolf, 342, 665, 786, 977, 1120, 1121
Schneider, Wolfgang, 465, 466, 517, 787

Schreiner, Oswald, 1033
Schröder, Gerald, 498
Schullian, Dorothy M., 56
Schultheis, Heinz, 182
Schütze, Sabine Knoll, 278
Schwamm, Brigitte, 518
Schwartzman, David, 888
Schwarz, Angelo, 1215, 1229
Schwarz, Holm-Dietmar, 222, 223
Sciortino, T., 727
Scott, J. R., 1063, 1064, 1065
Scoville, Wilbur L., 303
Segelman, A. B., 484
Segers, E. G., 1122, 1168
Seidlein, H. J., 436
Sevigny, David C., 889
Shannon, Michael C., 400
Shannon, Sam, 843
Sheehan, John C., 467
Shellard, E. J., 939
Shigeru, Nakayama, 581
Shimko, Phyllis, 1123
Short, Agnes Lothian, 1230
Shryock, Richard Harrison, 98, 468
Sigvard, Jacqueline, 1034
Silverberg, Robert, 1252
Silverman, Milton, 890
Simon, James E., 519
Simón, William J., 666
Simons, Corinne Miller, 42, 295
Sir William Henry Perkin, 325
Sivin, Nathan, 57, 58, 291, 528, 566, 581
Slinn, Judy, 187
Slocum, Robert B., 226
Smit, Pieter, 59
Smith, Carter, 1221
Smith, Dale C., 469, 667
Smith, Emilie Savage, 567, 668
Smith, F. A. Upsher, 236
Smith, George Winston, 401
Smith, Mickey C., 407, 669
Smith, R. L., 481
Smola, Gertrud, 788
Sneader, Walter, 670
Snelders, H. A. M., 282
Soldi, A., 728
Sommer, Francis E., 56

Sonnedecker, Glenn, 60, 61, 62, 99, 166, 309, 354, 729, 780, 789, 891, 978, 979, 980, 981, 982, 983, 984, 985, 986, 987, 988, 1035, 1036, 1124
Soubeiran, E[ugene], 402
Soupel, Serge, 1151
Sournia, J. C., 307, 1187
Southern, Walter, 1037
Spalding, James Alfred, 344
Spaulding, Mary, 1125
Spink, Wesley W., 671
Sprowls, Joseph B., 403
Srivastava, G. P., 142
Stabrawa, Anna, 1075
Stafski, Heinz, 1231
Stage, Sarah, 892
Stannard, Jerry, 306, 568, 569, 570, 571, 572, 573, 574, 790
Starks, Michael, 1232
Starr, Isaac, 336
Starr, Paul, 893
Stechl, Peter, 318, 470
Steele, I. K. (ed.), 404
Steinbart, Hiltrud, 1233
Steinegger, E., 353
Steudel, Johannes, 63
Stevenson, Lloyd G., 730
Stewart, Francis, 199
Stewart, Grace G., 520
Stieb, Ernst W., 121, 471, 731, 732, 733, 734, 905, 989, 990, 991, 992, 1089, 1090, 1095, 1126
Stoeckle, John D., 1234
Strichartz, G. R., 478
Strickland, W. A., 405
Stroud, Elaine C., 874, 1024
Strube, Irene, 346
Stuart, G. A., 575
Stürzbecher, Manfred, 735
Styran, Roberta, 64
Suñé Arbussa, José María, 736
Swain, Tony, 672
Swan, Harold T., 683
Swann, John P., 461, 472, 673, 674, 675, 894, 968, 993, 1038
Swanson Ben Z., Jr., 1127
Swarbrick, James, 372

Swazey, Judith P., 473, 676
Swintosky, Joseph V., 474, 1039
Taberner, P. V., 677
Tait, H. P., 1235
Talalay, Paul, 475, 521, 747
Tallis, Nigel, 1128, 1178
Tan, Sian Nio, 143
Tartaglia, Hrvoje, 168
Taylor, Frank O., 201, 202
Taylor, Frank Sherwood, 1040
Taylor, H. L., 994
Taylor, Norman, 678
Teigen, Philip M., 576, 577
Telle, Joachim, 141
Temin, Peter, 737, 895
Temkin, Owsei, 521, 578
Thomas, K. Bryn, 1129
Thomas, P. H., 333
Thomas, Ulrike, 269
Thompson, C. J. S., 1154
Thoms, Hermann, 65
Tom, J., 300
Trease, George Edward, 117, 896
Troupeau, G., 307
Tschirch, Alexander, 221, 476
Turner, Carlton E., 522
Turner, Helen, 1130
Tweedale, Geoffrey, 181
Tyler, V. E., 296
Tyler, V. M., 296
Ulmer, Bruno, 1236
Underwood, E. Ashworth, 849, 1237
Unschuld, Paul U., 124, 125, 579
Unschuld, Ulrike, 580
Urbanek, Beverly S., 522
Urdang, George, 66, 137, 167, 284, 286, 339, 791, 792, 844, 845, 846, 847, 996, 997, 998, 999, 1041, 1131, 1132, 1253, 1254
Vagelos, P. Roy, 192
Valverde, José Luis, 67, 68, 69, 70, 71, 523, 736, 738, 793, 794
Van Tassel, R., 524
Vandam, Leroy D., 477, 478
Vaughan, G. N., 106
Verg, Erik, 182
Vernia, Pedro, 158
Vernon, John, 868

Vershofen, Wilhelm, 1042
Vester, Helmut, 72
Vida, Maria, 1133
Vidal, Del Carmen, 71
Viel, Claude, 314
Vitta, Maurizio, 1172
Vliet, Elmer B., 179
Vogel, Morris J., 663
Vogel, Virgil J., 679
Vohora, S. B., 525
Vos, Rein, 680
Wagner, John G., 479
Wainwright, Milton, 681, 682, 683
Walker, Coy W., 522
Walker, Hugh D., 900
Wall, Cecil, 849
Wall, G. Michael, 522
Wankmüller, Armin, 73, 74
Ward, Patricia Spain, 684
Wardell, William M., 739
Warden, C. J. H., 488
Waring, Edward John, 75
Warner, John Harley, 480, 685, 686
Warthin, Aldred Scott, 1238
Washburn, Robert Collyer, 326
Watson, Andrew, 64
Watson, Gilbert, 526
Watson, Richard, 1134
Wear, A., 145
Weatherall, M., 687
Weber, A., 1239
Webster, George L., 910
Weinstein, Marvin, 1000
Welch, Henry, 740
Welch, Charles E., Jr., 967
Welch, Penny, 1125
Wertheimer, Albert I., 407, 657, 822
Weston, J. Fred, 865
White, Allen, 841
White, George Abbott, 1234
White, Paul Dudley, 434
Whitney, Harvey A. K., 916
Whitten, David O., 866
Whittet, T. Douglas, 741, 850, 851, 852
Wiggins, Steven N., 901
Wiley, Harvey W., 361
Wilkinson, Lisa, 251

Williams, Trevor I., 263
Williams, William H., 853
Wilson, Betty, 1136
Wilson, Bill, 1136
Wilson, Eugene, 122
Wilson, Robert Cummings, 1001
Wilson, William E., 390
Wimmer, Curt P., 351, 1002
Winkelmann, John P., 1003
Wittop Koning, Dirk A., 76, 1096,
    1122, 1137, 1138, 1139, 1161,
    1168, 1173, 1197, 1240, 1241,
    1242, 1243, 1244, 1245
Wolfe, H. George, 334, 355
Wolfe, Margaret Ripley, 742
Wood, Donna J., 902
Wood, G., 409
Wood, Joseph Remington, 1043
Woodruff, H. Boyd, 1044
Woodward, Grace Steele, 317
Wootton, A. C., 100
Wray, Susan, 688
Wrobel, Sylvia, 1004
Yoke, Ho Peng, 581
Young, Anne Mortimer, 1140
Young, Hugh, 297
Young, James Harvey, 689, 690,
    718, 729, 743, 744, 745, 746,
    747, 748, 903, 904, 1150, 1155
Young, L., 481
Youngken, Heber W., 227
Yu, Ching-mei, 512
Zaharans, V. I., 313
Zalai, K., 1005
Zaunick, Rudolf, 319
Zekert, Otto, 110, 228, 340
Zglinicki, Friedrich von, 1246
Zigrosser, Carl, 1247
Zopf, Louis C., 1006
Zupko, Ronald Edward, 1141, 1142
Zwettler, Gerhardt, 1174

For Product Safety Concerns and Information please contact our EU representative GPSR@taylorandfrancis.com
Taylor & Francis Verlag GmbH, Kaufingerstraße 24, 80331 München, Germany

www.ingramcontent.com/pod-product-compliance
Lightning Source LLC
Chambersburg PA
CBHW071801300426
44116CB00009B/1161